CARSON MCCULLERS: A Centenary Collection

# CARSON MCCULLERS:
## A Centenary Collection

Edited by

Carlos Dews, Saundra S. Grace,
& Sue B. Walker

MOBILE ALABAMA

*Carson McCullers: A Centenary Collection*
Copyright © 2022, Negative Capability Press

**Editors:** Dr. Carlos L. Dews, Saundra S. Grace, and Dr. Sue B. Walker
**Publisher and Founding Editor:** Dr. Sue B. Walker
**Editorial Assistance:** Bailey Hammond Robertson
**Book Design and Layout**: Jenni Krchak

Cover image: Library of Congress, Prints & Photographs Division, Carl Van Vechten Collection, [reproduction number, e.g., LC-USZ62-54231]

ISBN: 978-1-7378359-2-9

Negative Capability Press
150 Du Rhu Drive, # 2202
Mobile, Alabama 36608
(251) 591-2922

www.negativecapabilitypress.org
facebook.com/negativecapabilitypress

## Contents

**Sue Brannan Walker**   i
Conference. Correspondences.
Collaboration. Conjuring.

**Carlos Dews**   iii
Introduction

**Will Brantley**   1
Carson and Tennessee:
The Politics of a Literary Friendship

**Keith Byerman**   13
Blacks as Freaks in *The Heart Is a Lonely Hunter*
and *The Member of the Wedding*

**Sun Danping**   19
Why Amazon versus Blossomed Beauty?:
On Different Feminities in the Novellas
of Carson McCullers and Mo Yan

**Laura Virginia Gray**   39
What Should Be: McCullers's Craft of Longing
in *The Ballad of the Sad Café*

**Alessandra Grego**   49
The Spectacle of Monstrosity in *The Ballad of the Sad Café*

**Sarah-Marie D. Horning**   65
"Does Anyone Want Waiting On?": Love, Labor, Liquor
and the Utopian Function of Reproductive Work in *The Ballad
of the Sad Café*, an Ecofeminist Reading

**Katalin G. Kállay**   75
The We of Me: Senses of Longing and Belonging in
Carson McCullers's *The Member of the Wedding*,

*The Heart Is a Lonely Hunter*, and
*The Ballad of the Sad Café*

### Kerry Madden-Lunsford    85
Finding Carson McCullers in China

### James Mayo    97
"Except for this Queer Marriage": Taboo Pairings and Gender Restrictions in *The Ballad of the Sad Café*

### Liz Mayo    105
"Some Unheard-Of Thing": Performing Xenophobia and Gender Conformity in the Play *The Member of the Wedding*

### Annette Runte    117
"Angels, Tomboys, and Melancholy: Carson McCullers and the Swiss Writer Annemarie Schwarzenbach"

### Shannon Russell    157
Gothic Reverberations: Soundscapes in Ann Radcliffe and Carson McCullers's *The Ballad of the Sad Café*

### Emilia Salomone    171
The "Malady" Dr. Copeland Was Unable to Treat

### Mariarosaria Savino    179
Reading Carson in Italy—"Carson McCullers at Scampia": An Experience with Italy Reads

### Glenn Willis    187
Privileged Isolation: Narrative Interiority and Prejudice in the Novels of Carson McCullers

### Contributors    213

# Conference. Correspondences. Collaboration. Conjuring.

### Sue Brannan Walker

*Like a journey, every word a footstep that takes [us]*
*further into undiscovered lands.*
   —David Almond

*Like cosmic strings vibrating existence into being.*
   —Kristin Prevallet

In the photograph, Carson sits
 on a straight-back chair,
her feet in size eight shoes
 prominent beside piano pedals,
her fingers, long, thin, poised
 to write, to play,
converse, contingent upon
 convergence,
at a crossroads of collaboration
 & conjuring.

Listen.  The beloved and the lover
 conceived as uncertain ghosts
ply the clef of C,
 counterpoint, lover and beloved,
from different countries

composing cambiata
 in certain steps
collecting a chorus of voices.

# Introduction

## Carlos Dews

At the time of her fiftieth birthday in February of 1967, Carson McCullers was dreaming of Ireland. Her new friend and director of the film adaptation of her novel *Reflections in a Golden Eye*, director John Huston, had invited her to visit him at his manor house in St. Clerans, County Galway. Due to the myriad medical difficulties McCullers had faced during her life, mostly due to the lingering damage caused by a misdiagnosed and untreated case of childhood rheumatic fever, by 1967 McCullers was bedridden, with the loss of the use of the left side of her body. Travel, even from her home on the Hudson River in Nyack, New York, to nearby Manhattan had become almost impossible. But McCullers was determined to accept Huston's invitation. After celebrating her birthday on 17 February, McCullers traveled to the Plaza Hotel in Manhattan to receive friends and enjoy the services of the hotel. While there she granted an intimate interview to Rex Reed that would later appear in the *New York Times*. This trip to the Plaza was a trial to see if she could withstand the difficulties of travel. Having successfully completed this trip to New York, the meticulous planning for her visit to Ireland was put into motion. McCullers flew to Ireland in a first-class airline seat, adapted to allow her to recline during the entire flight, departing on 1 April 1967. When she arrived at the Shannon airport, she was then transported via ambulance, along with her housekeeper Ida Reeder, to Huston's estate. This trip, although arduous due to her medical difficulties, was perhaps the most joyous of McCullers's many international visits. Huston showered her with attention and affection, and her visit with him lifted her spirits and appeared to help relieve, or at least distract her from, much of the constant pain she suffered. After spending nearly two weeks there, almost all of the time in the bed of the lavish bedroom Huston had prepared for her in a ground floor room of his country house, she returned to her home in Nyack on 19 April 1967.

Although some friends and family probably suspected that McCullers was nearing the end of her life, McCullers would not have known that her fiftieth would be her final birthday and her trip to Ireland to see John Huston would be her final significant trip outside her home in Nyack. After returning home from Ireland to recount the splendors of the trip to anyone who visited her, McCullers suffered a major and final stroke on 15 August 1967. Comatose for forty-five days, she died in the Nyack hospital on 29 September 1967.

Now that her one-hundredth birthday has passed and the fiftieth anniversary of her death has been marked, it is perhaps time to provide a brief consideration of how McCullers's life and work have been recounted by biographers and literary critics as well as to take a look at her influence and resonance in popular and critical culture since her death more than fifty years ago.

The only biography of McCullers published during her lifetime was written by her friend Oliver Evans. The letters between McCullers and Evans as he was writing the biography are extant, and in them, one can see the extent to which the writer and his subject cooperated to ensure the accuracy of the book. The book was published both in the United Kingdom and the United States, but with different titles. The U.K. edition, published by Peter Owen in 1965, was titled *Carson McCullers: Her Life and Work*, and the U.S. edition, published in 1966 by Coward-McCann, was titled *The Ballad of Carson McCullers*.

As her papers were being assembled, cataloged, and prepared for sale (eventually they would be purchased from her estate by the Harry Ransom Humanities Research Center at the University of Texas at Austin), Carson McCullers's sister, Margarita Gachet Smith, was at work putting together a posthumous collection of McCullers's short stories, essays and articles, and poems. This collection, the title of which, *The Mortgaged Heart*, was taken from one of McCullers's poems, was eventually published in 1971, by McCullers's lifelong publisher Houghton Mifflin.

At roughly the same time, Carson McCullers's estate, administered by her former agent Robert Lantz, her former attorney Floria Lasky, her sister Rita Smith, and her former doctor Mary Mercer, looked for a scholar to write McCullers's authorized biography. They had been in touch with Virginia Spencer Carr, a professor at Columbus College in McCullers's hometown of Columbus, Georgia, who had written her Ph.D. dissertation on McCullers and was already at work on the biography that would become *The Lonely Hunter: A Biography of Carson McCullers*. The estate and Professor Carr did not develop a trusting relationship, and the estate not only did not select her to write a biography but also prevented her from consulting McCullers's papers in writing her biography and discouraged those close to McCullers from cooperating with Carr—three notable exceptions were McCullers's cousin Jordan Massee, Tennessee Williams, and the composer David Diamond, all three of whom helped Carr with her work. Once it was clear that Carr would be publishing a significant biography of McCullers, despite their lack of support of it, those controlling McCullers's estate ended their search for an authorized biographer. Carr's monumental biography of McCullers was published by Doubleday in 1975 and reissued by the University of Georgia Press in 2003. To date, Carr's book remains the most significant biographical work on McCullers.

Following Carr's 1975 biography, the next significant biographical work on McCullers was the translation of Josyane Savigneau's French biography of McCullers. Another monumental effort, originally published by Stock in French as *Carson McCullers: Un Cœur de Jeune Fille*, the English-language edition of which, translated by Joan E. Howard and titled *Carson McCullers: A Life*, was published in 2001 by Houghton Mifflin.

Jenn Shapland's *My Autobiography of Carson McCullers*, a mixed-genre memoir and biography, published in 2020 by Tin House Books, received critical acclaim and was a nonfiction finalist for the 2020 National Book Award. The publication of Shapland's memoir marks the most significant biographical contribution to the study of McCullers since Carr's biography in 1975.

In addition to the major biographies of McCullers written by Evans, during her life, and Carr and Savigneau, following her death, five additional briefer critical biographies have appeared. Dale Edmonds's pamphlet-length biography of McCullers was published in 1969 by Steck-Vaughn. Lawrence Graver, also in 1969, published a brief biography of McCullers as volume 84 of the University of Minnesota's Pamphlets on American Writers series. In 1975, Richard M. Cook published *Carson McCullers*, a critical consideration of McCullers's major works along with a brief biography of the writer. This volume was published by Frederick Ungar Publishing as part of their Literature and Life Series. Margaret McDowell's *Carson McCullers*, another longer book including some biographical information but mostly interpretations of her majors works, was published by Twayne in 1980. Similar to Cook and McDowell's books, Virginia Spencer Carr published in 1990, a brief critical biography of McCullers, *Understanding Carson McCullers*, as part of the University of South Carolina Press's Understanding Contemporary American Literature series.

Looking ahead, the American biographer Mary Dearborn is currently at work on a significant biography of Carson McCullers, to be published by Alfred A. Knopf sometime after 2021. A volume of McCullers's letters is currently under preparation and will be published sometime after 2022 by Houghton Mifflin Harcourt.

Another publication milestone for McCullers was the 1999 publication of the autobiography on which McCullers was at work at the time of her death. *Illumination and Night Glare: The Unfinished Autobiography of Carson McCullers* was published by the University of Wisconsin as part of their series Wisconsin Studies in Autobiography. This autobiography has been subsequently included in the 2017 Library of America edition of McCullers's complete work, although the University of Wisconsin edition includes a significant introduction and many more notes.

Since her death in 1967, McCullers's works have remained consistently popular and of interest to scholars of American literature. All of her novels have remained in print since their original publication dates, and the publisher of all her major works, Houghton Mifflin, has periodically reissued her works in new editions. Significantly, the Library of America published a 2001 volume including all of McCullers's novels and a second volume in 2017 that includes the rest of McCullers's published work, with the exception of the text of her 1964 book of children's verse, *Sweet as a Pickle and Clean as a Pig*. With their dedication to keep their volumes in print in perpetuity, the Library of America volumes ensure that McCullers's entire body of work will be available for future generations.

McCullers's continued popularity and importance can be demonstrated via the number of scholarly articles published with her as their major subject, the occurrence of her name in books published since her death, and the number of books with her as their subject that enter libraries worldwide. According to the Ngram search feature of Google Books, McCullers's name has continued to appear with significant frequency in books published since 1967, with a significant peak coinciding with the publication of Virginia Spencer Carr's biography of McCullers in 1975. According to the Modern Language Association's International Bibliography, from 1967 to 2019, there have been a total of 465 items, including books, articles, and dissertations written that include McCullers as a subject. And per the WorldCat catalog of library holdings worldwide, 2191 items related to McCullers have been added to libraries in the world between 1967 and 2019. Both the MLA International Bibliography and WorldCat statistics show a consistent entry of items into their databases across the years, with 10 items per year entering the MLA database and 52 items each year entering the WorldCat libraries.

Another indication of McCullers's continued cultural currency is how her personal story and her works have also inspired popular artists. A few examples might suffice. The 1987 song "Lock and Key" by the Canadian progressive rock trio Rush includes this verse: "Behind the finer feelings / This civilized veneer / The heart of a lonely hunter / Guards a dangerous frontier." The country and western singer Reba McEntire released a song in 1994 titled "The Heart Is a Lonely Hunter," inspired by McCullers's first novel, and the title of this novel appears in a 2019 video of the song "Crave" by the pop singer Madonna. The singer has often mentioned McCullers's work, in particular her first novel, as having influenced her significantly. Madonna also released a 1994 song, "Love Tried to Welcome Me," on her album *Bedtime Stories*, in which she incorporated "the heart is a lonely hunter" into the song's lyrics. The singer Nanci Griffith's 2001 album *Clock Without Hands* shares its title with McCullers's final novel, published in 1961. The singer and songwriter Suzanne Vega has produced a staged musical performance inspired by McCullers's life, *Carson McCullers Talks about Love*, and released a studio album *Lover and Beloved: Songs from an Evening with Carson McCullers* in 2016. It is not uncommon to hear actors and other celebrities mention McCullers as an inspiration or as one of their favorite writers, among them the comedian and talk-show host Rosie O'Donnell and the actor Julia Roberts. Oprah Winfrey, at the suggestion of Julia Roberts, chose McCullers's *The Heart Is a Lonely Hunter* for the book club associated with her talk show in April 2004.

With the exception of *Clock Without Hands*, all of McCullers's novels have been adapted as films. *The Member of the Wedding*, from her 1946 novel and 1950 stage play, was adapted for the screen in 1952, starring the original Broadway cast of Ethel Waters, Julie Harris, and Brandon de Wilde, and was directed by Fred Zinnemann. A film based on McCullers's second novel *Reflections in a Golden Eye*, directed by John Huston, starred Elizabeth Taylor and Marlon Brando and was released in 1967. The following year the film adaptation of *The Heart Is a Lonely Hunter*, starring Sandra Locke, Alan Arkin, and Brian Keith, directed by Robert Ellis Miller, was released. A number of McCullers's short stories have also been adapted as films or for television, including "The Sojourner" (1953), "A Domestic Dilemma" (2009), directed by Jonathan Demme, and "A Tree. A Rock. A Cloud." (1978 and 2017), the more recent directed by Karen Allen. Virginia Spencer Carr's biography of McCullers has been optioned multiple times for film adaptation, and although McCullers's life story seems ideal material for treatment in film, there has yet to be a feature biographical film based on McCullers's life.

McCullers's two plays, *The Member of the Wedding* and *The Square Root of Wonderful*, are both still produced regularly by professional and amateur theater companies, and a stage adaptation of her novel *The Heart Is a Lonely Hunter*, written by Rebecca Gilman, has seen multiple productions since its premiere in 2005. A stage play, *Carson McCullers (Historically Inaccurate)*, written by the novelist and playwright Sarah Schulman and co-produced by Playwrights Horizons and the Women's Project & Productions, was well-received when it was produced in New York in 2002. An operatic adaptation of *The Heart Is a Lonely Hunter* is currently being developed by Carey Scott Wilkerson and Robert Chumbley. A workshop performance occurred in 2021 with a full-scale production to follow in a year or two. Of note as well was the publication in 2017 by NewSouth Books of an epic poem, *It's Good Weather for Fudge: Conversing with Carson McCullers*, written by the poet, publisher, and McCullers scholar Sue Brannan Walker.

As an indication of her ongoing international appeal, BBC Radio has produced two documentaries on Carson McCullers. The first in 1996, titled *Carson McCullers: Love Me*, included interviews with

Eudora Welty and McCullers's cousin Jordan Massee, and the second was hosted in 2016 by the British singer Jarvis Cocker and was titled "Jarvis on McCullers."

Although it has now been superseded by the digital resources available to scholars, Adrian M. Shapiro, Jackson R. Bryer, and Kathleen Field's 1980 *Carson McCullers: A Descriptive Listing and Annotated Bibliography of Criticism* was an important resource for McCullers scholars. But 1995 saw the publication of what might well be considered the most important non-biographical book on Carson McCullers, Judith Giblin James's *Wunderkind: The Reputation of Carson McCullers, 1940-1990*, a comprehensive and exhaustive review of all the critical considerations of McCullers's from the publication of her first novel until 1990. This book, although in need of a supplemental edition to bring scholars up to the present, provides the most considered and detailed examination of how McCullers's work has been received. After Giblin James's review of McCullers's reception by critics and scholars, perhaps the most significant non-biographical monograph on McCullers is Sarah Gleeson-White's *Strange Bodies: Gender Identity in the Novels of Carson McCullers* published in 2003 by the University of Alabama Press. Another monograph that considers McCullers's most important works is Nancy B. Rich's *The Flowering Dream: The Historical Saga of Carson McCullers*, published by Chapel Hill Press in 1999.

Surprisingly few critical monographs on McCullers have been published, with collections of essays much more common; these include Beverly Lyon Clark and Melvin J. Friedman's *Critical Essays on Carson McCullers*, published by G.K. Hall in 1996, and Jan Whitt's *Reflections in a Critical Eye: Essays on Carson McCullers*, published in 2008 by the University Press of America. A significant new collection of essays, *Carson McCullers in the Twenty-First Century*, edited by Alison Graham-Bertolini and Casey Kayser, was published by Palgrave Macmillan in 2016. Graham-Bertolini and Kayser also edited a collection of essays, *Understanding the Short Fiction of Carson McCullers*, published in 2020 by Mercer University Press as the first volume in the press's series on Carson McCullers, with series editor Carlos Dews. Chelsea House has published two editions of their *Bloom's Modern Critical Views* collections on McCullers by Harold Bloom, the first in 1986 and the second in 2009. As well,

Chelsea House has published two of their Bloom's Guides collections of essays on individual works on McCullers's *The Member of the Wedding* and *The Ballad of the Sad Café*, both published in 2005.

The books mentioned in this introduction are those dedicated exclusively to Carson McCullers's life and work. In addition to these volumes, there have been a number of books published since 1967 that consider McCullers in a comparative context, especially in relation to her and fellow Southern writers, among them Katherine Anne Porter, Eudora Welty, and Flannery O'Connor.

In the years since her death, significant work has been done to preserve McCullers's legacy and promote scholarly consideration of her work and life. The Carson McCullers Society, a scholarly organization dedicated to the study of the life and work of McCullers, was founded by a group of university professors at the American Literature Association convention when it was held in Baltimore, Maryland, in 1997. This organization continues to publish an annual newsletter and awards an annual prize for the best conference paper on McCullers. The society maintains a website and also organizes sessions at various scholarly conferences, including the Modern Language Association, the American Literature Association, the Society for the Study of Southern Literature, and South Atlantic Modern Language Association.

Another milestone in the support of biographical and critical research on McCullers, as well as support for both writers and musicians, was the founding in 2001 of the Carson McCullers Center for Writers and Musicians. Based in her childhood home in Columbus, Georgia, the center was founded thanks to the generous donation of her childhood home at 1519 Stark Avenue to Columbus State University by local philanthropist and former university literature professor Thornton Jordan. The McCullers Center, per its mission statement, is "dedicated to preserving the legacy of Carson McCullers; nurturing writers and musicians, educating young people; and fostering literary, musical, artistic, and intellectual culture in the United States and abroad." The McCullers Center was the beneficiary of a generous bequest by Dr. Mary E. Mercer who, following her death in 2013, left it McCullers's home in Nyack, New York, and a significant collection of McCullers archival materials. With this gift and previous donations of manuscripts and archival materials, the McCullers

Collections, held in the archives of the Simon Schwob Memorial Library of Columbus State University, has become one of the top three most important resources for research on McCullers's life and work, along with the collection at the Harry Ransom Humanities Research Center at the University of Texas and the McCullers's collections at Duke University's David M. Rubenstein Rare Book and Manuscript Library.

To celebrate what would have been McCullers's one-hundredth birthday and to commemorate the fiftieth anniversary of her death, the Carson McCullers Center for Writers and Musicians, in 2017, sponsored a series of events both in her hometown of Columbus, Georgia, and in her adopted hometown of Nyack, New York. In Columbus, the celebration, *Carson at 100: The McCullers Centennial Celebration*, was held in the Bill Heard Theatre of the RiverCenter for the Performing Arts, part of Columbus State University, on 19 February 2017. The program included a dramatic representation of McCullers monologues compiled by Carey Scott Wilkerson, and accompanied by classical music. The event also featured the premiere of the film adaptation of McCullers's short story "A Tree. A Rock. A Cloud." directed by Karen Allen. In Nyack, New York, McCullers's 100th birthday was celebrated with events in both February and March 2017. On 19 February 2017 the Nyack Library hosted a performance of an original musical composition by former Columbus State University student Liliya Ugay (piano) accompanied by Paul Neubauer (viola) titled "After Carson's 'A Tree. A Rock. A Cloud.'" This performance was followed by a reading of the short story. On 25 March 2017, the Carson McCullers Center and Rivertown Film presented screenings of the film adaptations of two of McCullers's short stories, "A Tree. A Rock. A Cloud." directed by Karen Allen, and "A Domestic Dilemma," directed by Jonathan Demme.

Before the commemoration of her one-hundredth birthday, two major scholarly conferences dedicated to McCullers were organized. The first, at Columbus College (now Columbus State University), was titled *Reflections: A Carson McCullers Symposium* ran from 22-24 October 1987, and the second, *Carson McCullers: An Interdisciplinary Conference and 94th Birthday Celebration*, was held in February 2011, again at Columbus State University.

Perhaps most significant, because of its international and collaborative nature, also in celebration of McCullers's one hundredth birthday, the Carson McCullers Center, the Carson McCullers Society, and John Cabot University co-sponsored an international McCullers conference on the campus of John Cabot University in Rome, Italy. The conference, titled *Carson McCullers in the World: A Centenary Celebration*, was held from 14-16 July 2017, and included three exhibitions, performances, and screenings, as well as the presentation of scholarly papers. Participants in the conference came from Australia, Canada, China, Germany, Hungary, Ireland, Italy, Japan, Scotland, the United Kingdom, and the United States. The keynote address for the conference, "Grappling with Carson," was given by the novelist, playwright, and cultural critic Sarah Schulman.

The essays represented in the collection that follows were written by attendees at the conference but should not be seen as a simple reprinting of the pieces presented there. Conference participants selected to contribute to this volume were given time to expand and revise their presentations into the pieces included in the current volume. These essays were chosen to provide both a wide range of nationalities, points of view, subject matter, and genre. It is hoped that the pieces both reflect the current state of interest in McCullers and help to project that interest into the future.

# CARSON AND TENNESSEE: THE POLITICS OF A LITERARY FRIENDSHIP

## Will Brantley

Although Tennessee Williams did not meet Carson McCullers until 1946, she had been on his radar for some time. In *Tom: The Unknown Tennessee Williams*, Lyle Leverich cites a 1940 letter from Williams to publisher Bennett Cerf:

> I brought one novel down here [Acapulco] with me called *The Heart Is a Lonely Hunter* by a young girl named Carson McCullers. It is so extraordinary it makes me ashamed of anything I might do. Are you familiar with her work?—What a play she could write!—Let us hope that she doesn't—or that she does—however, it might deprecate other works in that field. (375-76)

At this early point, Williams could sense a rapport with the young Georgia writer, but it was McCullers's 1946 novel *The Member of the Wedding* that prompted a fan letter and an invitation to vacation with him in Nantucket. Their summer together was the beginning of a friendship that continued until McCullers's death in 1967. An ardent defender, Williams demonstrated great skill in protecting his physically and sometimes spiritually delicate friend and in promoting her work to others. Intertextually, McCullers's fiction may have more in common with the novels of William Faulkner than with the drama of Tennessee Williams, but no literary friendship was more crucial to her well-being than the one she shared with Williams.

Williams recounted that summer meeting on a number of occasions, but nowhere more evocatively than in "Praise to Assenting Angels," an unpublished essay cited at length in Margarita G. Smith's introduction to *The Mortgaged Heart*. Having convinced himself that he was dying, Williams did not want to miss meeting McCullers and therefore invited her to the house in Nantucket where he was staying with Pancho Rodriguez, his Mexican lover at the time, and a cat with newborn kittens. "Carson was not dismayed by the state of the house," he recalls:

> She had been in odd places before. She took an immediate fancy to the elated young Mexican and displayed considerable fondness for the cats and insisted that she would be comfortable in the downstairs bedroom where they were boarding. Almost immediately the summer weather improved. The sun came out with an air of permanence, the wind shifted to the South, and it was suddenly warm enough for bathing. At the same time, almost immediately after Carson and the sun appeared on the island, I relinquished the romantic notion that I was a dying artist. My various psychosomatic symptoms were forgotten. There was warmth and light in the house, the odour of good cooking and the nearly-forgotten sight of clean dishes and silver. Also there was some coherent talk for a change. Long evening conversations over hot rum and tea, the reading of poetry aloud, bicycle rides and wanderings along moonlit dunes, and one night there was a marvelous display of the Aurora Borealis, great quivering sheets of white radiance sweeping over the island and the ghostly white fishermen's houses and fences. That night and that mysterious phenomenon of the sky will be always associated in my mind with the discovery of our friendship, or rather, more precisely, with the spirit of this new-found friend, who seemed as curiously and beautifully unworldly as that night itself . . . (xxvi-xxvii)

Williams also said in this essay that the

> great generation of writers that emerged in the twenties, poets such as Eliot, Crane, Cummings and Wallace Stevens, prose writers such as Faulkner, Hemingway, Fitzgerald and Katharine Anne Porter, has not been succeeded or supplemented by any new figures of corresponding stature with the sole exception of this prodigious young talent that first appeared in 1940 with the publication of her first novel, *The Heart Is a Lonely Hunter*. (xx)

It is a view that Williams expressed on many occasions.

In 2000, I had the opportunity to appear with Carlos Dews and the late biographer Virginia Spencer Carr on a panel devoted to Williams and McCullers and their legendary friendship. I tried then to delineate the most significant affinities between the two writers, including their childhood illnesses (diphtheria in Williams's case, rheumatic fever in the case of McCullers); their overprotective mothers and absent fathers; their early feelings for the isolated individual—the afflicted, the freakish; their shyness, which was balanced by extremely strong wills; their unconventional expressions of sexuality; their alcoholism and periods of depression; their attachment to many of the same thinkers and writers, particularly to the poet Hart Crane; their intense loyalty to one another and to their friends; their ability to transform the events of their lives into autobiographical drama and fiction—a creative synthesis; their rejection of what Williams called the anarchy of modern society; their mastery of gothic humor; their acute sensitivity to negative appraisals of their work (each achieved early critical acclaim while their late work met with less success); their defense of themselves in self-reflective essays; and, finally, the poetic nature of their prose, which is both intensely lyrical and intensely symbolic. In short, the two writers shared a sensibility—and it was this sensibility that prompted Williams to write a fan letter that, in turn, initiated a life-long friendship.

With so many affinities, one wants to know if the two writers echoed one another in their works. If the question is: Did Williams write his own *Member of the Wedding*?, the answer is no, but he did encourage McCullers to bring her novel to the stage and even shared his agent, Audrey Wood. Still, one can discern McCullers's presence within Williams's writing—in, for instance, the character of Hannah Jelkes in *The Night of the Iguana*. McCullers and Hannah are different, to be sure, but one telling thread connects them. In her self-reflective essay, "The Flowering Dream," published in *Esquire* in 1959, and included in *The Mortgaged Heart*, McCullers provides one of her most frequently cited remarks:

> Symbols suggest the story and theme and incident, and they are so interwoven that one cannot understand consciously where the suggestion begins. I become the characters I write

about. I am so immersed in them that their motives are my own. When I write about a thief, I become one; when I write about Captain Penderton, I become a homosexual man; when I write about a deaf mute, I become dumb during the time of the story. I become the characters I write about and I bless the Latin poet Terence who said, "Nothing human is alien to me." (276-77)

In Williams's play, which appeared two years later, Hannah recounts for Mr. Shannon two incidents from her "lovelife," including the time that she covered for a man who attempted to grope her in a theatre, and the time when another man requested she remove a piece of her clothing and turn the other way as he "satisfied" himself. Shannon calls the incident "dirty," but Hannah, with a resolve that rivals that of McCullers, says she was merely a bit confused: "I'd known about loneliness—but not that degree or depth of it." Hannah then echoes McCullers's well-known comment from "The Flowering Dream," adding her own twist: "Nothing human disgusts me unless it's unkind, violent. And I told you how gentle he was—apologetic, shy, and really very, well, *delicate* about it" (*Plays* 418). Williams and McCullers were drawn to other-worldly misfits, to characters such as Hannah Jelkes; their preoccupation with such characters permeates their drama and fiction.

Williams's and McCullers's letters are spread over a dozen or more libraries and archives, so readers can be grateful to Joyce Durham for citing some of the most quotable letters between the two writers in her *Mississippi Quarterly* article from 2005, "Portrait of a Friendship: Selected Correspondence Between Carson McCullers and Tennessee Williams," letters culled from the collection at Duke University. On February 14, 1948, two years after their summer idyll in Nantucket, McCullers confides: "Wish I could talk with you . . . . I imagine us swimming in the Mediterrean [sic]. Without my imaginary life—in which you play a leading part, *I would go crazy*" (8). Writing in August of 1952, seven years after their summer together, Williams would also pine for that special season. "Two plays that didn't make money and, brother, you're on the skids! I wish we could spend a week or two working quietly together this summer, the way we did that wonderful summer in Nantucket, when you did 'Member' and I did 'Summer,'" which he subsequently dedicated to McCullers. "The presence of someone else doing creative work is a comfort and a stimulation I think, for it is a lonely business" (7).

Like the true Southerners they were, the two loved to gossip and share impressions of fellow writers. After meeting Gore Vidal in Italy, March 1948, Williams wrote to McCullers:

> Vidal is 23 and a real beauty. His new book 'The City and the Pillar' I have just read and while it is not a good book it is absorbing. There is not a really distinguished line in the book and yet a great deal of it has a curiously life-like quality. The end is trashy, alas, murder and suicide both. But you would like the boy as I do: his eyes remind me of yours! (9)

The two writers confided their illnesses to one another, but Joyce Durham may be right to suggest that McCullers was generally more reticent on this score, perhaps because of the bond that Williams drew between her and his sister Rose. One of Williams's nicknames for McCullers was, affectionately, "Sister Woman." Here is one exceptional letter from 1949 in which McCullers does not hold back:

> This last year has been unspeakably difficult. My health has failed steadily. I can't walk more than half a block, can't play the piano of course or type, can't smoke too much or, alas, get drunk. And neuritis has set in—the damaged nerves are constantly spastic and painful.... But Tenn, why do I have to suffer so? What have I done? I want to cry out for help—and there is no help possible. (13)

Williams seems to have been a good counselor, advising his friend to refrain from a mode of thinking that would hinder her recovery.

> I am a vulnerable person, but it frightens me to see how even *more* vulnerable *you* are," he wrote. "Is there no way you can defend and spare yourself, learn how to live not so acutely, and still be yourself and an artist?. (14)

Both writers supported one another publicly. In 1948, McCullers wrote a letter to the editor of *Life* regarding an article by a psychiatrist who saw similarity in the two writers' treatment of psychic disorders and fights for survival. McCullers said that her friend was "not only an artist and genius, but also one of the most wholly beautiful human beings she had ever known" (Carr 299). In 1950, Williams wrote an introduction to the New Directions re-issue of McCullers's *Reflections in a Golden Eye*, a piece that has become central in the critical discourse on McCullers's writing. Although the official topic is McCullers and her second novel, Williams used the occasion to account for his artistic vision as well. Williams implicitly acknowledges that he and McCullers share a mysterious sense of dread that typifies the work of many modern artists, and that the often-misunderstood *Reflections* "is one of the purest and most powerful of those works which are conceived in that Sense of The Awful which is the desperate black root of nearly all significant modern art, from the *Guernica* of Picasso to the cartoons of Charles Addams." Williams surveys each of McCullers's novels up to that time, with specific praise for *The Ballad of the Sad Café*, "assuredly among the masterpieces of our language in the form of the novella" (*Where I Live* 46- 47).

This public support took a comic turn on at least one occasion. In 1954, McCullers convinced Williams to appear with her at the Poetry Center of the 92nd Street Y. Donald Spoto provides this amusing account of that evening:

> She had been invited to speak on "Twenty Years of Writing" at the Poetry Center . . . and she thought that Williams—much stronger and the better reader—should accompany her. He agreed, on condition that a pitcher of martinis be set at his elbow. His intolerance for any substantive quantity of alcohol, and her generous refilling of her own glass, resulted in a strange event. Two of American's most famous writers sat for the evening, interrupting one another, stumbling, and slurring over their words, perversely relishing one another's boozy humor as much as they were oblivious to the uncomfortable audience. (194)

A well-known photograph of the two writers at this event would appear to support at least the first part of Spoto's description; the audience's discomfort might be more difficult to prove.

In 1961, Williams provided another public assessment, this time in *Saturday Review*. Suppressing his reservations about McCullers's final novel, *Clock Without Hands*—according to Gary Richards, he tried to convince McCullers to delay publication (159)—Williams rendered instead this assessment: "If I hadn't known before that Carson is a worker of miracles, this work would surely have convinced me of it. . . . Here was all the stature, nobility of spirit, and profound understanding of the lonely, searching heart that make her, in my opinion, the greatest living writer of our country, if not of the world" (*Where I Live* 136).

After her death in 1967, McCullers's attorney Floria Lasky, her psychiatrist and friend Mary Mercer, her agent Robby Lantz, and her sister Margarita G. Smith all refused to speak with Virginia Carr as she researched her biography. Williams, however, broke with this group and shared his memories of McCullers. Williams permitted Carr to conclude her biography, *The Lonely Hunter*, with a poem that he had written for his friend—"Which Is My Little Boy?"—and he supplied Carr with a preface, in which he contends that "Carson McCullers is what I would call a *necessary* writer: She owned the heart and the deep understanding of it, but in addition she had that 'tongue of angels' that gave her power to sing of it, to make of it an anthem." In his prefacing remarks, Williams insists that McCullers must be measured by the quality rather than the quantity of her work, and that her lonely heart "was graced with light that eclipsed its shadows" (xviii-xix).

Clearly, the two writers were devoted to one another, but the public utterances in essays and lectures should be read in light of the more private ones that we now encounter in published letters to other writers and friends. Writing to Donald Windham in 1948, Williams called McCullers "a continual problem, however lovable." Williams was disturbed that McCullers's "new stories are not quite stories and she is so hypersensitive that I don't dare talk frankly about this. I believe she really wrote all but one of them at least 10 years ago, the quality is so immature. PLEASE don't speak of this!!! It is terribly upsetting" (225). Of course, Windham did more than speak of the matter; much to Williams's displeasure, he published the correspondence between the playwright and himself.

Williams was not unaware that some of his friends were not so taken with McCullers. Maria St. Just, who would become the executor of Williams's estate, found it taxing to be in McCullers's company, nicknaming her Choppers since her cheeks reminded St. Just of lamb chops. With St. Just, Williams could be candid about his frustrations and could even resort to the demeaning nickname:

> Choppers [Carson McCullers] just now hauled her freight out of here. . . . Key West was not for Choppers. She was here sitting for about two weeks, in Havana sitting for about five days, all the time swilling my liquor and gobbling my pinkie tablets in such a way that I reeled with apprehension. I was about to run out of pinkies. Two a night for Choppers, content with no less! Fortunately I was able to buy some without prescription in Havana. I had hoped that Chops would start bobbing with creative activity. After two days of dictating a short play [*The Square Root of Wonderful*] to me, she scuttled up [to] her ivory tower and bolted the door! Said she could not be rushed into writing, had to think and dream a long time first. Since we pursue opposite methods, she thought she'd better go home and germinate there till she got the whole thing in her chops and then start writing. So off went Choppers this morning on the nine-forty-five plane to Miami. (112-13)

Williams's tone then changes. He becomes more reconciled and even apologetic: "I am worried over Choppers. I feel that she is dreaming herself away. I was very unkind." Williams tells St. Just that he cares most about his own work, which he hopes will enable him to give "more love to more people." Needing the friendship of both women, Williams employs St. Just to reach out to his other friend: "Will you call her in Nyack? She needs every little bit of attention or affection, real or make believe, that anybody can give or pretend to give her" (113). When *The Square Root of Wonderful* did not meet with a favorable critical reception, it was Williams who helped her weather the disappointment. "As Tennessee Williams once told me," she remarked in an article for the *Philadelphia Inquirer*, "'It takes a tough old bird to work in the theatre'" (5).

In her own way, McCullers was equally defensive of Williams. Novelist and playwright Jess Gregg recounts an incident that speaks to the intensely supportive nature of their friendship. An assistant to Elia Kazan during the often-volatile rehearsals for and pre-Broadway opening of *Cat on a Hot Tin Roof*, Gregg published a reminiscence of that experience in 2011. Williams was, Gregg writes, surrounded by an assortment of visitors—"The Williams One-Note Singing Family"—who were there to lend their support to the playwright even though few expected his elusive play to last for long on Broadway:

> Of all who came to prejudge the out-of-town show, the most memorable was a figure who limped into the dim theatre almost every day. At first one of the assistants tried to turn her out, thinking she was a bag woman who had strayed in from the street. She was possibly still young, her hands wrapped in soiled gauze bandages, her partially paralyzed face fiercely contorting in an effort to smile. She had to be helped up the stairs. Doors had to be opened for her. Doors *did* open for her, for she was Tennessee's close friend, the Southern novelist Carson McCullers.

Gregg underscores McCullers's importance to Williams at this juncture in his creative life. It was McCullers who understood that the play's open-endedness and lack of resolvability is in fact its true meaning:

> It was she, a woman of great inner radiance, whom I first heard use a particular phrase in Philadelphia. In defense of the increasingly evident flaw of the play, she said gently, "But it's the truth." Or more gently answered any suggested solution: "Ah, but that's not the truth." Soon it became the rallying cry of the Williams One-Note Singers. *Up the truth!* One afternoon I asked Mr. Kazan why he had restored a certain scene when the play seemed clearer without it. He met my eye somberly, then shrugged, "Tennessee says it's the truth," he replied. "Maybe it is, I dunno." (38-39)

Since she predeceased him by sixteen years, Williams had the opportunity to reflect on the emotional space that McCullers had assumed in his life. The passage of time brought some new perspectives and enabled him to say what he could not have said when McCullers was still alive. Although he never failed to acknowledge her importance, Williams could be more forthright about the demands that she had placed on his attention, as when he told Rex Reed, in 1971—and in one of his more hyperbolic moments—that "the only *real* writer the South ever turned out was Carson . . . She was no angel, ya know. Or if she was, she was a black angel. But she had infinite wisdom. Ours was a deep relationship that spanned many years" (Devlin 199).

The image of McCullers that emerges from Williams's 1975 *Memoirs*, however, is clearly revisionary, as if Williams needed to separate himself from earlier and more effusive pronouncements. He recalls McCullers in the contexts of three memorable exits and even notes that he ejected her from his apartment when she attempted to comfort him following one of these departures; he claims at this point to regard Jane Bowles as "the finest writer of fiction we have had in the States," with praise for a sensibility that he "found even more appealing than that of Carson McCullers" (91); he notes that while Carson was once the only writer who could work along with him in the same room, he is able to compose now with a young male "prodigy" whose "warm and dreamy presence" nonetheless recalls that of McCullers (238); and he recounts his sister Rose's impatience with Carson's self-absorption before suggesting, indirectly, that McCullers, with her "relentless illnesses," was nonetheless a survivor on at least one front: she managed to escape from her sad and haunted husband Reeves, who had arranged for the two to end their lives together (70). It's a bitchy portrait, but most readers know that Williams also indicts himself in *Memoirs*. The portrait of McCullers is disturbing, but no less so than Williams's depiction of his own darker moments.

*Cat on a Hot Tin Roof* may provide a better key to understanding the friendship of McCullers and Williams, for it's a play about competing truths. There's Maggie's truth, Brick's truth, Big Daddy's truth, and Big Mama's truth. Williams even supplied Elia Kazan with a version of the third act that satisfied *his* sense of the truth (and then notoriously published the two competing acts together). If we wish to understand the friendship of McCullers and Williams, we must look at all the truths available—truths gleaned from essays, letters, interviews, memoirs, biographies, gossip, photos. We may discover a slightly more shaded relationship than previously acknowledged. In a letter included in Donald Windham's volume, Williams told Kenneth Tynan in 1955 that Carson made "something very light" happen within him; that lightness seems to have darkened with Carson's absence. But none of the truths I've uncovered negate Williams's remark, again to Tynan, that he had been the recipient of two "providential accidents," or, rather, "two great friendships," one with Frank Merlo—his "Good Man Friday"—and the other with ... Carson McCullers (306).

# Works Cited

Brantley, Will, and Virginia Spencer Carr, Carlos L. Dews, and Barbra Ewell. "Exotic Birds of a Feather." *Tennessee Williams Annual Review,* vol. 3, 2000, pp. 69-90.

Carr, Virginia Spencer. *The Lonely Hunter: A Biography of Carson McCullers.* Doubleday, 1975.

Devlin, Albert J. editor. *Conversations with Tennessee Williams.* UP of Mississippi, 1986.

Durham, Joyce. "Portrait of a Friendship: Selected Correspondence Between Carson McCullers and Tennessee Williams." *Mississippi Quarterly,* vol. 59, nos. 1-2, Winter-Spring 2005-06, pp. 5-16.

Gregg , Jess. "Kazan and *Cat.*" *Tennessee Williams Annual Review,* vol. 12, 2011, pp. 27-43.

Leverich, Lyle. *Tom: The Unknown Tennessee Williams.* Norton, 1995.

McCullers, Carson. *The Mortgaged Heart.* Edited and introduced by Margarita G. Smith, Houghton Mifflin, 1971.

---. "Playwright Tells of Pangs." *Philadelphia Inquirer,* 13 Oct. 1957, sec. B, pp. 1, 5.

Richards, Gary. *Lovers and Beloveds: Sexual Otherness in Southern Fiction, 1936-1961.* Louisiana State UP, 2007.

Spoto, Donald. *The Kindness of Strangers: The Life of Tennessee*

*Williams*. 1985. Da Capo, 1997.

Williams, Tennessee. *Five O'Clock Angel: Letters of Tennessee Williams to Maria St. Just, 1948-82.* Knopf, 1990.

---. *Memoirs.* Doubleday, 1975.

---. *Plays 1957-1980.* Library of America, 2000.

---. *Tennessee Williams' Letters to Donald Windham, 1940-1965.* Edited by Donald Windham, Holt, 1977.

---. *Where I Live: Selected Essays.* Edited by Christine R. Day and Bob Woods, New Directions: 1978.

# Blacks as Freaks in *The Heart Is a Lonely Hunter* and *The Member of the Wedding*

## Keith Byerman

The freak, in Carson McCullers's fiction, is primarily known by physical traits. Rachel Adams explains, such characters are "constrained by corporeal anomalies that defy the imposition of normative categories of identity." She continues, "These freaks suffer an alienation from their bodies that parallels their experiences of estrangement within and alienation from the society of others" (552). The most obvious marker of difference in the South of McCullers's time was race. The key question for this analysis, given her generally liberal social views, is whether blackness is for her an inherently freakish quality. Beyond this issue is the deeper question of how she values racial difference. After all, the most sympathetic characters in many of her works are freaks, so to have a random mark of difference is not necessarily negative. But, if blacks *are* freaks, then we must ask how she is using that designation. I want to suggest that it, in fact, compromises her social and political views by reducing the options for black self-expression.

In *The Heart Is a Lonely Hunter*, the emphasis with black characters is the quality of voice. Early on, we are told that Willie (William) stutters when he is excited. Biff claims that he cannot understand him when he tries to explain Blount's strange behavior. Portia, his sister, is said by Mick Kelly to demonstrate "n----- craziness" when she tries to tell a story. Doctor Benedict Copeland, their father, proves eloquent when speaking formally, but chokes on words when trying to express emotion. Of course, in a novel with a deaf-mute at its center and the need and failure to communicate as its theme, three of its characters showing these traits is not surprising. However, the family relationship and the color of their skin suggest that there may be a "racial" aspect to this version of the problem. After all, there is a long history of whites labeling black speech as gibberish or illiterate dialect or proof of intellectual incompetence.

For this reason, we need to attend to the conditions under which these patterns occur. When William is trying to tell Biff about Blount, his speech is nearly incomprehensible. But near the end of the book, when he is in a black environment, even when responding to Blount, there is virtually no hesitancy. Similarly, though Portia apparently tells the same story over and over in the Kelly's kitchen, when she faces the stress of telling her father about William's traumatic experience, the narrator points out that she takes time to sort out the story before she tells it. In both cases, the environment, a space controlled by whites, renders their voices "freakish." Outside of that alienated place, in a black space, their speech is perfectly normal.

Dr. Copeland is a much more complicated case. He reflects many of the qualities associated with W.E.B. Du Bois, a renowned scholar, a founder of the NAACP, and, by 1940, a political radical who identified himself as a Marxist. The relevance of the connection is Copeland's association with all three of the Du Bois features. He is a member of a national civil rights organization, a reader of history and sociology, and a supporter of Marxism. Most pertinent to the narrative is that Copeland, like Du Bois, is a believer in racial uplift. Du Bois contends that a select group, which he refers to as the Talented Tenth, have the skills and opportunities to rise significantly above the black masses. But when they do so, they have the obligation to help raise those left behind because of the effects of slavery and the racist restrictions and violence of segregation. When Copeland refers repeatedly to "the one true purpose," uplift is what he means. This is seen by not only his words, but also his actions and his criticisms of other blacks.

Copeland's problem is that he feels acutely his unusual situation, his freakishness. On the one hand, he is the intellectual superior of most if not all the whites in the town; he reads Spinoza, though McCullers is careful to point out that he is not certain that he understands what he is reading. He indicates that he feels or intuits rather than intellectually grasps the philosopher's message. But he is caught in a society that does not respect his intelligence or dignity. He winds up beaten and jailed primarily because the sheriff considers his speech and behavior to be "uppity." His very existence, not his anger or his frustration, make him unacceptable in a white supremacist world.

On the other hand, he cannot resist a condescending attitude toward other blacks, including his family. We learn that his wife, Daisy, was so resistant to his efforts to educate her and change her behavior that he beats her. She then takes the children, named Karl Marx, Hamilton (presumably for Alexander), Portia, and William (for Shakespeare), and returns to her illiterate father's farm. While he is highly respected in the black community for his medical skills, they pay no attention to his advice on birth control or other matters that might enhance their well-being. They will name their children after him, but they have no understanding of what he is trying to do for them. He refuses to speak their language and they cannot speak his. Even his own children make no effort to use him as a model. Those who do follow his lead, such as the pharmacist, are typographically mocked in the text. In a conversation with Blount about William's experience, Marshall Williams's multi-syllable words are italicized, and Blount finally tells him to speak clearly.

This representation suggests an ambiguity on McCullers's part about Copeland. On the one hand, he is the one truly tragic character in the book. Despite his nobility and sacrifice, he still misses the mark due to the flaw of pride. On the other hand, the author points insistently to his anger and bitterness. She goes so far as to give him a lingering disease, tuberculosis, that is often associated in literature with melancholy (Sontag 20). The crucial point is that McCullers, like other Southern liberals and moderates, often sympathized with black suffering but saw the impatience of activists as a sign of bitterness that was counterproductive. Making Copeland's failure to achieve "the one true purpose" the result of his flaws rather than the intransigence of white racism suggests the limits of the author's understanding. In fact, she seems to make Portia the model of black possibility meaning, in effect, that she sides with those who always say, "Wait."

*Member of the Wedding* is a simpler text for this analysis since it has fewer significant African American characters and no Doctor Copeland. There is just the set of three that parallel Willie, Portia, and her husband Highboy. Here it is Berenice, TT Williams (her current boyfriend), and Honey Brown, her foster cousin.

Of these, Berenice is the only major black character, though Honey is potentially the more intriguing figure. He is most often seen with a book, and he seldom speaks, though, like William, he goes out to socialize with others. He is also marked by a sense of personal style in his attire. But, like Copeland, he has an internal disorder that in his case makes him ineligible for military service. This small fact in the narrative reinforces the sense that intelligent black men do not belong in McCullers's fictional world. Even the preadolescent Frankie recognizes that Honey belongs somewhere else. In addition, his status as a young black man puts him at legal risk. The last time he is seen in the story, he is headed to Fork Falls for the night. Later, he is reported to be doing eight years on the chain gang. Such a penalty would be the result of a violent crime, probably against another black man. It would seem that McCullers cannot quite escape the stereotype of black men as violent, even when they are more sophisticated than those around them. They are ultimately freak in the sense of being incapable of living submissively in a Southern environment.

The final character is Berenice Sadie Brown, who is also the best known. Next to Frankie, she is the most frequent speaker in the text, but her role is ambiguous. She is the mother figure for both Frankie and John Henry, but at times, it is difficult to distinguish her speech from theirs. Even when she demonstrates maternal wisdom, Frankie defies her as often as she listens. In other words, Berenice has no true authority within this white space. The three of them make a strange, freakish trio. John Henry runs the gamut from a gender-fluid infant to a wise / crazy old man; Frankie is obsessed with being the third member of her brother's wedding.

Berenice is physically distinctive, having a brown, normal eye and a blue glass one. Frankie points out that the black woman is often out of her mind in her personal narratives, a comment very similar to one Mick Kelly makes about Portia. Berenice claims, for example, to be beautiful, though the white girl asserts that her eye, her dark skin, and her oily coils of hair disqualify her from anybody's sense of beauty. Significantly, the narrative does not reject the child's claim.

But there is a deeper sense in which race makes Berenice freakish. She has been married four times and the first relationship occurred when she was thirteen. This is the same age as Frankie at the end of the novel. There is no indication that she is ready for anything other than a normal, rather bland adolescence. The difference here is embedded in the racial history of the South. Slave girls were expected to be sexually active at as early an age as possible in order to return a profit in children for their master's investment in them. They were considered breeders to enhance wealth in black bodies. After emancipation and certainly into McCullers's lifetime, domestic servants were subject to sexual assault by their employers, with no recourse to the law. Such white male behavior came to be justified by a claim that black girls matured much earlier than white ones and became irresistible temptresses.[1]

The final point about Berenice is the superstitious nature of her marriage narratives. Her great love is Ludie Freeman, whose one physical flaw is a smashed thumb. When he dies, she is heartbroken until she sees another man with a similar thumb. She marries him, but the relationship fails. Then she meets a man wearing a coat that once belonged to Ludie, which she had sold to pay for his funeral. Not surprisingly, she marries him as well, again with no success. We are not told what part of Ludie she finds in the fourth husband, but he is the one who gouges out her eye. This series is a parody of the romantic convention of always looking for a replacement of the first, best love. That this perspective is assigned to a black woman suggests a belief in a level of magical thinking that was conventionally associated with African Americans.

What does this set of observations tell us about Carson McCullers? Certainly not that she was a virulent racist. After all, it is the same Berenice who talks about the special entrapment of blacks in the famous conversation about being caught and loose. And her representation of Doctor Copeland's views on race accurately captures a radical version of the philosophy which guided the civil rights movement. What it does indicate is an understanding that the dominant American racial ideology is in part premised on the assumption that blackness equals freakishness; after all, each of these characters offers some form of excess, whether it is speech, bitterness, or superstitious thinking. Black intelligence is a fraud; black manhood and womanhood are not to be taken seriously; and young black adulthood is inherently criminal. Carson McCullers, as a Southern white woman, would be especially conditioned by this ideology. That she could see through some of it is to her credit. But even those efforts are qualified by the power of white supremacist thinking. She, like all of us, is caught in the prison house of race.

*Notes*

¹ According to very recent research, this view of premature black female sexuality is still held by a majority of white Americans. See Epstein et al.

# WORKS CITED

Adams, Rachel. " 'A Mixture of Delicious and Freak': The Queer Fiction of Carson McCullers,"*American Literature,* vol. 71, no. 3, 1999, pp. 551-83.

Du Bois, W.E.B. "The Talented Tenth." *A W.E.B. Du Bois Reader.* Edited by Andrew G. Pashal, 1903, Macmillan, 1971, pp. 31-51.

Epstein, Rebecca, Jamilia J. Blake, and Thalia Gonzalez. "Girlhood Interrupted: The Erasure of Black Girls' Childhood." Georgetown Law Center on Poverty and Inequality, 2017. www.law.georgetown.edu/academics/centers-institutes/poverty-inequality/upload/girlhood-interrupted.

McCullers, Carson. *The Heart Is a Lonely Hunter* (1940) in *Complete Novels*. Edited by Carlos Dews, Library of America, 2001.

---. *The Member of the Wedding* (1946) in *Complete Novels*. Edited by Carlos Dews, Library of America, 2001.

Sontag, Susan. *Illness as Metaphor*. Farrar, Strauss, and Giroux, 1978.

# WHY AMAZON VERSUS BLOSSOMED BEAUTY? ON DIFFERENT FEMININITIES IN THE NOVELLAS OF CARSON MCCULLERS AND MO YAN

## Sun Danping

This essay compares the femininity of two heroines in Carson McCullers's *The Ballad of the Sad Café* (1951) and Chinese Nobel-Prize winner Mo Yan's *Folk Music* (1983). Under the influence of McCullers's novella, Mo develops a specific Chinese heroine in his imitative literary creation. Despite similarities related to plot and narrative in the two texts, different characterizations, especially the diverse femininities of the two heroines, are worth noticing and highly reflective of a more comprehensive socio-cultural context. This essay examines the underlying basis of these similarities and differences.

As one of the most famous contemporary Chinese writers, Mo Yan (1955, birth name Guan Moye) has attracted worldwide attention since his first collection *Explosions and Other Stories* was introduced to the United States in 1992. M. Thomas Inge made the prediction: "Mo Yan promises to step onto the larger stage of literature in the twenty-first century as a world-class author" in 2000 (501). It comes true twelve years later with Mo's winning the Nobel Prize in literature. This highest accolade, received by Mo stimulated academic research in China in a dramatic way as compared to Chinese interest in him in 1986. According to the China National Knowledge Infrastructure (CNKI)[1], the first decade of the new century witnessed an upsurge of academic publication on Mo Yan from an average of 430 per decade to 2,212. During the 2010s, this number soared to 7,486. Among these papers and articles, about one-third focus on the translation of his fiction, another one-third is concerned with his writing style such as hallucinatory realism, and no more than 30% is on thematic issues such as humanism and ideology. It is worth mentioning that Chinese scholars find many commonalities between Mo Yan and William Faulkner, on which the research amounts to 1.26%.

For reference, McCullers's studies in China emerged from the 1970s. According to the CNKI database, the first Chinese critical article on McCullers appeared in 1979 when her novella, *The Ballad of the Sad Café* (*Ballad*) was translated and introduced in China for the first time.[2] Since then, Chinese McCullers's studies started to take shape: from 1979 to 2016, 440 articles, 193 MA theses, and two doctoral dissertations on McCullers have been published.[3] Concerning issues in which Chinese scholars engage, Professor Lin Bin, in her thorough and in-depth review of Chinese McCullers studies, observes "What strikes Chinese readers most about McCullers's fictional work is her scathing representation of loneliness" (209). Nonetheless, research on other topics does exist, for instance, comparative studies between McCullers and other Chinese writers.[4]

It may seem dubious to parallel Mo Yan and Carson McCullers, whose life stories share no similarities. However, comparability does exist in their writing, most notably, in novellas. Mo once admitted his short story was inspired by *Ballad*: ". . . the story is mine, though, the intuition of language is under the other's influence. Since the intuition has been caught, the story itself could develop itself" (Yang 69).[5] This self-evolving story takes place in Masang, China near Gaomi, where the wineshop proprietress Jasmine accommodates and then falls in love with a blind man who specializes in playing traditional Chinese musical instruments and hence attracts more customers to the wineshop for amusement as well as purification of their souls. Respected and loved by people around him, the blind man nevertheless chooses to leave the town due to Jasmine's proposal. After being turned down, Jasmine runs after the blind young man to somewhere nobody knows. The story ends with the folk tune hummed by road builders resting beside the highway.

Similar plots and characterizations between this story and *Ballad* are easily noticed, especially the image of the two heroines: both own properties and run a profitable enterprise; both are divorced and fall in love with physically challenged vagrants; both live a relatively untraditional life and hence catch the attention of the whole town. However, these two women present different femininities despite the similarities.

## 1. How Different?

Due to the disputable concept of "femininity", it is necessary to make a brief review of its definition which goes through several stages with different denotations and connotations. *The American Heritage Dictionary* (1982) defines "femininity" as "the quality or condition of being feminine; womanliness", while "feminine" as "of or belonging to the female sex" ("Femininity"). According to this definition, female sexuality is the decisive factor for the formation of femininity. Since Simone de Beauvoir's declaration that "One is not born, but becomes a woman" (267) which "clarifies its physiological nature and social / cultural features. . . " (Liu 91), the concept of "gender" is of primal importance to understand what femininity connotes. In other words, it is a social and cultural embodiment rather than the anatomical structure that defines femininity. On the basis of a sociologist concept of gender which refers to "the structure of social relations that centres on the reproductive arena, and the set of practices that brings reproductive distinctions between bodies into social processes" (*Gender* 11), Raewyn Connell regards both masculinity and femininity as "processes of configuring practice through time, which transform their starting-points in gender structures" (*Masculinities* 72). According to Connell, femininity can be understood as a dynamic process during which one's personality and gender identity keep being molded and constructed under the impact of the discourse, ideology, culture, and institutions of the human society where one lives. In addition, its interaction with gender structure, in which relations of power, production, emotion and symbolic meanings between male and female, male and male, and female and female, must also be taken into consideration. Therefore, the heroines' different femininities this article intends to compare, not only refer to their personalities and gender identities, but also to the gender structure of the society in which they live.

As far as Amelia's femininity is concerned, the modifier "Amazon" is an expressive delineation not only for its denotation of appearance, but also its connotation of social and cultural features. At first, critics stress the explicit masculine traits of Amazons to interpret Amelia's femininity: Griffith compares Amelia to "an Amazonian queen" who is "strong and domineering" (48), while Millichap addresses Amelia directly as "The big-muscled Amazon" (333). Then the word's implication of a specific type of gender identity that formed through interactions between sociocultural norms and individuality is foregrounded by other McCullers scholars. For example, Louise Westling interprets it as a type of "transgression of conventional sexual boundaries" which "brings catastrophic male retribution" ("Nightmare" 472), and later develops it into a representation of a grown-up tomboy "without any concessions to social demands for social conformity" (*Sacred* 119). According to Westling, Amelia's Amazonian androgyny is not only a courageous transgressive attitude toward taboos of sexuality, but also a brave practice against traditional gender roles assigned by the society, albeit doomed to futility. By contrast, Gleeson-White holds a more positive attitude toward Amelia's Amazonian femininity, of which she regards as "a carnivalesque process in which supposedly contradictory elements are juxtaposed in the one body, in the form of the double-voiced hybrid" (116). This form of hybridity, according to Gleeson-White, is more than the traditional concept of androgyny in which femininity and masculinity compound regardless of the sexual differences. Amelia's hybridity "defies the limits of the discretely gendered classical body to displace stable gender formation in terms of either / or" (117), the significance of Amelia's Amazonian femininity thus extends to identity. In sum, discussion on Amelia's femininity is based on physical, social, cultural and psychological issues relevant to her ambiguous sexuality, as a deconstructing force which heterosexual binary critics may dispute though, its rebellious and subversive stance is mostly affirmed.

In contrast with the zeal for Amelia's ambiguous femininity, Jasmine's femininity in Mo's *Folk Music* has not raised much concern in academia. To date four papers discuss this issue from different aspects: Zhang Changcheng criticizes Mo's neglect of the female character's subject and desire, and argues that Jasmine is delineated as a meaningless signifier of traditional patriarchy and hence has been blurred into a background against which the versatile blind young man's selfless pursuit for the promotion of folk music and folk culture is underlined.[6] On the contrary, Wang Yusong reaches the opposite conclusion after a general review of the cultural context of the 1980s when this novella was created. Wang praises Mo's characterization of the suburban woman Jasmine, who courageously faces life and pursues her love with awakened subjectivity.[7] While the previous two articles center on female gender practice in social discourse, Zhang Yitian, in comparing images of Amelia and Jasmine, stresses Jasmine's gender identity and believes she identifies with her feminine physiological features, and presents her sexual appeal with no reluctance.[8] Shi Ying's chronological study of women's images considers important female characters in Mo's main works, among which Jasmine is also analyzed as an innocent and benevolent pure-love pursuer.[9] Similar to Wang's conclusion, Shi also emphasizes the character's relatively assertive attitude toward life in the personal layer of their gender practice configuration. Studies of Jasmine's femininity focus more on her heightened awareness in leading her own life as an autonomous woman. However, her prominent feminine feature and appearance are not so unconventional as Amelia's ambiguity.

In general, discussion of Amelia's femininity covers almost every aspect of gender, among which gender relation and gender structure, i.e., the social and cultural construction of her gender identity, and her masculinized gender identity, provokes the greatest attention. Studies of Jasmine's femininity, to some extent, converge to the evaluation of her personal gender practice, especially when embodied in the dimension of emotional relations. Since different research objectives can reflect different significances of the text, how differed significances have been brought by the author, i.e., what makes these two authors create such similar but also different figures in their works is intriguing.

## 2. Why Different?

To figure out the contributing causes of the artist's creation, an investigation of the artist's personal life, and the historical and cultural context of the work is indispensable. This article intends to answer the question of why different femininities are embodied in Amelia and Jasmine from three aspects: the author's relevant personal experience, the author's living environment, and the author's special reading experience in their creation.

## Influence of Personal Life

As Thomas Wolfe states, ". . . all serious creative work must be at bottom autobiographical, and that a man must use the material and experience of his own life if he is to create anything that has substantial value" (14). For McCullers and Mo Yan, their experience of life becomes a rich source for their creative process of *Ballad*, as recorded by the biographer Virginia Spencer Carr, has been greatly influenced by her own life: "The situation that Carson was fantasizing daily at her typewriter, *The Ballad of the Sad Café*, which she told David Diamond was for him, was reminiscent of her own experience" (171). McCullers, like Amelia, was trapped in a love triangle with David Diamond and her husband Reeves when she conceived of the story. Furthermore, her androgynous sexuality is regarded as a cause for Amelia's ambiguous femininity. Lynne Greeley noticed that "In addition to the cultural context of her writing, McCullers's own body became a literal expression of her sexual ambiguities" (157). Whether a lesbian or not, McCullers's own disputable gender identity is regarded as one of the decisive reasons for complex and labyrinthine characters in her work as far as gender relation is concerned.

McCullers's personal attitude towards Southern patriarchal doctrines is regarded as another reason for her creation of masculine women and feminine men in her stories. The behavioral norm of "The Southern Lady", for example, was rebelled against by McCullers in her personal gender practice of dressing. Anaïs Nin, in her journal of 1943, recalls her first impression of McCullers: "I saw a girl so tall and so lanky I first thought it was a boy. Her hair was short, she wore a cyclist's cap, tennis shoes, pants" (270). Nin's observation of McCullers's taste for dressing "highlights Carson's attire as a way of remaining adolescent, of refusing to join the ranks of women rather than a provocative display of sexual preference" (Savigneau 73). It is obvious that McCullers is a determined grown "tomboy" who disdains and mocks doctrines for "The Southern Lady" as being fragile, virtuous, obedient, beautiful, and hence "feminine". Her scorn has been well exemplified in female characters like Miss Amelia, who wears her hair like a man, dresses like a man, and even her bones and muscles resemble a man. In addition, it is also noted that McCullers's career ambitions are embodied in Amelia's success in making money which, according to Westling, "are the psychological equivalents for the physical assertiveness of the tomboy, and again the requirements of submissiveness and restraint for the Southern lady have traditionally discouraged the pursuit of professional, artistic, or political goals" ("Tomboy" 157). McCullers's satire and disapproval of the traditional image of "The Southern Lady" is hence represented both in female characters' physical and psychological features. In conclusion, Carson McCullers's own ambiguous sexuality and disagreement with the gender structure in Southern society help the cultivation of Amelia's masculine femininity to a great extent.

Like McCullers, Mo Yan's own life is also resourceful and inspiring for his composition. He once quoted Wolfe's statement in his essay "Transcending Hometown" and emphasized the dialectic relationship between his own experience and his literary creation (11). Mo believes that stories must be constructed on the author's personal experience, particularly his / her emotional experience. His characterization of female images is highly relevant to his own emotional attachment to women in his life.

Mo's mother, as is depicted figuratively in his novels and literally in his memoirs, set a role model for all women when he was very young that affected his attitude toward women throughout his life. His respect and love for his mother stems not only from a son's sense of thankfulness and obligation, but also from a man's esteem and sympathy for a woman who maintains virtues of traditional Chinese femininity. After recalling a great many of his mother's sufferings and sacrifices in detail to explain his creative motive for the famous *Big Breasts and Full Hips*, Mo attributes it to his mother and all mothers in China with grief: "Women of the same generation with my mother, are regarded as both the tool of reproduction and the labor of material resources production; as both the servant of parent-in-law and the appendage of her husband. Nevertheless, mothers made all the sacrifice, willingly" (32). It is hence safe to infer his stance as a eulogist for women as he declares: "I have no reason to refrain my compliments of women, because they could be our grandma, mother, wife, lover, daughter and bosom friend. Actually I can still make them represented in a better way. It's a pity for me" (9).

In spite of the humble statements above, Mo's consideration of a contemporary woman's living situation is still remarkably reflective in his work, as in the case of Jasmine's story. Mo has confessed and blamed himself for his biased view of divorced woman in an interview:

> It demonstrates that though I was young then, the feudal ideology has been solidly constructed in my mind. According to the traditional standards of value, only incompetent men would marry divorced women. This discrimination against women, especially against divorced women, as well as other influences of the feudal culture, still exist in my hometown, and will not disappear even after a decade. (Mo and Wang 47)

Under such circumstances, the great risk it needs to take and the price it needs to pay for Jasmine, in Mo's *Folk Music*, which is written 21 years before this interview, in order to initiate the divorce with her handsome and powerful bureaucrat ex-husband is not beyond comprehension. Besides, the reason Jasmine gives for the divorce is such a striking contrast with the pressure she faces in the future: "It was said the only reason for Jasmine's wanting a divorce was her husband's having 'loved her as if she were a court lady and he an emperor'. This was far too baffling for the townspeople" (44). Nevertheless, she did it and then displayed her love for a blind man. Therefore, the progressiveness of Jasmine's image appears even more precious in her subjective, courageous, unconventional and righteous views of life. It is apparent that Mo's own respect and sympathy for women have been well exemplified through Jasmine's pursuit of equal power with man in gender relations.

In conclusion, McCullers's own gender identity and attitudes towards traditional patriarchal doctrines of women facilitates the formation of her literary creation of female masculine femininity as in Amelia's case. Similarly, Mo's experience in his life, i.e., his love, respect and sympathy for women, is also embodied in the female characters in his stories. Both Amelia's masculine femininity and Jasmine's unconventional femininity bear great significance and progressiveness considering the social and cultural context embedded in which the two authors still broke confinement of conventional patriarchal ideology and made implicitly and explicitly their rebellious gestures against discriminations in gender structure.

**Causality of the Social and Cultural Context**

As femininity is cultivated and transformed in the structure of society and the configuration of gender relations, the social and cultural context in which fictional figures are created is by no means far-fetched; on the contrary, its causal effect is remarkable and significant.

In 1941, McCullers worked on *Ballad* as well as *The Bride and Her Brother* (later entitled, *The Member of the Wedding*) from June to August, when she visited Yaddo Artists' Colony in Saratoga Springs. On June 22, the European Axis powers launched an invasion of the Soviet Union, which opened the largest land theatre of World War II. 1941 witnessed the introduction of conscription for women and the end of marriage bar—a policy that prevented married women from being employed in white-collar occupations. Under such circumstances, numerous women joined the workforce. Michelle Abate points out: "Whereas the Depression era had insisted that a woman's place was as a feminine wife and mother in the home, the war years asserted that during this time of national crisis she served best as a tomboyish worker in a factory" (145). Those tomboyish workers have been embodied in the tough image of Rosie the Riveter, an icon for women who lived during the war time. Showing her muscular arm and fierce look, Rosie's masculine features are highlighted as in Amelia's case. While working on *Ballad*, McCullers also wrote an essay to express her stand and attitude toward the war: "And we Americans will fight to preserve it [democracy]. We have clenched our giant fist; it will not open until we are victorious" ("Banners" 230). It is safe to infer that the masculinized Amazon-like Amelia embodies both McCullers's determined will against the war and the call of the country; women must be strong enough to make themselves qualified warriors and soldiers while facing fascist invasion.

Similar to the effect of temporal context, Amelia's femininity is also under the influence of spatial context—McCullers's cultural inheritance of the Deep South. While comparing three Southern writers—Eudora Welty, Carson McCullers, and Flannery O'Connor, Westling remarks: "Despite obvious differences, all three of these writers share preoccupations with feminine identity which are shaped by the traditional Southern veneration of the lady" (5) on whom the previous section discusses as "The Southern Lady". The old image of femininity put too much burden on Southern women writers like McCullers in that they "inherited an acute consciousness of what they could not be, of how the past had jilted their mothers and grandmothers. They would take the more difficult next step to discover who they were" (37). The social and cultural context of the Deep South, especially considering ideologies of gender, partially contributes to McCullers's personal and fictional disdain and satire of the Southern lady's femininity and the unconventional practice and experimental creation of a more masculine femininity both in her life and works.

Although Mo Yan was born almost four decades later than McCullers, the social and political situation he faces is by no means less complicated or less stressful. China witnessed a severe famine from 1959 to 1961 when Mo was a little boy, followed by the ten-year turbulence of the "Cultural Revolution" of 1966. Struggling with hunger for food throughout his childhood, Mo also experienced a hunger for books as a youngster. Due to the poverty and ideological control, novels and books to read were a luxury. For a poor peasant boy living in a village, Mo could only find stories of "The Red Classics" (including "revolutionary model operas" and in works reflecting political campaigns and the daily life of the alliance of worker / peasant / soldier / classes under the guidance of the Communist Party of China) or "The Seventeen-year Literature" (referring to literary works created from 1949 to 1966, between the founding of the People's Republic of China and the Cultural Revolution), which distinguished the specific political aims of class struggle and highly stylized images and plot development. While talking about the influence of "The Red Classics" on Chinese literature in the 1980s, Mo comments:

> I personally believe this is a backwash of 'The Red Classics' that once occupied the dominant position of literary discourse in China. Writers realized it is of course not valueless, but it is problematic at the same time. . . . The creative environment in the 1980s allows us to observe and write about people from a more unconventional point of view. We are permitted to treat and delineate the enemy from exploiting classes as human beings. (Mo and Wang 50)

The humane treatment and characterization of the "enemy" is no doubt a practice of ideological emancipation for Chinese writers. Everything humane can be openly taken into consideration in their writings, including the sentimental and romantic love affairs which used to be criticized as "Petty-bourgeois sentiments" in the previous decades. Therefore, as early as 1981 when Mo presented a free spirit like Jasmine, he quickly gained praise from critics and other famous writers. His work answers the call of time.

Mo's inheritance of local culture also helped him form his characterization of Jasmine. He was born in Shandong, the hometown of Confucius and many chivalrous outlaw heroes in Chinese history. People in Shandong are known for their protocol-consciousness and sense of righteousness. Women brought up in such a culture share common traits such as high self-esteem, frankness, and unstrained boldness. It is among such women that Mo led his life in his young age. Even images of women, in his favorite traditional Chinese literary works, are created by an ancient Shandong writer named Pu Songling, a superb master in the mystery novel. Mo recalls that, "among all those unforgettable women images in literature, I prefer . . . those vixenish ghosts in Pu's work. Some of them are fun-loving and smile often. Each has a unique, otherworldly, unassuming, and unstrained feature. Their purity is permeated with alluring enchantment as well" (158-59). Obviously, the bold, unpretentious, and straightforward personality embodied in women of his hometown, both in real life and in the literary world seem more beautiful and lovely to Mo. Jasmine, for instance, is delineated by Mo as a beautiful and enchanting woman: "Judging by her appearance, Jasmine was nothing more than a skittish, beautiful woman. Her slight squint added a liveliness to her expression, and her charming, moist lips were extremely inviting . . ." (44); "Even her smiles had given one the shivers." (51) Nevertheless, Mo endowed her with Shandong women's common traits: "A pretty woman like Jasmine, bold and independent, would sometimes make decisions that shocked even herself, not to mention strangers. Her divorce from her ex-husband was an example." (51) The influence of local culture and regional personalities of Mo's hometown is apparently reflected from his characterization of Jasmine's femininity.

As discussed above, there is evidence of a causal relationship between the temporal / spatial context and works of McCullers and Mo Yan, specifically the background of world war and patriarchal doctrines of the Southern town from which stems the Amazon Amelia in McCullers's *Ballad*. The emancipating creative environment of 1980 in China, after the ideological control of the Cultural Revolution and the traditional culture of the "hometown of Confucius", especially its cultivation of Shandong women's personality, produces female images like Jasmine, the free spirit who pursues love with no consideration of conventional values. How then can writers accomplish their mission of serving the needs of the time? The voice of readers should not be neglected.

**The Effect of the Author's Reading Experience**

As for the reader's impact on literary creation, H. R. Jauss declares: "In the triangle of author, work, and public, the last is no passive part, no chain of mere reactions, but rather itself an energy formative of history. The historical life of a literary work is unthinkable without the active participation of its addressees" (19). Jauss's assertion of the reader's active participation in the reading procedure as well as the creating procedure is enlightening for this study's comparison between McCullers and Mo Yan.

McCullers pays great attention to the reader's response. Her biographer, Carr, recorded her reaction towards a fan's blame for her mocking of a Jew in *Ballad* in an anonymous letter: "Instead, her whole being was thrown out of kilter. She wrote many frantic letters seeking advice" (237). Though it is obvious that the fan's accusation of McCullers is, in fact, too incredulous for her to be indifferent, her unsettledness is convincing enough to show her concern for the reader's reaction and response. Correspondingly, her literary creation can never take place in a vacuum of the artist's imagination regardless of her contemporary readers' voices.

It is worth noting that McCullers herself was a voracious reader whose experience of reading was "predominantly masculine" (Westling, *Sacred* 56). The problem of this masculine reading experience is, as Virginia Woolf put it: "It is strange to think that all the great women of fiction were . . . not only seen by the other sex but seen only in relation to the other sex. And how small a part of a woman's life is that" (89). Female readers would no doubt keep imagining and trespassing the gender boundary in the masculine fictional world with curiosity. As both reader and writer, McCullers must have recognized the function of a literary work which:

> awakens memories of that which was already read, brings the reader to a specific emotional attitude, and with its beginning arouses expectations for the 'middle and end,' which can then be maintained intact or altered, reoriented, or even fulfilled ironically in the course of the reading according to specific rules of the genre or type of text. (Jauss 23)

With such prescriptions, it is not impossible for McCullers to expose her readers (especially female readers) with woman's androgynous identity to obtain power in the fictional discourse during her composition of *Ballad*, as far as Amelia's femininity is concerned.

As McCullers comments in one essay, the impact of readers and critics should be dealt with in an artist's own aesthetic standards and judgement in the final stage of creation:

> Unfortunately, it must be recognized that the artist is threatened by multiple pressures in the commercial world of publishers, producers, editors of magazines. . . . The professional writer may accede to these demands and concentrate on the ball and the bleachers. But once a creative writer is convinced of his own intentions, he must protect his work from alien persuasion. ("Vision" 269)

The reader's expectation, therefore, exerts a relatively dynamic influence on McCullers's literary creation. On issues she is convinced are significant, for example the androgynous gender identity, McCullers adheres to her aesthetic standards and creative philosophy with little consideration of the reader's criticism and skepticism.

Mo's special consideration of readership, as in the case of McCullers, derives from his sense of responsibility as a writer:

> It was the early 1980s, the so-called 'golden age of contemporary Chinese literature'. An enthusiastic readership inspired writers to become passionate about literature. People were no longer content to create or read stories written in traditional styles. Readers demanded that we be more creative, and we dreamed of nothing but becoming more inventive. ("My 3 American Books" 473)

Mo, in fact, does make strenuous efforts to become more inventive and creative, not only with respect to the art of writing but also to the ideological connotation of the work. While commenting on the impact of "The Seventeen Year Literature", Mo confesses his experiences as a reader—clearly remembers every detail of love stories but almost forgets all the other parts. He then ascribes this to authors of these works:

> writers just strive for elaborating the Party leader's ideologies. However, when they are describing love with really limited length, they can put the work of elaboration aside. Only these chapters and parts can reflect writers' remaining personalities in fact. ("Seventeen" 37)

Mo's reading experience enables him to recognize the importance of the author's unique, independent, and profound reflections on common issues of all human beings, which has also been well practiced in his own literary creation.

Take Jasmine as an example. While depicting a young and beautiful widow who enjoys a rich and influential life in the prosperously expanding town, Mo also highlights her daringness in giving up her seemingly perfect marriage, living her life by herself and rebuffing a vagabond who intends to take liberties. Additionally, her hardworking spirit and smartness in business have not been weakened or blurred. Such an attractive personality as Jasmine is hence fully shown in the novella, with Mo's unique observation of women, which may relieve his sense of pity in "The Seventeen Year Literature" authors' repressed expression and lack of uniqueness. Furthermore, Jasmine's unconventional love story echoes Mo's own reading experience. Those unforgettable and lingering memories and sentiments of a reader still drive him to develop his own imagination and creativity as a writer.

It is also noted that Mo Yan's description of women, especially in his long novels, is positive, affective, and representative enough to draw critical attention. There was an academic conference held in 2014 that focused on "Mo's Literary Creation in the View of Woman's Culture" in China, and some 60 scholars contributed their ideas and comments respectively delineating Mo's female imagery, his awareness of gender in writing, and his construction of woman's culture. It should also be stressed that Mo's creation of female imagery goes through different stages. *Folk Music* was finished years before his writing matured (as seen in *The Transparent Carrot* published in 1985), when he drew inspiration from his personal life stories and reading experiences. The impact of reader's response and expectation in Mo's literary creation is therefore worth considering.

Both McCullers and Mo Yan wove their experiences as readers into their works. McCullers responds to her reading experience as a woman in the Southern patriarchal culture and the masculine literary tradition, constructing her female characters with masculine femininity to rebel against the traditional women images in the Deep South and to assert her own influence as a writer. Mo Yan's treatment of his reading experience is reminiscent of his own enjoyable memories of beautiful and lovely women. He endeavors to be more inventive not only in style but also in themes. Female characters like Jasmine in Mo's works are described as beautiful and charming, as well as unconventional and independent.

After a comparison of the different heroine's femininity in *Ballad* and in *Folk Music*, considering both authors' personal life, social and cultural context, and their response to the reader's expectation, this study hopes to answer the question of "why different?" on the basis of the comparability between these two novellas. What makes the finding of this research interesting, despite these different causes and influencing factors, are the many similarities that have been found between these two writers with different backgrounds. Both writers show their strong sense of locale; both rely on imagination in their literary creation and both express concern for the defectiveness of human beings, physical or mental. This comparative study of Mo's imitation of McCullers's renowned novella seems to show their similar aesthetic standards and creative norms. This has led to a resonant dialogue which aims to communicate, rather than compete, between two different cultures in two different eras.

*Notes*

¹ CNKI (China National Knowledge Infrastructure) is the largest and most used academic online library in China. The data was collected at the library database of Guangdong University of Foreign Studies, on May 28, 2017.

² *The Ballad of the Sad Café* is included in the book *Collection of Contemporary American Short Stories* 《当代美国短篇小说集》, translated by Li Wenjun (李文俊, and published in 1979.

³ The data was collected at the library database of Guangdong University of Foreign Studies, on November 10, 2016.

⁴ In my essay entitled "From 'Seeking Similarities' to 'Reserving Differences': A Review of Comparative Study between Carson McCullers and Chinese Writers" (2017), a general trend of the comparative study between Carson McCullers and Chinese writers is foregrounded. In comparing Eileen Chang and McCullers, scholars stress their similarities from many different aspects. Studies of Su Tong and McCullers demonstrate certain common ground between their writings;. in comparing Mo Yan and McCullers, Mo's innovation is emphasized, while his imitation of McCullers's writing is also noted. This essay also advocates for more concern for the comparative study, especially when compared with its notable research significance and prospect.

⁵ Mo further explains his imitative creation in the early stage of his writing career in the same interview: "My writing went through several stages. Before enrolling in the People's Liberation Army Art Academy, most of my published novellas, probably a dozen, were imitative". See Yang Qingxiang, "Avant-garde, Folk and Underclass". All quotations from Chinese books and articles in this essay are translated by the author.

⁶ See Zhang, Changcheng. 《论莫言小说中的性别盲区》 ["The

Gender Blind Spot of Mo Yan's Fiction"]. 《厦门教育学院学报》 [*Journal of Xiamen Educational College*], vol. 1, 2003, pp. 39-41.

[7] See Wang, Yusong. 《莫言与麦卡勒斯——以小说<民间音乐>、<透明的红萝卜>和<伤心咖啡馆之歌>为中心》 ["Mo Yan and McCullers: Focusing on *Folk Music*, *The Transparent Carrot* and *The Ballad of the Sad Café*"]. 《世界文学评论》 [*World Literature Review*], vol. 2, 2014, pp. 73-76.

[8] See Zhang, Yitian. 《<民间音乐>与<伤心咖啡馆之歌>之比较》 ["Comparative Study on *Folk Music* and *The Ballad of the Sad Café*"]. 《文艺争鸣》 [*Literature and Art Forum*], vol. 2, 2016, pp. 140-143.

[9] See Shi, Ying. 《莫言小说中女性形象的嬗变》 ["On the Change of Women Images in Mo Yan's Novels"]. 《吉首大学学报》 [ *Journal of Jishou U* ], vol. 6, 2012, pp. 173-176.

# WORKS CITED

"Femininity." *The American Heritage Dictionary*. 2$^{nd}$ ed., 1982.

Abate, Michelle Ann. *Tomboys: A Literary and Cultural History*. Temple UP, 2008.

Carr, Virginia Spencer. *The Lonely Hunter: A Biography of Carson McCullers*. Doubleday & Company, 1975.

Connell, Raewyn. *Gender: In World Perspective*. 2nd ed., Polity Press, 2009.

---. *Masculinities*. 2nd ed., U of California Press, 2005. de Beauvoir, Simone. *The Second Sex*. Translated by H.M. Parshley, Vintage Books, 1989.

Gleeson-White, Sarah. *Strange Bodies: Gender and Identity in the Novels of Carson McCullers*. The University of Alabama Press, 2003.

Greeley, Lynne. "Carson McCullers: Young, Gifted, and Odd." *Theatre History Studies*, vol. 22, 2002, pp. 155-76.

Griffith, Albert J. "Carson McCullers' Myth of the Sad Café." *The Georgia Review*, vol. 1, 1967, pp. 46-56.

Inge, Thomas M. "Mo Yan: Through Western Eyes." *World Literature Today*, vol. 74, no. 3, 2000, pp. 501-06.

Jauss, H.R. *Toward an Aesthetic of Reception*. 7$^{th}$ ed., U of Minnesota P, 2005.

Lin, Bin. "Seeking the Meaning of Loneliness: Carson McCullers in China." *Carson McCullers in the Twenty-First Century*. Edited by Alison Graham-Bertolini and Casey Kayser, Palgrave Macmillan, 2016.

Liu, Yan. 《西方文论关键词：第二性》["The Second Sex: A Keyword in Critical Theory"].外国文学》 [*Foreign Literature*] 4, 2016, pp. 88-99.

McCullers, Carson. "The Vision Shared." *The Mortgaged Heart*. Penguin Books, 2008, pp. 268-71.

---. "We Carried Our Banner—We Were Pacifists, Too." *The Mortgaged Heart*. Penguin Books, 2008, pp. 227-32.

Millichap, Joseph R. "Carson McCullers' Literary Ballad." *The Georgia Review,* vol. 3, 1973, pp. 329-339.

Mo, Yan. "Folk Music." *Chinese Literature,* spring 1988, pp.41-59.

---. "My 3 American Books." Translated by Sylvia Li-chun Lin. *World Literature Today*, vol. 74, no. 3, 2000, pp. 472-6.

---.《我看十七年文学》["My Views On 'The Seventeen Year Literature'"]. 《莫言研究资料》[*Research Materials on Mo Yan*]. Edited by Yang Yang, Tianjin,, Tianjin People's Publishing House, 2005.

---.《丰乳肥臀解》["Notes on *Big Breasts and Full Hips*"].《莫言研究资料》[ *Mo Yan: Research Materials*]. Edited by Kong Fanjin and Shi Zhanjun, Jinan, Shandong Publishing House of Literature and Art, 2006, pp. 30-35.

---. Preface.《红高粱》 [*Red Sorghum*]. Beijing, People's Literature Publishing House, 2007, pp.1-11.

---.《超越故乡》["Transcending Hometown"].《莫言散文新编 [*A New Compilation of Mo Yan's Essays*]. Beijing, Culture and Art Publishing House, 2009, pp. 1-20.

---.《什么气味最美好？》[*What Smells Best?*]. Haikou, Nanhai Publishing Co, 2002.

Mo, Yan and Wang Yao.《从<红高粱>到<檀香刑>》 ["From *Red Sorghum* to *Death by Sandalwood*"].《莫言研究资料》[*Mo Yan: Research Materials*]. Edited by Kong Fanjin and Shi Zhanjun, Jinan, Shandong Publishing House of Literature and Art, 2006, pp.44-63.

Nin, Anaïs. *The Dairy of Anaïs Nin: 1939-1944*. Harcourt, Brace & World, 1969.

Savigneau, Josyane. *Carson McCullers: A Life*. Translated by E. Howard. Boston, Houghton Mifflin, 2001.

Westling, Louise. "Carson McCullers' Amazon Nightmare." *Modern Fiction Studies,* vol. *28,* no. 3, 1982, pp. 465-73.

---. *Sacred Groves and Ravaged Gardens: The Fiction of Eudora Welty, Carson McCullers, and Flannery O'Connor*. U of Georgia P, 1985.

---. "Tomboys and Revolting Femininity." *Critical Essays on Carson McCullers*. Edited by Beverly Lyon Clark and Melvin J. Friedman, G.K. Hall and Co., 1996. pp. 155-65.

Wolfe, Thomas. "The Story of a Novel." *Saturday Review of Literature* 14 Dec.1935: 3+. Web. 20 Jun. 2017. <www.unz.org/Pub/SaturdayRev-1935dec14>.

Woolf, Virginia. *A Room of One's Own*. Grafton, 1977.

Yang, Qingxiang. 《先锋·民间·底层》["Avant-garde, Folk and Underclass"]. 《南方文化论坛》[*Southern Cultural Forum*], vol. 2, 2007, pp. 68-73.

# WHAT SHOULD BE—MCCULLERS CRAFT OF LONGING IN *THE BALLAD OF THE SAD CAFÉ*

## Laura Virginia Gray

The unique way Carson McCullers crafts a collective narrative in *The Ballad of the Sad Café* both emphasizes and includes readers in the deep sense of loneliness made manifest in this work. She makes society complicit in the division and barriers to intimacy. While some important work focuses on determinations of the narration, ultimately, a reading of the novella does not detract (for me) from the narration in relation to the chain gang specifically or more generally, even from labeling the narration into specific parts or voices. Poet-scholar, Edward Hirsch, notes that American work songs, and as further examination, the chain gang songs, are tied to this novella while Darren Millar examines the call and response patterns within the form and structure.

In the article, "And Every Day There Is Music: Folksong Roots and the Highway Chain Gang in *The Ballad of the Sad Café*," Daniel Patrick Barlow explores how the use of musicality is closely tied to that of a ballad in this work. While there is debate about the chain gang as the defining narrative device, this exploration informs the call and response patterns. In the careful attention to and division of the narration into what she defines as two distinct voices, Mary Ann Dazey offers a close reading of the grammar, form and design within McCullers's work. Barlow sees the chain gang as being bound to each other, so symbolically, this liberates the story from mundane work in song to historical hyperbole and an allegorical tale. If we examine, beyond the boldly grotesque and Gothically-exaggerated characterizations, McCullers builds a subtle and complex narrative frame that looms as large and as invisibly unimportant (so as to be overlooked?) as Miss Amelia's home, in the very center of things. This consideration shifts our understanding from the applaudable technical virtuoso toward a more complicated telling form that extends from the page and includes the reader as a culpable participant. The story can be understood from the point of view of outsiders imagining life beyond their own entrapments, and this includes each reader who becomes an onlooker on the story's pages. I will examine McCullers's narrative technique in terms of our inclusion both within and without the plot structure in *The Ballad of the Sad Café*, namely its effects and demands on the reader.

To demonstrate the subtleties of McCullers's approach, I will show how form and this narrative approach might correlate. There is not much in our human experience that can feel more isolating or lonesome than being studied, summed up and made sense of by others rather than being joined, listened to, accepted, and understood. Intimacy admits another into revelation in a surprising moment or honest turn, and reveals the complexities, strengths, and vulnerabilities within. This state of being with another is a unifying state of immediacy. It is closeness in the metaphysical space that leaves neither time nor distance to stand apart and reason separately about or to make of one the "other." Without removing oneself into interior headspace to search for causes within one's own reasons and experiences, without dividing a moment of revelation to further include and imagine oneself as the experiencer, intimacy is a state of being with another in acceptance as another shares with you. The other person is allowed opportunities to break preconceived patterns to be or do or have experiences and realizations in that union that are outside the onlooker's expectations.

The spiritual state of wholeness is sacred and in becoming whole, each of us is often surprised when we evolve into behaviors that mark maturation and growth. One cannot be both intimate, experiencing revelation of another, and apart, studying him / her, at the same time. One is either present and listening, or to varying degrees, is mentally removing himself / herself to think and judge the other. The problem with the temporal mind in much of McCullers's work becomes a theme, but, in particular McCullers's *Ballad* places readers directly in contact with an experience of these two states of being that do not and cannot occur at the same time. It is these varying degrees of distance created within relationships that McCullers captures so well in her work. It is human nature to reason and judge others—and try to understand why they might do what they do. But, unchecked, this pinning down power of the mind creates a damning divisive dynamic of observer and observed that can lead to a-partness. (I am interested in the division here not so much thematically, but especially in terms of the shifts in narrative perspective, though formally, there is much mirroring between form and idea in this story.) These shifts create much of the tension in the rising action that resounds within readers long after denouement because we become as guilty as the onlookers in town, as guilty as Cousin Lymon and Marvin Macy, as they reject and abandon Miss Amelia, and guilty in our own responses to make sense of why these characters do as they do. It is this complicated use of the technique that distinguishes McCullers from other Southern writers of her time.

In *"The Ballad of the Sad Café,"* the collective and limited-omniscient narrative distance demonstrates how separations can occur within a community and within intimate relationships. Not only Miss Amelia, but the whole town suffers, what it ultimately means to part ways from another. McCullers comes to conclusions she's found before: what can we truly know and share with others? The genius of this work is that it highlights the ways human nature divides based on differences, and in 1943 when her story first appeared in *Harper's Bazaar*, shows the inequalities we create via externalizing roles and expectations assigned to gender, race, physicality and status that remain important considerations today. The *Ballad* shows that no one is immune from meanness of judgment, and much awareness is required to see the many ways we stand apart from one another, so that we may overcome "othering" our neighbors. Within the first four paragraphs of the story, we have been told the beginning and end of the café, and the central players involved, so we trust we will be guided by what we need to know in any actions as the story unfolds. Throughout the narration, McCullers blends kinds of knowledge and the ways this knowledge can be obtained. The narration reasons at general and particular affairs of the heart: what happens to the hearts of orphan children (28) and what happened to the hearts of the specific orphaned Marvin and Henry Macy (29). Some of this information is worldly; some, provincial. Since some information is speculative, and some, delivered like gossip, we cannot be sure of its source or veracity. Some comes from deepest compassion for the situations the characters are in. Some information would be known both to citizens outside the café and some only to those insiders in the mill town, closest to the real answers.

One of the most profound things that McCullers's narrative technique does is to place readers within the open spaces left within the narration itself. For example, when Cousin Lymon arrives in the town at midnight, he is quickly accepted by Amelia. The narration moves in time between what is occurring in the story with the hunchback's arrival to the narrative telling details of Amelia's life: "Miss Amelia listened with her head turned slightly aside. She ate Sunday dinners by herself; her place was never crowded with a flock of relatives, and she claimed kin with no one (7)." McCullers creates a scene with a character that we are primed to assume will NOT accept Lymon for all her solitary and odd ways. There is a slight exception in her studying him, a pause, and then, the narration follows with details that she *might* be lonely. But further, we, as readers, are forced to reason *why* she might be making this choice. It is subtle but notable in her craft. Millar, examining the affect within the characters, concludes that to McCullers, love represents social hope, and even in the tragedy of unrequited love, a vision of a progressive utopian society is made possible by its opposite. But it is in the failings of Miss Amelia, Cousin Lymon, and even Marvin Macy, and in the ways the world does not or has not yielded to them as noted by Sarah Gleeson-White, in *Strange Bodies*, physical deformities become manifestations of the characters' limitations and markers.

To better understand the narrative distances, we must examine where we begin to enter this text. Millar states: "As a form, affect cannot be qualified; it makes the difference between the blur of Miss Amelia's becoming and the particular event of Miss Amelia falling in love with a dwarf." I would say that also in the blur is McCullers's beauty where her narrative crafting of loneliness occurs. The uncertainty McCullers creates is on whom the responsibility of the failing of any union lies. Some culpability rests within the gaps in narration and thus, on us, the onlookers, because the weight of the dissolutions sits like a heavy deformity by the story's end. For all the possible prejudices, divisions and learned judgments against differences, it is not clear that an individual like Miss Amelia, whom readers are led in the general narrative descriptions to imagine, could very easily by experience and nature have internalized judgments around her so that love, affirmation, and finally a happy union, do not succeed, but Miss Amelia does not seem so inclined in her actions, and this defiance, causes the reader to wonder. The narration does not enter her space, and we, as readers, can see her fierce struggle for love and continuance of her life with Cousin Lymon and the café, which builds tension.

In order to make sense of this union, we, as readers, become complicit in the same acts that become a distancing stance within the community McCullers deftly shines light upon, ultimately warning of the grave dangers in doing this. The fault of distancing leaves the town without the café, and it becomes "dreary" and yet the story seems to suggest a fatalistic worldview that there is nothing else that can be done. It leaves us without a happy ending. Millar says: "These lyrics are meant to alleviate the atmosphere of suffocating boredom that frames *The Ballad* proper by suggesting that one 'might as well' go listen to the singing of the chain gang at work on the Fork Falls highway just outside of town." There is a vast distance in the intimacy and interior sharing that we are set up to hope for. For all the boredom, the narration repeatedly suggests that studying others and situations might be an easy and natural pastime. As we read *The Ballad of the Sad Café*, it requires the same act as if we were a part of the community, watching others' lives unfold outside our own. As readers encountering the enigmas within the plotting, we try to fill in the narrative gaps, so that in trying to get closer to understanding, we are as guilty as the townsfolk in making our own separations from what really might go on in the hearts and minds of Miss Amelia, Cousin Lymon, and Marvin Macy. We thus follow a kind of narrative call and response pattern as we read in that there are suggestions to which we form generalizations in or about love, small towns, the South, ugliness and companionship.

Meaning occurs in relation to specific behaviors or words. It is McCullers's narrative technique that precludes any state of redemption and connection, keeping it from possibility because of the ways the characters are viewed by others, but also because of the ways we imagine they might conceive of the world and themselves in their interior lives. McCullers builds more questions into the plotting than are answered through the action. With only a light framing usually found by creating a natural progression of events that develop or reveal characters' weaknesses, Miss Amelia appears *in medias res*, and outside of the routine we are given. Her choices make little sense regarding Cousin Lymon and Marvin Macy. In other words, the plotting is purposefully inexplicable. If it is not completely unclear on all counts, it is at least murky as to why Miss Amelia takes in Cousin Lymon, treats him with such care and affection, opens the café outside of a goal of money, and turns away Marvin Macy, her attractive and devoted husband of ten days or fights him in the end. The reasons are vague as to why Cousin Lymon follows Macy around after such ill treatment by him. We are left to wonder what is in it for Lymon and just what is it they might be doing those long hours in the secrecy of the swamp that would pull him away from the luxury and good treatment he has received from Miss Amelia? It is not a given that Macy would even return to the town with such hostility. Aside from our own speculation as readers, which at times, puts us in the most prurient of places from which to make these claims—for example, just how much physical intimacy transpires between Amelia and Lymon. How close did her wedding come to being consummated? McCullers makes use of the unknowns of the bedroom, and the fact that the house has rooms on the second floor means that spying eyes cannot look in to know. We, like townspeople, can only guess.

McCullers points to physical onlooking as a way of knowing. Readers are left to wonder what occurs between Lymon and Macy, are left to guess important happenings or rely on guessing or gossip. McCullers's gaps in the plotting enables intimacies and exchanges to occur off the page. Humanity is not self-focused and selfish as the narration suggests and shows that human nature can be dangerous for anyone vulnerable or disadvantaged. The way we make sense of the fight with Miss Amelia at the end of the novella is through generalizations about her lack of decorum and attention to the rules for being a proper lady and perhaps to assume something transpired that was abhorrent to her with Macy or deeply safe and connective with Lymon.

The wisdom of the narrative voice goes beyond the mill town and its particulars, and into generalizations about the heart and world. Whereas parts of the narration, a ballad maker and a lamenter of the tale, follow a kind of call and response, I conclude that rather than these superficial forms, McCullers makes a kind of collective mind to tell this story that knows the things a townsperson would know (and is limited by what might be seen or not seen through private spaces) and that knows human nature and invites us to join there. The generalizations and the particulars that she defines in two distinctive parts could also be understood as holistic poetic tools used in both song and in lyricism to create tension and interest, and while they mimic symbolically the call and response of the chain gang or work-music, the narration sometimes seems to operate in this divided way, as the story itself notes when there is a question within the text like "What sort of thing then, is this love?" The narration then proceeds to answer. I assert this could also serve as a mimicry of conversation and interior study, and in that, a tool to suggest multiplicity that counters the plain, straightforward dimness pervading the setting, the monotony of the town prior to and after the café. Once Lymon leaves, there is no more conversation for Amelia, however disconnected that conversation was.

Dialogue is limited in this story. To ascertain motivations, readers must respond to the narrative calls. For example, when Miss Amelia shares with Lymon the significance of the acorn she values because she found it on the day her father dies, and his response is "What a peculiar reason to keep it (35)," we have to judge how he understands the import of this intimacy she is sharing with him, and how much she assigns to his response. His level of compassion to her, for all her care and consideration of him, seems to be lacking. He does not understand what it could mean, and he does not cross into accepting or appreciating her feelings. Since in the narrative technique in *The Ballad of the Sad Café,* McCullers makes much of speculating about the inward lives of her characters, this suggests that the problems of the human heart are not only created by externals such as racism, gender bias or other societal prejudices, but are also considerations, individually and apart. To also register distance and the sensory range of the narration, it can and does overhear intimate words, in a few rare instances like the one between Amelia and Lymon in front of the fire in their private upstairs parlor, but it cannot see any actions outside of them sitting in front of the parlor talking. It does show their intimacies as physical beyond one caring touch on Lymon's humped shoulder. The narrative technique is limited to what might be seen from outside the home or from outsiders, even as the home is an open store and café. In keeping with the historical time and societal rules of a Southern mill town, and Miss Amelia's status, the possibilities of physical intimacies with Cousin Lymon are not addressed outright but seem to be speculated about indirectly.

To make sense of the tragedy and lack of union at the end, the narration further complicates the points of view of internal and external forces. Miss Amelia, by her solitary nature, works hard. Her life is meted out in the commercial exchanges with the town, and this is softened by the arrival of Lymon. "It was said that if Miss Amelia so much as stumbled over a rock in the road she would glance around instinctively as though looking for something to sue about it (5)." This judgment, while humorous, is both defensive and righteous. A more sociable person might well go on about her business. In the humor, there is admonition characteristic of a reasonable collective view of a snap judgment. Amelia's response to a trivial issue defines a character flaw that, at least from the point of view of the narration, contributes to her isolation.

In analyzing Amelia's options after her father passed, Marvin Macy would be thought to be the perfect male specimen for marriage, both in looks and height. He *changed* his "bad boy" ways for love of Miss Amelia when he had his pick of beautiful, more socially normalized, straight-visioned women, and yet, he married her: "Then finally, at the age of twenty-two, this Marvin Macy chose Miss Amelia. That solitary, gangling, queer-eyed girl was the one he longed for. Nor did he want her because of her money, but solely out of love (27)." The narrative distance is far outside Marvin Macy's feelings and the stance of one who might have deeper compassion. There is no reasonable excuse for him choosing her, but she is the object of strangeness. Thus, as the plotting follows, she rejects him, while the reader is left to consider, why is it that she could not accept his love and feel it is acceptable because: "There, for a few hours at least, the deep bitter knowing that you are not worth much in the world could be laid low (55)." This line describes a feeling of liberation in the café that also captures the failing of an individual.

The café is metaphor and manifestation of Miss Amelia's love for Lymon and hope for community. The state of forgetting for those who go there also is significant in letting go of insecurities and the perceived perceptions of individual flaws and lack of worthiness that work within the narrative to define what keeps us all separated, real or imagined, even if, in the end, it does not seem to matter.

If an individual cannot hold the conception of worthiness, of intimate knowing, then disruption and dissolution are the only narrative possibilities left. We, as participants in the unfolding, are left feeling somewhat bereft in experiencing the questions and gaps through this carefully planned structure.

# Works Cited

Barlow, Daniel Patrick. "'And Every Day There Is Music': Folksong Roots and the Highway Chain Gang in *The Ballad of the Sad Café.*" *The Southern Literary Journal*, vol. 44, no.1, fall 2011, pp. 74-85.

Dazey, Mary Ann. "Two Voices of the Single Narrator in *The Ballad of the Sad Café.*" *The Southern Literary Journal,* vol. 17, no. 2, spring 1985, pp. 33-40.

Gleeson-White, Sarah. *Strange Bodies: Gender and Identity in the Novels of Carson McCullers.* U of Alabama P, 2003.

Hirsch, Edward. "Reverberations of a Work Song: A Column." *The American Poetry Review,* vol. 28, no. 2, 1999, pp. 43-47. *JSTOR.* July 2017.

McCullers, Carson. *The Ballad of the Sad Café and Other Stories.* Houghton Mifflin, 2005.

Millar, Darren. "The Utopian Function of Affect in Carson McCullers's *The Member of the Wedding* and *The Ballad of the Sad Café.*" *Southern Literary Journal,* vol. 41, no. 2, 2009, pp.87-166. *ProQuest.* January 2019.

# THE SPECTACLE OF MONSTROSITY IN *THE BALLAD OF THE SAD CAFÉ*

## Alessandra Grego

*The peculiarity of the organic monster is that s/he is both Same and Other. The monster is neither a total stranger nor completely familiar; s/he exists in an in-between zone; I would express this as a paradox: the monstrous other is both liminal and structurally central to our perception of normal human subjectivity. The monster helps us to understand the paradox of 'difference' as a ubiquitous but perennially negative preoccupation.* (Braidotti 292)

Carson McCullers's characters call each other, and sometimes themselves, freaks. This is mostly a term of endearment, a manifestation of empathy for human frailty, and at the same time, an invitation for the reader to side with this frail humanity. The sense of community that is created between maladjusted character and empathetic reader is built on the rejection of the racism, sexism, and hypocrisy of the American South in which McCullers's novels and short stories are set. Her readers find, like Biff Brannon, that they like freaks, and that they may well be freaks themselves.

In the mimetic style of realism, neither the individual and deviant point of view of the characters identified as freaks, nor the reader's sympathy, allows for an alternative representation of the material conditions of life in the South.[1] Both deviance and conformity lead to unhappiness in McCullers's novels, in which the normative society is an invisible, mostly remote force preventing change. Indifferent to the characters' condition of isolation, society refuses to tolerate the characters' difference, occasionally making violent or repressive interventions to reassert this rejection. From this dominant group, narrated as morally wrong, readers are invited to distance themselves, while knowing that the freaks will have to finally adapt or succumb, and that society will not change. In the end, the experience of isolation is transferred to the readers who distance themselves from the collective incomprehension and mistrust for otherness in the American South.

Scaling down these large political issues to represent them in the miniature of everyday life in the South is a common feature in the literature by Southern women writers. McCullers was praised by Gore Vidal for the way in which using the small scale, the relations of human beings at their most ordinary, [McCullers] transcends her milieu and shows, in bright glimpses, the potentiality that exists in even the most banal of human relationships, the 'we' as opposed to the meagre 'I' (Schmidt 751).

Vidal's choice of words, "small scale," "ordinary," "banal . . . human relationships," reflect the common opinion that McCullers's topic is domestic and subjective, and not political, because it concerns itself with the private lives of those who are excluded from political action: children, misfits, freaks, blacks, as they uneventfully unravel in and around homes, often in kitchens. But in 1942, in a letter to her friend and unrequited love, the Swiss journalist and author Annemarie Schwarzenbach, Carson McCullers writes:

> *The Member of the Wedding* is about a third way done. And now I cannot go on with it. In the last year I have suffered and known too much. *The Member of the Wedding* is too restricted, it is beautiful in itself, but too small for me just now. Writing it is like working on a very complex, charming, and small entaglio [sic] and what I want to do is to strike out with all my fury. I want to howl to the Lord Almighty from the bottom of my night.
>
> And a new book as [sic] come over me.[2]

The letter was written on June 13, 1942 (Augustin), and the idea for a book that is preventing her from continuing *The Member of the Wedding* is most likely *The Ballad of the Sad Café*, since other publications by McCullers, and the publication of *The Member of the Wedding* in 1946, are very short stories of two to three pages, of which she would have been unlikely to say, as she writes in this letter, "I want to throw into this work all of my passion. It is a tremendous book . . . [sic] and just now I feel very weak and small. The book will very likely take about two years, or more."³

The wording of the letter suggests that McCullers is feeling the strain of working within the medium of realism which limits her possibilities to the probable and the known and is thinking in terms of size; the minute intaglio and her own perceived smallness are in direct contrast to the largeness of the protagonists of *The Ballad of the Sad Café*.

> The giant is represented through movement, through being in time. . . . In contrast to the still and perfect nature of the miniature, the gigantic represents the order and disorder of historical forces . . . and while our daydream might be to animate the miniature, we admire the fall or the death, the stopping, of the giant. (Stewart 86)

The difference is not merely one of size, but of perspective. The giant is not represented subjectively; she is the spectacle, and the reader is not expected to empathize with the giant Miss Amelia, or the deformed dwarf, Cousin Lymon, and the morally deformed Marvin Macy, who, though named and highly individualized characters, are only seen from the outside. The reader knows nothing of their motivations and feelings and is only told what the town has deduced about them. Much remains unexplained, contradictory, and essentially unknowable. On the contrary, the town is an entirely known quantity, familiarized through the expression of its prejudices and expectations, its intimate feelings of frustration and worthlessness, its cowardly potential for group violence and even more cowardly tendency to submit to power. It is less flattering to the reader, to be asked to recognize him / herself in the ordinary humanity of the town, but there is no possibility of identification with Miss Amelia.

The point of view is consistently that of the first-person narrator. Though a few town- dwellers are named, we are invited to "[t]hink of them as a whole" (*Ballad* 408, 412). A collective voice embodying the nameless and anonymous Southern mill town where the story unfolds, the narrator asks the readers to "see" (*Ballad* 416) and "remember," (*Ballad* 418, 424) and sometimes to "imagine" (*Ballad* 403) what the town has seen, what it remembers, and what it has imagined. In other words, the narrator requires the reader to share the town's fascination with the spectacle of the three differently monstrous characters destroying each other.

Mary Ann Dazey, claiming that the story of Miss Amelia requires a form of its own, has pointed out the existence of two narrative voices in *The Ballad*. The first narrator is the lamenting or mournful voice that uses the present tense, complex syntax, and employs generalizations to place "the characters and their actions in the mainstream of human existence" (Dazey 34). The other and dominant narrator is the "objective voice of the literary ballad maker" (Dazey 36) who tells the story of Miss Amelia in the past tense using simplified syntax and short assertive sentences with frequent repetitions of adverbs and conjunctions.

These narrating voices are in contrapuntal relation with each other. To narrate Miss Amelia, McCullers devises a realist frame which will act as a diaphragm between the mythical quality of the three central characters' narrative and the reader's commonsensical systems of interpretation. I suggest that this stylistic shift is made necessary because Miss Amelia, Cousin Lymon, and Marvin Macey are not narrated as freaks, but as monsters, and as such, in their mythical function, they enter the realist narrative to disrupt it and cannot be effectively narrated by it. In *The Ballad of the Sad Café,* McCullers is no longer offering the reader a sad intimacy with the freak, seen as intensely human, but rather as a liberating opportunity for imaginative escape by means of "an impossibly distant body through which a repressed mind might dream its freedom" (LeGoff 197).

I argue that this shift in perspective and in style is determined by McCullers experimenting on her preferred subject of the conflict between non-conforming characters and community by reversing it, representing the non-conforming character as the indifferent focus of the community's curiosity, fascination, and desire. Instead of representing Miss Amelia as a commonsensical impossibility, McCullers allows her to appear in the text as a non-realistic possibility. If it is true that "through the body of the monster fantasies of aggression, domination and inversion are allowed safe expression in a clearly delimited and permanently liminal space" (Cohen 17), it can be said that in McCullers's novel, the clearly delimited space is the stylistic precinct of the ballad.

Miss Amelia's body fascinates and repels the town. A massive woman who appears impermeable to gender restraints that bind women in the American South to effective social invisibility and silence, Miss Amelia appropriates male and female characteristics, recognizes no authority superior to herself, cannot be controlled by social conventions, much less by individuals, and lashes out to attack anyone who attempts to do so, both physically and through the law.

Amelia's gender ambiguity has been interpreted as a grotesque parody of femininity—what Sarah Gleason-White has called "a harsh mockery of Southern womanhood" (Gleason-White 52). This has been the focus of critical attention as a leitmotif that runs through McCullers's production. It allows us to read Miss Amelia as the older incarnation of other McCullers's characters who struggle with the gendered expectations of their society, most famously, Mick Kelly and Frankie Addams, "young girls, both with masculine names," who, according to Louis Rubin, "remain fixed in pre-adolescence; when they have to become women, as they must, they are, as characters, all but destroyed" (Rubin). But while gender identity, or at least the limited boundaries of socially acceptable femininity, is a central issue for the protagonists of *The Heart Is a Lonely Hunter* and *The Member of the Wedding*, both relatively conforming women can re-enter society (although their conforming is written as defeat). Amelia seems to have no intimate doubt about herself that the reader is allowed to share, and she has made no compromises for social acceptance.

It is the town's opinion that Amelia is an unnatural woman because of her height and manners, but she doesn't appear to be ill at ease or in any way uncomfortable in her skin. She refuses superficial femininity. She doesn't shave her legs and her body is muscular and strong; she is not petite or demure, and the red dress she occasionally dons looks ridiculous on her. But surely to deny she is a woman because she does not conform to the petite, fragile, well-groomed, and well-dressed ideal of the period would be a peculiar form of feminist critique. All the more, when she is connoted by powers typically associated with female mythical characters, she is a healer who understands nature's remedies and is nurturing towards the sick, especially sick children, both physically and psychologically. She makes things, and makes things work. She improves, mends, builds, and restores, understanding nature as well as man's law. "With all things which could be made by the hands Miss Amelia prospered"

(*Ballad* 398).

Most symbolic of Amelia's mythical powers is the whiskey she produces at her still, a liquor that has truth-revealing powers and the ability to awaken commonsensical, practical minded, or hopeless men from the repetitive squalor of their existence to beauty and awe: "Such things as these [...] happen when a man has drunk Miss Amelia's liquor. He may suffer, or he may be spent with joy—but the experience has shown the truth; he has warmed his soul and seen the message hidden there" (*Ballad* 403).

Miss Amelia is not a realistic character; she is larger than life, more effective, more powerful, more knowledgeable, and less needy of human companionship. But she is a woman. She is dangerous and must be addressed with respect and caution because she is a powerful woman. And she is the fulcrum of social life in the small town. Even before the arrival of Cousin Lymon, men gravitate toward her because of the whiskey, of course, but also because they are attracted to the only free individual in town. She is a beneficent, terrifying, community-creating mythical character, associated with spring-like regeneration, healing, fertility, and industriousness, and the narrative shows that when such a woman is allowed to live according to her own rules, when she is unshackled by definitions, she brings prosperity—both material and spiritual—to the community.

*The Ballad of the Sad Café*, however, is not solely the story of Miss Amelia; it is the story of how the town reacted to Miss Amelia, and how it is doomed, like Coleridge's Ancient Mariner and innumerable other literary witnesses of the incomprehensible, the sublime, the other, to eternally repeat its story, haunted by the awareness of having failed through fear. The narrator focuses on the town-dwellers' reaction to having such a woman in their midst, on how she upsets their certainties and defies their conventions, on their misapprehension of her quality, on their attempt to constrict her, and on their awakening to the loss her demise constitutes for them, understanding only when it is too late that by embracing her difference, the town had found a liberating force which strengthened the community, brought prosperity and gave the town-dwellers a sense of worth that countered the perceived cheapness of their existence. Too late does the town learn to correctly read the sign that was Amelia's body.

> The monster's body [. . .] incorporates fear, desire, anxiety, and fantasy, giving them life and an uncanny independence. The monstrous body is pure culture. A construct and a projection, the monster exists only to be read: the monstrous is etymologically 'that which reveals,' 'that which warns,' a glyph that seeks a hierophant. (Cohen 4)

But monsters are also

> harbingers of a category crisis [. . .] disturbing hybrids whose externally incoherent bodies resist attempts to include them in any systematic structuration. And so the monster is dangerous, a form suspended between forms that threatens to smash distinctions. (Cohen 6)

Evidently, in *The Ballad of the Sad Café*, McCullers is writing about a culture that is afraid of women. As Patricia Yaeger has shown, "gargantuan women" frequently appear in literature by Southern women: "mountainous women who take on the role of un-domesticating Southern fiction, claiming vast physical as well as literary-historical space" (Yaeger 115). Size, as Yaeger argues, is a recurring feature because imagining gigantic bodies helps the Southern woman writer contrast the cultural and social battle that takes place over the female body used as a conceptual barrier to protect white persons from racial, social, cultural contamination. Even if the texts do not overtly engage with politics, the scale of the characters disrupts the narrative, as mythical characters do when they are inserted into realist forms.

Miss Amelia's monstrosity goes beyond mere size. She crosses every boundary set up to contain and separate; she is a hybrid from every point of view—gender, race, culture, and in this sense, is a composite of the Southern town's fears, an impossible and unthinkable composite which is at once terrifying and compelling, and which tears the town between revulsion and desire. Unable to tolerate its own desire for change, the town initially reads Amelia as a freak who must be contained within the framework of traditional Southern femininity. And because no town-dweller has any actual power over her, the attempt to contain her is purely narrative, trying to bind her within traditional plots that have been known to work in reducing unconventional women to their accepted social role—plots of marriage, of illicit love, and, finally, of monster slaying. To contrast Amelia, the town conjures up two commensurate male monsters with historical credibility and a long literary tradition.

Employing the contrapuntal relationship between the realist narrative and the ballad, the narrator recalls how the town gradually identifies and projects its own desire for change and liberation from this dreary existence onto Miss Amelia, transforming her from a potential freak into the embodiment of a new law. But the male monsters the narrative has liberated cannot be stopped, and the town has to bear silent and powerless witness as the Teratomachia—or battle of the monsters—runs its inevitable course. The monsters destroy each other, and the momentary embodiment of the town's liberation that was Miss Amelia, is turned back into the knowable and inevitably defeated freak of the realist text.

The first male monster the town envisages is a modern type: the morally depraved, physically attractive man, a creation of modernity's preoccupation with the danger of invisible moral evil, the libertine serial seducer and occasional murderer, handsome and corrupt.

> ... Marvin Macy was the handsomest man in this region—being six feet one inch tall, hard-muscled, and with slow grey eyes and curly hair. He was well off, made good wages ... From the outward and worldly point of view Marvin Macy was a fortunate fellow; he needed to bow and scrape to no one and always got just what he wanted. (*Ballad* 418)

Marvin Macy is a rapist and murderer, as per tradition, and, as a Southern addition to the type, a racist and a Klan member. Adored by the "gentle young ladies he degraded and shamed" (*Ballad* 419), the narrator explains that "Marvin Macy was not a person to be envied, for he was an evil character" (*Ballad* 418). His proclivity for evil and similarity to the devil is explained in town by the light of his harsh childhood, which caused his heart to shrink to a stone after he was abandoned by his parents. Seeing him as a victim of ill-usage has produced the opposite effect in his brother Harry, who became painfully sensitive and feminine through suffering. The town is inclined to justify and possibly rather admire Macy and certainly root for him, when he casts himself in the role of the reformed rake who falls inexplicably in love with Miss Amelia. ". . . [L]ove changed Marvin Macy" (*Ballad* 419), and the town "counted on the marriage to tone down Miss Amelia's temper, to put a bit of bride-fat on her, and to change her at last into a calculable woman" (*Ballad* 421).

What the town doesn't understand is that Macy's monstrosity is internal, secret, invisible; he is an incarnation of male violence. Why is he attracted to Amelia? Because she is the most powerful woman in town, and so, his natural antagonist. Marvin Macy tries to bring down the female monster by the customary procedure of marriage, performing in a grotesque version of the reformed rake. Casting Amelia as an unlikely embodiment of female virtue who has succeeded in making him change his ways, Macy becomes the town's champion, the man who will restore Amelia to comprehensibility and resize her into the role of a wife. But her reaction to his attempt to turn her into a "calculable woman" by offering her the illusion of having power over him is first to marry Macy and accept all his gifts, and then to strike him any time he attempts physical contact. In other words, she refuses him what the law and the town see as legitimately his right, marital sex, thus effectively emasculating him. "The town laughed a long time over this grotesque affair" (*Ballad* 424), as the narrator tells us. Amelia makes the town laugh at the practices and the narratives of Southern masculinity, in a real act of collective liberation, in which Amelia has ignored the romantic narrative surface, and directly addressed the underlying violence of male prevarication that the narrative conceals, reducing Macy from the gallant character of the reformed rake to an impotent figure of ridicule.

In a carnivalesque reversal of its original expectations, which were to see Macy's power confirmed, "the town felt the special satisfaction that people feel when someone has been thoroughly done in by some scandalous and terrible means" (*Ballad* 423). And yet, Macy remains in the consciousness of the town, "like a troubling undertone beneath the happy love of Miss Amelia and the gaiety of the café" (*Ballad* 424).

The second male monster conjured up by the town in its attempt to contain Miss Amelia within a narrative is more complex and much older. The physical opposite of the giantess, the hunchback dwarf is an ancient mythical figure, associated with jollity and entertainment, luck and prosperity, which also has a darker side of greed, debauchery, and gratuitous evil. In modernity, the hunchback dwarf is frequently represented in association with power, especially with the female power of Queens and Empresses. Apparently weak and grotesquely innocent, perpetually childlike in size, cherished and spoiled like a human pet, the dwarf must be politically adept at navigating the dangerous environment of courtly life. "Enigmatic figures because of their monstrous status and marvelous attraction, they nonetheless lived and worked at the epicentre of power" (Ravenscroft 147). A sexually ambiguous figure, the dwarf enjoys a physical intimacy with the powerful protector from which others are purposefully excluded. Cousin Lymon plays such a character to Miss Amelia in her role of community leader. Attracted by her power, like Macy is, his immediate intention seems to parasitically benefit from it by more convincingly performing weakness than Macy was able to do, and most likely, by excluding sexual intimacy which Amelia seems to read as an act of physical prevarication. Received by Miss Amelia as a gift— possibly the gift of a child?—he is welcomed into her house, dressed, fed, pampered, allowed where no one else has ever entered, and initially brings her happiness through her ability to make him happy which radiates throughout the town.

As the original source of the community spirit which grows around the café, Miss Amelia's happiness breaks the spell of worthlessness that has been keeping the town-dwellers captive. In a radical reversal of the town's expectations to see Miss Amelia subdued by a man, or by the violence of her own passions, her incomprehensible feelings of affection actually improve the living conditions of the town.

> There is a deeper reason why the café was so precious to this town. And this deeper reason has to do with a certain pride that had not hitherto been known in these parts. To understand this new pride the cheapness of human life must be kept in mind [. . .] no value has been put on human life, it is given to us for free and taken without being paid or. What is it worth? [. . .] Often [. . .] there comes a feeling deep down in the soul that you are not worth much [. . . .] [T]here, for a few

hours at least, the deep bitter knowing that you are not worth much in this world could be laid low. (*Ballad* 443)

Through the ancient literary form of the ballad, the narrator tells the story of the town that dreams of its own escape from a miserable, dreary, and worthless existence, an escape which can only take place through change by imagining an oversized and powerful woman who escapes enforced gender conformity. The town, however, projects both its desire for change and its fears for change by creating the male monsters to contrast the female one.

The story becomes thus a metaphor for the impossibility of change because of a lack of credible narratives; there is no previous narrative about a successful community building, gender defying female giant that does not end with her slaying. And *The Ballad of the Sad Café* is no exception. Once the male monsters have been created, they cannot be stopped, and the terrible conclusion that the lamenting narrator has been anticipating, must inevitably come to pass with the staging of a *Teratomachia*, a battle of the monsters.

This battle is initiated by Macy's return to the town, which has "brought bad fortune" in contrast to the prosperity produced by Amelia's happiness: "it was a time of waste and confusion" (*Ballad* 440). Macy's monstrosity, and similarity to the devil, is visible to all. "There was about him a secret meanness that clung to him almost like a smell. Another thing—he never sweated, not even in August, and that surely is a sign worth pondering over" (*Ballad* 440). And the similarity between Lymon and Macy, the fact that they are made of the same mettle and will form an allegiance to bring down the female monster, becomes clear to the town from their very first encounter.

[The hunchback] and the man stared at each other, and it was not the look of two strangers meeting for the first time and swiftly summing up each other. It was a peculiar stare they exchanged between them, like the look of two criminals who recognize each other. (*Ballad* 436)

In contrast to Amelia, the male monsters are sterile in this story. Violent and impotent, they operate indirectly and complicitly. When one fails to contain the female monster by the customary procedure of marriage, the other tricks her by impersonating a monstrous child, to whom she tenders lovingly, feeding him, rubbing him with oil, putting him to bed at night. It seems the male monsters agree that the female monster must be slain through love. It takes two of them to bring her down. One uses love to weaken her because she is physically stronger than the other, and it is interesting that it is her 'maternal' love for Lymon that finally defeats Amelia.

The battle itself is staged like a sacred performance between figures who have quite dropped their human mummery and are now appearing as monsters before the powerless and dumbstruck town that can only look on fascinated by the spectacle, until finally the giant Amelia is brought down by the dwarf who flies through the café to attack her when she has beaten Macy. She is thus symbolically slain by Lymon's betrayal and shrinks into impotence.

As the story ends, the narrator is still searching for the communitarian experience that the café and Miss Amelia's liquor produced. And the only place where he can find something like it is in the magic of the chain-gang's singing whose harmony of voices gives the illusion

> that the sound does not come from the twelve men on the gang, but from the earth itself, or the wide sky. It is music that causes the heart to broaden and the listener to grow cold with ecstasy and fright . . . and what kind of gang is this that can make such music? . . . Just twelve mortal men who are together. (*Ballad* 458)

Should we conclude, then, that McCullers's attempt to "strike out with all her fury" as she writes in the letter to Schwarzenbach, fails? Not entirely. Although Miss Amelia is now a powerless, sexless, cross-eyed face peering out of the window of a rundown ex-café, this Southern town—the real protagonist of *The Ballad*— has succeeded in dreaming of its own prosperity and narrating pleasure and community life as an ambition and a possibility that can only become reality through the rejection of the dominant practices of Southern masculinity.

As the Chinese artist Liu Di says, in describing his digital images of giants in metropolitan environments, it is "[b]y violating the rules of common sense, we can break the hypnotic trance induced by familiar reality" (Liu). In shifting the focalization of the novella from the characters onto the town, *The Ballad* illustrates the function of narrative in allowing to re-think reality in new ways.

*Notes*

[1] On McCullers's brand of Southern Gothic as a fusion of realism and a romantic conception of the carnivalesque, much has been written. See, for instance, Dara Downey's "The Gothic and the Grotesque in the Novels of Carson McCullers," *The Palgrave Handbook of the Southern Gothic*, Edited by Susan Castillo Street and Charles L Crow. London, Palgrave Macmillan, 2016, pp. 365-378.

[2] I am grateful to Carlos Dews for showing me this currently unpublished letter, held in the Schweizerischen Literaturarchiv in Bern, Switzerland.

[3] According to Vinciane Moeschler's romanced biography of Annemarie Schwarzenbach, the Swiss author received this letter in 1941, while she was writing her novel *Das Wunder des Baums (The Miracle of the Tree)* and interpreted it as sign of intimate spiritual connection between them: "A travers les mots de Carson, je devinais que son sentiment envers moi était toujours éveillé et tenace. Elle me révéla une chose très étrange. Alors qu'elle se consacrait à l'écriture de Member of the Wedding, elle ressentit l'étrange besoin d'interrompre son écriture pour passer à une autre nouvelle, qu'elle appela "A Tree, a Rock, a Cloud." Or, il se trouvait par un fait extraordinaire et inexplicable que l'histoire et les aboutissements de ce récit relataient les mêmes sentiments que j'écrivais dans mon dernier roman." (Moeschler)

# Works Cited

Augustin, Bettina. "Spiegelbild im Augen der Anderen." *Neue Zürcher Zeitung*, 2 July 2005. nzz.ch/articleCT58W-1.154639, accessed October 20, 2017.

Bloom, Harold. *Carson McCullers*. New ed., Bloom's Literary Criticism, 2009.

Braidotti, Rosi. "Signs of Wonder and Traces of Doubt: On Teratology and Embodied Differences." *Feminist Theory and the Body. A Reader*. Edited by Janet Price and Margrit Shildrick, Routledge, 1999, pp. 290-301.

Cohen, Jeffrey Jerome, editor. *Monster Theory: Reading Culture*. University of Minnesota Press, 1996. ProQuest Ebook Central.

Dazey, Mary Ann. "Two Voices of the Single Narrator in 'The Ballad of the Sad Café.'" *The Southern Literary Journal*, vol. 17, no. 2, 1985, pp. 33–40. JSTOR.

LeGoff, Jacques. *Time, Work, and Culture in the Middle Ages*. Translated by Arthur Goldhamer. University of Chicago Press, 1980, p. 197, qt. in Cohen, Jeffrey Jerome. *Of Giants: Sex, Monsters, and the Middle Ages*, University of Minnesota Press, 1999. ProQuest Ebook Central.

Liu, Di. whiterabbitcollection.org/artists/liu-di. Accessed October 20, 2017.

McCullers, Carson. "The Ballad of the Sad Café." *Carson McCullers, Complete Novels*. Edited by Carlos Dews, Library of America, 2001, pp. 395-458.

---. Unpublished letter to Annemarie Schwarzenbach, Schweizerischen Literaturarchiv, Bern, Switzerland.

Moeschler, Vinciane. *Annemarie S. Ou Le Fuites Éperdues. Roman d'une Vie*. Lausanne, L'Age d'Homme, 2007. Qt. by Jean Moncelon, *Carson McCullers et Annemarie Schwarzenbach*, moncelon.fr/mccullers.htm. Accessed October 17, 2017.

Ravenscroft, Janet. "Dwarfs—and a Loca—as Ladies' Maids at The Spanish Habsburg Courts," in *Politics of Female Households. Ladies-in Waiting Across Early Modern Europe*. Brill, 2013. ProQuest Ebook Central.

Rubin, Louis D. "Carson McCullers: The Aesthetic of Pain." *Virginia Quarterly Review*, vol. 53, no.2, pp. 265-283, 1977. vqronline.org/essay/carson-mccullers-aesthetic-pain.

Schmidt, Michael. *The Novel: A Biography*. Belknap Press of Harvard University Press, 2014.

Westling, Louise. "Carson McCullers's Amazon Nightmare." *Modern Fiction Studies*, vol. 28, no. 3, pp. 465-473, 1982.

Yaeger, Patricia. *Dirt and Desire: Reconstructing Southern Women's Writing, 1930-1990*, University of Chicago Press, 2014. ProQuest Ebook Central.

# "Does Anyone Want Waiting On?" Love, Labor, Liquor, and the Utopian Function of Reproductive Work in *The Ballad of the Sad Café*: An Ecofeminist Reading

Sarah-Marie D. Horning

Carson McCullers has often been described as the literary queen of human loneliness. Literary critics have frequently examined the theme of loneliness as a way to explain her isolated and grotesque characters. The dust jacket for the 1987 Bantam edition of *The Ballad of the Sad Café* describes her fiction as a "voyag[e] into the depths of the spiritual isolation that underlies the human condition." Even Tennessee Williams, McCullers's close friend and frequent defender, described the theme of her fiction, in his introductory note to Virginia Spencer Carr's biography of her, as "the huge importance of the nearly insoluble problems of human love" (xviii). But as much as Carson McCullers might be called the literary queen of human loneliness, her readers (and critics) might also see her as the queen of friendship or the queen of community. In *The Ballad of the Sad Café*, Miss Amelia produces medicine for sick children, spiritually powerful liquor, and comfort food, among other earthly goods, as a natural healer who resists changing "internal chemistry"[1] and who is afraid of exercising too much power over other bodies and souls.

Would questioning the theme of loneliness reveal Carson McCullers as a writer concerned with friendship? Instead of reading Miss Amelia as grotesque or amazon-like (though these readings have been productive, too) and defeated, what if we read her as a connected, loving healer, and as a maternal and homeopathic medicine woman?

McCullers's investigations of loneliness and isolation include friendships that are powerful for the ways they resist or transcend loneliness. Singer and Antonapoulos, Frankie and John Henry, Mick Kelly and Singer, and Miss Amelia and Cousin Lymon all share (at least for a time) deep friendships. In *Ballad*, especially, McCullers's narrator breaks away from telling us Miss Amelia's story to reflect on love. Virginia Spencer Carr called these passages McCullers's "love thesis." Carr suggests the "concept of the 'immense complexity of love'—a phrase from her short story 'A Domestic Dilemma'—surfaces repeatedly in McCullers's various writings, especially in her domestic tales that reflect many aspects of her life with Reeves" (xii). The love thesis begins by suggesting that "the sensible people" of the town came to the conclusion that "if [Miss Amelia and Cousin Lymon] had found some satisfaction of the flesh between themselves, then it was a matter concerning them and God alone" (26). The narrator asks, "What sort of thing, then, was this love?" and proceeds to sketch out a thesis for successful love (26). Though McCullers's fiction is filled with lonely characters, it also yearns for and pictures free, connected spaces united by bodily, earthly pleasures.

I am drawing on the ecofeminist ideas and works of Patrick D. Murphy[2] and Patricia Yaeger to frame my understanding of ecofeminism for this paper. From these authors, I paraphrase ecofeminism's relationship to literature as a method of critical reading that interrogates the connections between the environment or natural resources, the exploitation of women's bodies, and reproduction. *Ballad* is full of moments worth questioning that are otherwise unexplainable, ambiguous oddities. Miss Amelia keeps an acorn in her pocket as a talisman. Later, she gives Lymon her kidney stones as a gift. Might these natural products turned bodily keepsakes be stand-ins for mothering and childbirth otherwise absent in the novella—one an attempt or hope to make something grow, the other a bodily sacrifice? They are indications that McCullers makes Miss Amelia into a character whose body is not only seen as social, but also as a materially ecological being connected with both human and nonhuman materials.

In her analysis of the connections between grotesque bodies and their (Southern) environment, Patricia Yaeger reframes McCullers's "grotesque" girl characters. She asks, "What happens if we refuse to think of the grotesque as the objective correlative for civic decay? Are there other ways to digest the sideshow wonders that could pass for politics in McCullers's stories? What happens to readers of Southern fictions as they continue to encounter these repetitious bodies?" (229). Yaeger asks readers of McCullers's fiction to examine the strange bodies of her characters for the ways they do more than operate as lived consequences for the sin of slavery. Specifically, *Dirt and Desire* calls on critics to consider how those bodies are connected to the environment.

Ecofeminism resists the idea that humans are superior to nature, as it works to resist the domination of women's bodies that results from their culturally devised link to nature. Ecofeminism also illuminates the ways women's bodies are connected to nature through their shared history of exploitation upheld by dualistic rhetoric based on culture / nature man / woman dyads, and especially for the ways that women's connection to nature is productive. Asking how women are productively connected to nature is what interests me about *Ballad*.

Throughout the novella, many of the bodily pleasures described are closely tied to the Earth and to nature, and to materials that Miss Amelia produces using natural resources. The most explicitly described pleasures (the warmth of the café, food, liquor, tobacco, Miss Amelia's "cures," and her physical doting on Cousin Lymon with good clothes and food) have connections to things Miss Amelia has produced by dint of her agricultural savvy. Patricia Yaeger might say that Miss Amelia's gardens, livestock, stills, remedies, and acorn are her desires brought about by working in the dirt. I see Miss Amelia's desire as a longing for connection to people and bodies through quasi-maternal nurturing and healing. In this way, McCullers creates possibilities for characters to connect through bodily pleasures that are enmeshed with nature.

> That autumn was a happy time. [. . .] After the long hot summer the first cool days had a clean bright sweetness. Goldenrod grew along the dusty roads, and sugar cane was ripe and purple [. . .] sweet potatoes bedded in the ground [. . .] [Miss Amelia] was looking forward greatly to the first frost [because she] intended to make much barbecue, chitterlins, and sausage. [. . .] She laughed often, with a deep ringing laugh, and her whistling had a sassy, tuneful trickery. She was forever trying out her strength, lifting up heavy biceps. (McCullers, *Ballad* 45)

This scene and its description of natural abundance is a vivid pastiche of Southern bioregionalism. Sugarcane echoes of the exploitation[3] of crops and bodies in the American South and in the South Atlantic. Goldenrod, though we now think of it as an irritant, is still widely consumed as an herbal tea remedy. These plants, though they are connected to the institutions of slavery and medical science, are neither produced nor consumed as economic products in Miss Amelia's utopic town. Other summer crops such as sweet potatoes and pork—the production of which are accomplished by Miss Amelia on her own and for herself, are not turned to economic commodities. Miss Amelia's production is not for profit. With the people of the town, Miss Amelia barters: "she had traded for three tremendous hogs" (45) and when the weather turned cold, Amelia drew on her community to produce the pork by-products:

> people began to come in from the country to find out what Miss Amelia thought of the weather; she decided to kill the biggest hog, and word got around the countryside. The hog was slaughtered and a low oak fire started in the barbecue pit. There was the warm smell of pig blood and smoke. . . . Miss Amelia walked around giving orders and soon most of the work was done. (46)

Miss Amelia's productions are connected to the Earth rather than to the economy, as she produces food to share with others. She doesn't hoard what she grows and creates, rather she operates in a gift economy of bartered goods for labor. Her community agrees to help with the hog because they will share in the pork they make. Her care for the town is tied to nourishment, to the production of bodily goods and pleasures. She does this production of food, liquor, and medicine without expectation of remuneration. This nourishment is Miss Amelia's selfless generosity and love in keeping with "the love thesis."

The love thesis describes several ways love operates from the different perspectives of lover and beloved and ends with a caution that love becomes painful when the lover is "forever trying to strip bare the beloved" (27). With this warning, the love thesis concludes with the cautionary advice for the reader to avoid transactional relationships. McCullers models, in her failed and successful loves, relationships that "strip bare," those that are "strange, intense" and create new worlds.

The strangeness and intensity for Miss Amelia is inscribed on the body and creates a utopic world in the town and (for a time) in the café. The café, and especially Miss Amelia's liquor, are instruments of "unpredictable [bodily] events"[4] that forge social friendships, kindness, and love. Once she converts her storefront into a café, Amelia does not exploit the space as leisure-for-profit: "For in order to come to the café you did not have to buy the dinner, or a portion of liquor" (54). Food and liquor are essential pleasures of the body which the narrator describes as particularly important, capable of delivering deep personal insight: Imagine that the whiskey is the fire and that the message is that which is known only in the soul of the man—then the worth of Miss Amelia's liquor can be understood (10).

The bodily pleasure of alcohol is liberating since Miss Amelia's liquor, it seems, produces a drunkenness which reveals knowledge available "only in the soul of the man" and not accessible by means of medicinal, psychiatric, or scientific discourse. Amelia does not economically exploit her medical services: "for an ordinary treatment she did not hesitate, and no disease was so terrible but what she would undertake to cure it. [. . .] [P]eople trusted her. She charged no fees whatsoever and always had a raft of patients" (17). Miss Amelia refuses to treat "female complaints." As a medicine woman who resists turning women's bodies and natural resources into economic objects to regulate, she resists not only economic benefit from her medicine, but also from intervening in female reproduction.

Perhaps one of the most tragic and perplexing ambiguities of the novella is why Lymon and Macy destroy Miss Amelia's life. The fight scene has been interpreted from many angles—as Lacanian *jouissance*, Lymon as trickster figure, Lymon as Quasimodo. Reading *Ballad* as a story about the exploitations of women and natural resources leads to a different understanding of Lymon's and Macy's motives. From this perspective, Amelia's powers of production are threatening. She doesn't follow the marriage plot to become a "calculable woman," but she also does not uphold masculine economies of the slaveholding, agrarian South. When Miss Amelia leaves Marvin Macy, she cuts up his Klansman's robe to cover her tobacco plants.

Though the tobacco crop is described as flourishing that season, Miss Amelia has few enough tobacco plants to be covered by the shredded robe. Miss Amelia's co-op style of governance, and her ability to satiate the town of Forks Falls outside of the large-scale plantation economy of the South is threatening, and this is why Macy and Lymon destroy the café, the store, her still, and eventually her body. At the close of the novella, Miss Amelia's body is withering and grey. She is no longer productive and the "peach trees seem to grow more crooked every summer." Once the productive center of her community, Miss Amelia becomes a shut-in after she is beaten by Lymon and Macy.

Reading *Ballad* as an optimistic tale of community and sustainable ecology helps move McCullers out of the "loneliness" realm and into the "love thesis" space of bodies and ecology. In the same way that Patricia Yaeger's *Dirt and Desire* weaves feminist readings of Southern women whose bodies are productively and pleasantly (though often grotesquely) connected to nature, I suggest that McCullers's Miss Amelia, and especially her "love thesis," can serve as a productive assessment for new feminist, ecocritical, or postcolonial readings of "loneliness" that doesn't passively lament the inevitability of social estrangement, but resists with good food, good liquor, friendship, solidarity, and love.

With its utopian dimension, *Ballad* provides a tempting space to think about the work Miss Amelia does, what she produces, her relationship to nature as healer, cook, farmer, moonshiner, and general store owner. Ecofeminist ideas of community, nature, and reproductive work help to reimagine *Ballad* as a reflection of a South where cooperative and ecocritical ideals of community (rather than kinship) and sustainability help build successful relationships, friendships, and social spaces. These ecofeminist and ecocritical ideas offer possibilities for further examination of the bioregional details in McCullers's fiction. The isolation of the town and Miss Amelia's egalitarian agricultural work create friendships and social cohesion by bringing disparate groups together for the production and consumption of locally produced food and liquor. Miss Amelia serves as a model for building (horizontal) friendships that nourish and produce in the face of social forces of mass production and slavery which otherwise fracture, isolate, and demolish.

*Notes*

¹ This quote comes from a letter McCullers wrote in 1941 to her therapist friend, Sydney Isenberg. In the letter, she describes a recent hospitalization which causes her to question the validity of psychotherapy. She reflects on her own experiences before asking Isenberg if, as a therapist, he worries about having too much power over his patients. Finally, she concludes that, for herself, she intends "to maintain my grasp of my own soul—however fragile that grasp might be as long as possible" (Letter III).

² In *Nature, Literature, and Other: Ecofeminist Critiques*, Patrick D. Murphy writes that "ecology is not only a viewpoint on the 'natural world' but a viewpoint on humanity's participation in that world as one of its natural elements as well. . . . Love is human, certainly physical as sensual pleasure and procreative power . . . ecology and love are intertwined, if not in a particular poem, then throughout a volume, in such a way that to ignore one is to fail to appreciate the other" (84-85).

³ See Kao, Grace Y. "The Universal Versus the Particular in Ecofeminist Ethics." *The Journal of Religious Ethics*. vol. 38, no. 4, 2010, pp. 616-636. "While not monolithic, a central premise shared by most ecofeminists is that there are important connections between the exploitation of women and the exploitation of nature" (617).

⁴ This phrase comes from *Foucault's History of Sexuality*. Though Carson McCullers has long been thought of as the "pilgrim of human loneliness," contemporary scholarship has deployed Foucault to imagine the ways in which McCullers's fiction is instead picturing free, connected spaces united by bodies and pleasures. Temple Gowan asserts firmly that "Bodies and pleasures" are key to McCullers's queer post humanist resistance to the normalizing effects of biopower" (130); Kristen Proehl credits McCullers with anticipating Foucault, writing that her "specific interest in the relationship between friendship and queerness anticipates the groundbreaking scholarship of Michel Foucault and Lillian Faderman, as well as more recent studies of queer friendship" (146); and Miho Matusi's recent essay, which uses Foucault's idea of the "normalizing gaze" to read *The Ballad of the Sad Café* for the ways that Miss Amelia works to dodge the regulatory purview of the town's collective surveillance is an example of the ways in which scholarship on McCullers has

used Foucault and his ideas about sexuality and power to revisit her fiction and to disrupt the idea that her work is consumed with "the problem of human loneliness."

# WORKS CITED

Alimo, Stacy and Susan Hekman. *Material Feminisms*. U of Indiana P, 2008.

Bin, Lin. "Seeking the Meaning of Loneliness: Carson McCullers in China." *Carson McCullers in the Twenty-First Century*. Edited by Alison Graham-Bertolini and Casey Kayser. Palgrave Macmillan, 2016, pp. 209-233.

Carr, Virginia Spencer. *The Lonely Hunter: A Biography of Carson McCullers*. Doubleday, 1975.

Davis, David A. "Southern Modernists and Modernity." *The Cambridge Companion to the American South*. Edited by Sharon Monteith. Cambridge UP, 2013, pp. 83-103.

Dews, Carlos. "'Impromptu Journal of My Heart': Carson McCullers's Therapeutic Recordings, April-May 1958." *Carson McCullers in the Twenty-First Century*. Edited by Alison Graham-Bertolini and Casey Kayser. Palgrave Macmillan, 2016, pp. 21-48.

Foucault, Michel. *The History of Sexuality: An Introduction*. Vintage, 1990.

Gowan, Temple. "'To be a Good Animal': Toward a Queer-Posthumanist Reading of Reflections in a Golden Eye." *Carson McCullers in the Twenty-First Century*. Edited by Alison Graham-Bertolini and Casey Kayser. Palgrave Macmillan, 2016, pp.127-142.

Matsui, Miho. "Queer Eyes: Cross-Gendering, Cross-Dressing, and Cross-Racing Miss Amelia." *Carson McCullers in the Twenty-First Century*. Edited by Alison Graham-Bertolini and Casey Kayser. Palgrave Macmillan, 2016, pp. 157-174.

---. McCullers, Carson. *The Ballad of the Sad Café*. 1951. Houghton Mifflin, 1986.

---. *Collected Stories of Carson McCullers*. Edited by Virginia Spencer Carr. Harcourt, 1998.

---. "Letter to Dr. Sidney Isenberg (Letter III)." *Dr. Sidney Isenberg*

*Collection on Carson McCullers Papers, 1948-71*. Washington and Lee University Library. Murphy, Patrick D. *Literature, Nature, and Other: Ecofeminist Critiques*. State University of New York P, 1995.

Oksala, Johana. "Archaic Bodies: Foucault and the Feminist Question of Experience." *Hypativa,* vol. 29, no. 4, 2004, pp. 99-121.

Proehl, Kristen. "Coming of Age in the Queer South: Friendship and Social Difference in *The Heart Is a Lonely Hunter*." *Carson McCullers in the Twenty-First Century*. Edited by Alison Graham-Bertolini and Casey Kayser. Palgrave Macmillan, 2016, pp.143-156.

Rountree, Stephanie. "An 'Archeology of [Narrative] Silence': Cognitive Segregation and Productive Citizenship in McCullers's *The Heart Is a Lonely Hunter*." *Carson McCullers in the Twenty-First Century*. Edited by Alison Graham-Bertolini and Casey Kayser. Palgrave Macmillan, 2016, pp.189-208.

Yaeger, Patricia. *Dirt and Desire: Reconstructing Southern Women's Writing: 1930-1990*. U of Chicago P, 2014.

# THE WE OF ME: SENSES OF LONGING AND BELONGING IN CARSON MCCULLERS'S *THE MEMBER OF THE WEDDING*, *THE HEART IS A LONELY HUNTER* AND *THE BALLAD OF THE SAD CAFÉ*

Katalin G. Kállay

In *The Member of the Wedding*[1], the teenage heroine Frankie explains her feelings toward her brother and his bride with a peculiar sentence: "They are the *we* of me". This phrase has a special significance in Carson McCullers's works; the shift from first person singular to first person plural indicates the lonely speaker's longing for and the importance of a real or imaginary community. It is precisely the singularity of the isolated and solitary characters that somehow reaches a desired plurality in the expression; therefore, the center of the fictive relationship can only remain the isolated self.

In examining this shift—a sudden expansion of spiritual dimension—in three works by the author, I compare the phrase with the notion of "the inside room" in *The Heart Is a Lonely Hunter* with the famous difference between the attitudes of "the lover" and "the beloved" in *The Ballad of the Sad Café*. I experiment with a change of word order and ask whether the sentence "We are the *they* of me" could make sense in the context of the characters, to what extent it could be seen as the opposite, and to what extent it could enlarge the scope of the first expression.

Long after having submitted this abstract of my paper entitled "The We of Me" did I realize how popular the phrase has become: it is the title of a powerful essay by Elizabeth Freeman (*Women and Performance* 111-135); it is in the title of Joyce Carol Oates's review of *Illumination and Night Glare* in the *London Review of Books* (15-16); it is in the title of a short writing by Cece DuBois in a 2015 issue of an online magazine called "Rebelle Society"; it is the title of a song in Suzanne Vega's album *"Lover, Beloved: Songs from an Evening with Carson McCullers"*, released in 2016; the title of the

2017 exhibition in the Yarbrough Gallery of the Columbus Museum, celebrating the centenary anniversary of the author's birth, as well as the title of several blog entries and visual works of art. It seems that this is one of the most famous quotes, and among people familiar with responses to the works of Carson McCullers, "the we of me" as a phrase is commonplace.

Carson McCullers was a master at turning commonplaces into communicative spaces, in the literal and physical sense. In *The Ballad of the Sad Café*, a common and quite unpoetic store is turned, by the power of Miss Amelia's love and the narrator's diction, into a welcoming café of a created community. In terms of language, the example could be "A Tree. A Rock. A Cloud", where the much used and abused common phrase "I love you" becomes so disturbingly meaningful in light of the speaker's strangely narrated personal history and "science of love". It is worth examining what makes "the we of me" so catchy, so memorable, and in what way this wording differs from other senses of "we", from other ways of expressing the first person plural.

In a study entitled "Three Forms of the First Person Plural"[2], Matthias Haase calls attention to

> the crucial distinctions between the different *logical* roles that 'we' can play in a sentence: it can figure as [. . . ] 'Distributive We' with which I refer to a set of which I am an element, as a 'Communal We', with which I refer to a community of which I am a member and, finally, as a 'Generic We' with which I articulate the form of which I am a bearer. (231)

He argues that in the case of the 'Distributive We', the 'I' is an element of a set that is observable and verifiable from the outside, for example, "we are those who have red dots on their noses", thus the 'I', despite quantitatively belonging to the group, cannot contain the others and does not necessarily have to agree with them (245). This relationship is based on observation. In the case of a 'Communal We', there needs to be an agreement, a "mutual attunement to one another" in order to form (or rather perform) the first-person plural, for example, "we are dancing the tango with each other". Haase points out that only a *"plural subject"* can fall under this concept; dancing the tango can only be done together with another person (249). This relationship is based on participation. The third form of the first-person plural, the 'Generic We', is regarded to be more fundamental by Haase than the other two; the example for this is the utterance of a native speaker of English saying, "we use this expression so-and-so". In this case, Haase claims, despite belonging to a group of native speakers, "I speak not about or *for a group*, but rather articulate the general form whose *exemplar* or 'bearer' I am" (254). These types of judgments are "*generic self-predications*", making them a means "to understand oneself, in virtue of the *form* of one's judgment, as an exemplar of something general, of which there are also other exemplars" (255).

It becomes an exciting question where to put McCullers's "the we of me". In *The Member of the Wedding*, it comes to Frankie as a revelation, while talking to John Henry in the evening:

> The darkening town was very quiet. For a long time now her brother and the bride had been at Winter Hill. They had left the town a hundred miles behind them, and now were in a city far away. They were them and in Winter Hill, together, while she was her and in the same old town all by herself. The long hundred miles did not make her sadder and make her feel more far away than the knowing that they were them and both together and she was only her and parted from them, by herself. And as she sickened with this feeling a thought and explanation suddenly came to her, so that she knew and almost said aloud: *They are the we of me* (35).

It seems that from the point of view of longing, Frankie's 'we' is communal. She wishes to be a member of a community; to share the experience of her brother and the bride to name herself F. Jasmine, in order to join the JA-group of Jarvis and Janice, to be a member of the wedding in the most intimate and absolute way possible, so to say, to become a part of their body. However, from the point of view of belonging, her 'we' is rather generic. The expression seems to be more of a self-predication through which she is beginning to understand herself. "For it was just at that moment that Frankie understood. She knew who she was and how she was going into the world.

Her squeezed heart suddenly opened and divided. Her heart divided like two wings. And when she spoke her voice was sure (38)."

There is a discrepancy between Frankie's sense of longing and her sense of belonging, exactly along the lines of the two types of 'we'. But what she experiences is a spiritual expansion that is far from being logical. How could it ever occur to her that she could become one of them? Get married to them? Go with them on their honeymoon? And as what kind of third party to the bride and bridegroom? Not as their child or parent, but as an equally important member of a trinity. Despite the surrealistic aim, the expansion of her heart and consequently the feeling of self-assurance is real, with an absolute spiritual certainty. Therefore, she is desperate, feeling somehow cheated when in the end, they, of course, refuse to take her along.

It is the tension between the logical discrepancy and the spiritual certainty that causes the pain that McCullers's characters inevitably feel, which accompanies or follows the expansion of the heart. One could put it more simply, in commonplace phrases: this is the nature of falling in love. Or, in the case of Frankie: this is the experience of growing up. Yet, the expansion of the heart is never a commonplace experience. It comes suddenly, by surprise, and no matter how safely one can categorize it, either in religious or sexual terms, one is always exposed and vulnerable when it happens. Quite paradoxically, it is precisely the exposure and the vulnerability that provides the experience with a fragile and exquisite beauty. It seems that the power of "the we of me" is not in "who" or "what" one is longing for, but the "how" of this feeling, which is unmistakable yet illogical, out of the ordinary or familiar world of the 'I'; it must be therefore a transitory feeling, leaving the 'I' in painful isolation, but providing one with a different sense of belonging, even to the ordinary or familiar world, and, generically, to oneself. I return to this idea after briefly examining an earlier and a later work by Carson McCullers.

In *The Heart Is a Lonely Hunter*[3], the author's first novel, Frankie's literary predecessor, thirteen-year-old Mick Kelly experiences the expansion of the heart first through listening to music:

> ... Wonderful music like this was the worst hurt there could be. The whole world was this symphony, and there was not enough of her to listen.

It was over, and she sat very stiff with her arms around her knees. Another program came on the radio and she put her fingers in her ears. The music left only this bad hurt in her, and a blankness. She could not remember any of the symphony, not even the last few notes. She tried to remember but no sound at all came to her. Now that it was over there was only her heart like a rabbit and this terrible hurt.

. . . She was not trying to think of the music at all when it came back to her. The first part happened in her mind just as it had been played. She listened in a quiet, slow way and thought the notes out like a problem in geometry so she would remember. She could see the shape of the sounds very clear, and she would not forget them.

Now she felt good. She whispered some words out loud: 'Lord forgiveth me, for I knoweth not what I do.' (93-94)

For Mick, something like the 'we of me' is what she calls 'the inside room', inhabited by her thoughts on music and only one person, Mr. Singer, the deaf-mute engraver who rents a room in their house. She feels closer to Mr. Singer than to anybody in her family. "For some reason it was like they had a secret together. Or like they waited to tell each other things that had never been said before" (185). In her daydreams, she wishes to be an orphan living with Mr. Singer: "just the two of them in a foreign house where in the winter it would snow" (186). The charm of Mr. Singer is in his ability to pay attention, although he cannot talk and cannot understand much of what he can read from the lips of others. He becomes the 'we of me', a grotesque father confessor, almost a god-like figure not only for Mick, but for three other characters, Biff Brannon, the owner of the New York Café with a quite feminine tender heart, Dr. Copeland, the African American medical doctor with a strong purpose and Marxist consciousness, and for Jake Blount, the troubled anarchist stranger. For Mr. Singer, however, the "we of me" is not the company he keeps in the small town, but his mute friend, the corpulent Greek Antonapoulos with sleepy eyes who he used to live with, until his friend developed kleptomania, showed antisocial behavior, and was finally sent by his

Greek nephew to a lunatic asylum.

For all the characters, including Mr. Singer, being understood by the person they confide in does not really matter; what matters is the expansion of their hearts and their trust in self-expression. Here, too, there is a logical discrepancy between longing and belonging: the community they long for is temporary and fragile, and finally, all of them remain isolated, belonging, generically, only to themselves. Apart from Mr. Singer, who commits suicide after the death of his Greek friend, the other characters somehow manage to survive the shock of losing the relationship that was most important for them, and the end of the novel is not utterly hopeless, in the words of the grown Mick, who is about to start working in the ten-cent store, there is "some good" (270) for them in the future.

In the author's later work, *The Ballad of the Sad Café*[4], however, sadness is already in the title. The circular structure of the narrative emphasizes the initial and the final isolation of not only the main character, Miss Amelia but her house as well, which is "boarded up completely and leans so far to the right that it seems bound to collapse at any minute" (7). The house is out of balance and so are the grotesque relationships—Miss Amelia Evans, the cross-eyed, bony, and masculine owner of the house and the store of the Southern small town, mysteriously falls in love with a stranger, a bird-like hunchback who claims to be her cousin Lymon. As a result of this, the store is turned into a café, creating a lively community in the otherwise dull and dreary town. But Cousin Lymon, in turn, is carried away by Amelia's ex-husband, the criminal Marvin Macy as soon as he gets back from the penitentiary, and the two of them take revenge on Miss Amelia (the only person Macy had ever truly loved but by whom he was brutally rejected during their absurd ten-day marriage). No matter how unbelievable this strange love-triangle is, one must take the feelings seriously. It is the "we of me" that Amelia believes when telling Lymon all the stories about her father, showing him the treasures (like her kidney stones, or an acorn she picked up when her father died) she stores in the cabinet of curios. It is the "we of me" that Marvin Macy believes when he prepares himself spiritually for two long years, getting rid of his laziness and evil habits, before proposing marriage to Amelia. It is the thought of the "we of me" that makes Cousin Lymon follow Marvin Macy, trying to im-press him by rapidly moving his ears. The "we of me" is betrayed when Amelia brutally strikes her newlywed husband, or when Cousin Lymon helps Macy win the fight against Amelia. Again, we see the logical discrepancy between longing and belonging. In McCullers's philosophy of love, there is hardly any chance for reciprocity:

> There are the lover and the beloved, but these two come from different countries. Often the beloved is only a stimulus for all the stored-up love which has lain quiet within the lover for a long time hitherto. And somehow every lover knows this. He feels in his soul that his love is a solitary thing. (33)

Here, too, it is emphasized, that it is the "how" that really matters, and not the object of the longing:

> The beloved may be treacherous, greasy-headed and given to evil habits. Yes, and the lover may see this as clearly as anyone else—but that does not affect the evolution of his love one whit. A most mediocre person can be the object of a love which is wild, extravagant, and beautiful as the poison lilies of the swamp. A good man may be the stimulus for a love both violent and debased, or a jabbering madman may bring about in the soul of someone a tender and simple idyll. Therefore, the value and quality of any love is determined solely by the lover himself.
>
> It is for this reason that most of us would rather love than be loved. (33)

The narrative, however, is not out of balance: it follows the expansion and the shrinking of Miss Amelia's heart, turning indifference into beauty and beauty into pain, and in the final coda, entitled "The Twelve Mortal Men", pain into beauty again. A special type of first-person plural is observable in the final song of the chain gang. At first sight, one could say that they are the perfect example for Haase's 'Distributive We', since they belong together on a visible, observable basis. Still, as the song unfolds, the relationship of the singers grows into a 'Communal We', creating a community of the prisoners, and even reaches the 'Generic We' if we take it as an example of the *conditio humana*, the human condition:[5]

> One dark voice will start a phrase, half-sung, and like a question. And after a moment another voice will join in, soon the whole gang will be singing. The voices are dark in the golden glare, the music intricately blended, both somber and joyful. The music will swell until at last it seems that the sound does not come from the twelve men on the gang, but from the earth itself, or the wide sky. It is music that causes the heart to broaden and the listener to grow cold with ecstasy and fright. Then slowly the music will sink down until at last there remains one lonely voice, then a great hoarse breath, the sun, the sound of the picks in the silence. (84-85)

The novella ends on the note of the word "together", despite the first shown and the last suggested image the reader gets of Miss Amelia:

> It is a face like the terrible dim faces known in dreams—sexless and white, with two grey crossed eyes which are turned inward so sharply that they seem to be exchanging with each other one long and secret gaze of grief. (7-8)

Is this the prospect of what becomes of the "we of me" once the magic is over? The only community remaining for Miss Amelia is to be shared by her two crossed eyes.

I would not like to leave it at that, but to return instead to the thought of the "ordinary" or the "familiar", which is the neutral or unwanted starting and final point for the characters examined. Instead of a 'we', in the familiar world they think of themselves as alienated, even if they are in company, about to say something like "we are the they of me". For Frankie, this "they" company would be the trio of herself, Berenice, and John Henry; for Mick, her own family, and for Miss Amelia, her two crossed eyes. In this sense, the change of the word order creates a complete opposite of the original phrase.

However, if in the expression "we are the they of me", the word "we" designates the unity of longing, the word "they" might refer to the objects of longing, now within the self-predication of the generic, solitary belonging. That is, for Frankie, such a sentence could expand to say "we (the three JA-s) are the they (Jarvis and Janice) of me (the grown Francis)". For Mick, it could say "we (Mr. Singer, music and I) are the they (Mr. Singer and music) of me (the grown Mick, about to work in the ten-cent store). Miss Amelia's case is the most complicated, since in her "we" of such a sentence, besides Cousin Lymon, both her father and Marvin Macy would have to be included. What allows me to think so is the way she talks about her father as a primary reference in her life, and the way she relates to Macy during the preparation for the fight, as well as the possible interpretation of the fight itself as a strange consummation of their wedding night. In her case, the sentence would mean: "we (Cousin Lymon, my father, Marvin Macy and I) are the they (Cousin Lymon, my father and Marvin Macy) of me (Amelia, sad, like the sad café).

The experience of the expansion and shrinking of the heart, that is, the experience of transient beauty inevitably indicates growth in the first two cases: Frances and Mick literally grow up to be adults. But can grief and ruin be interpreted as growth? Does Miss Amelia reach a spiritual adulthood? Her situation is tragic, and, for her, it can only be seen in terms of growth through some kind of profound aesthetic experience, as if, with her crossed eyes, she were able to read and reflect on her own beautiful and tragic story. Is this not the way in which literature might offer itself as a "we of me" for its readers, giving an opportunity for self-predication, for reflection on our generic, solitary belonging to the *conditio humana,* the human condition?

*Notes*

[1] All references to the novel are based on the following edition: Carson McCullers. *The Member of the Wedding*. Houghton Mifflin Company, 1946.

[2] Matthias Haase: "Three Forms of the First Person Plural." *Rethinking Epistemology*. Vol. 2, p. 231.

[3] All references to the novel are based on the following edition: Carson McCullers. *The Heart Is a Lonely Hunter*. Houghton Mifflin Company, 1940, 1967.

⁴ All references to the novella are based on the following edition: Carson McCullers. *The Ballad of the Sad Café*. Penguin Books, Ltd., Harmondsworth, Middlesex, England, 1963, 1982. (First published in Great Britain by the Cresset Press, 1953)

⁵ Blaise Pascal has a relevant image in *The Pensées*: Imagine a number of men in chains, all under sentence of death, some of whom are each day butchered in the sight of the others; those remaining see their own condition in that of their fellows and looking at each other with grief and despair await their turn. This is an image of the human condition. (199) [http://www.gutenberg.org/files/18269/18269h/18269-h.htm#SECTION_II],downloaded 08.07.2017.

# Works Cited

DuBois, Cece. "Living the We of Me: Seeing Ourselves As Two Different People." *Rebelle Society*, 13 July 2015. Web, 20 January 2019.

Freeman, Elizabeth "'The We of Me': *The Member of the Wedding*'s Novel Alliances." *Women and Performance*, vol., 8 no. 2, 1996, pp. 111-35.

Haase, Matthias. "Three Forms of the First Person Plural." *Rethinking Epistemology: Volume 2*. Edited by Günter Abel and James Conant. Berlin: De Gruyter, 2012, pp, 229-256.

McCullers, Carson. *The Ballad of the Sad Café*. London: Penguin Books, 1982.

---. *The Heart Is a Lonely Hunter*. Houghton Mifflin, 1967.

---. *The Member of the Wedding*. Houghton Mifflin, 1946.

Oates, Joyce Carol. "You are the We of Me." Review of *Illumination and Night Glare by Carson McCullers*. *London Review of Books*, Vol. 21, no. 17, 2 September 1999, pp. 15-16.

Pascal, Blaise. *Pascal's Pensées*. E. P. Dutton, 1958. Project Guttenberg, 27 April 2006. Web, 8 July 2017.

Vega, Suzanne. "We of Me." *Lover, Beloved: Songs from an Evening with Carson McCullers*. Amanuensis Productions, 2016. CD.

# FINDING CARSON IN CHINA

## Kerry Madden-Lunsford

*It was the year Frankie thought about the world. And she did not see it as a round school globe, with the countries neat and different-colored. She thought of the world as huge and cracked and loose and turning a thousand miles an hour.* The Member of the Wedding

**C is for China.** It is 1987 in the emerald rice fields in Ningbo, China where I teach English with my husband, Kiffen. We are newly married, teaching at a university eclipsed by rice fields where the Number One Teaching Building rises up against a slate sky like a Salvador Dali painting. I sometimes hold classes by the river where a ship sails by each night on its way to Shanghai. We wave to the passengers, but I secretly long to sail away too. *Wait for me!* A water buffalo frolics in a rice paddy when not tethered to its farmer. My goal has been to come to China to have an adventure before real life had to begin and not be encumbered with a lot of history or information—I would make up my own mind about China—in other words, ignorant.

There are few books here except for what we've brought. I have the letters of Isak Dinesen and some short story collections, but the university is so new, there is no library yet.

Then a miracle—the University purchases the entire Penguin Paperback Collection. One title catches my eye called *The Member of the Wedding*. I know Carson McCullers was a Southern writer, but I have worked so hard to escape the South. Yet, annoyingly, I remain homesick. I pick up the novel, and soon realize I am Frankie Addams wandering around Ningbo's green rice fields the way she wandered around her hot Georgia town.

But I don't see the irony of having escaped the South to teach English in China while finding solace in the words of Carson McCullers. Kiffen reads me her stories aloud at night under our mosquito net, since the television only plays old episodes of *Columbo,* and *Mickey Mouse* dubbed in Chinese. BBC Radio and the Voice of America only air once a day. Carson escaped Georgia for New York, but we've escaped Georgia for China, and now we are caught.

> *"I know, but what is it all about? People loose and at the same time caught. Caught and loose. All these people and you don't know what joins them up."* - The Member of the Wedding

I, too, am not connected to anything except for being different and foreign, but Kiffen doesn't worry about such things and finds each day full of possibility. He brings home wire and sculpts it into flowers. He teaches the engineering students and names them Lincoln and Washington, Picasso, and Van Gogh. He studies Chinese and picks up the Ningbo dialect, which comes in handy when we ride our bikes into town on Saturdays to the market where they sell live eel, chickens, and crickets.

**E is for English.** We have no idea how to teach English and no one tells us. We are given a thin boot-leg textbook of English readings and exercises, and after weeks of slogging through an abridged version of "Kon Tiki," I decide that my three classes of twenty-five English majors will write their own plays in groups of five. One student will direct the play, and they will all write it together and create as many characters as there are students in the group. During the first hour of class, we read the boring text and do grammar, and in the second hour of the class, we write plays.

While they write their plays, I orbit from group to group to help them shape the plots and characters. If they can't think of another character for a student to be, I tell them to make a narrator or maybe a stage manager like in "Our Town." We talk about "Our Town," and I try to not speak too fast in my nervousness. After all, I have an MFA in Playwriting. It is my specialty.

But one day, Ms. Xing, our colleague, who is clearly the boss of the English faculty, comes to see me in our room at the Foreign Guest House. She wants to have a "lively conversation" about my responsibilities teaching "Extensive and Intensive English." At first, I am excited to talk to her about the progress the students are making, and then she says, "Perhaps, you are too tired, Mrs. Kerry. Perhaps the students are too tired. It is your responsibility only to teach English.

Extensive English and Intensive English—not to make the theatrical plays."

"I am not too tired," I tell Ms. Xing. "They are learning English by writing plays. They are writing dialogue. They are learning about heroes and villains and conflicts and survival. One play is set at the North Pole."

"Yes, I see," Ms. Xing smiles. "But it is your job to teach extensive and intensive English."

"Look, they are writing stage directions and memorizing lines. They write everything longhand and they type up the plays." I get carried away when it's clear she's not actually listening. "Carson McCullers wrote plays. Tennessee Williams wrote plays. I am teaching them about the world through theatre and film."

"But perhaps it is not extensive and intensive English."

"But what does that even mean?"

We go round and round. I try to not to cry. Ms. Xing never stops smiling. She doesn't back down. I don't back down. She does not care that I intend to make the students see a world beyond Ningbo even while the Bourgeois Liberalism campaign is all the rage and students are forced to attend military classes. I never do learn the difference between either one.

In the end, we have a night of fifteen one-act plays in the spring on the Chemistry Lab Stage with windows wide open, but there are no screens in the windows, so giant lunar moths and buzzing cicadas flutter in from the rice fields to watch the performances too, floating like fairies above the heads of the audience. For the finale, the students gather and sing, "Imagine" which Kiffen blasts on the boom box.

\* \* \* \* \*

But I am still lost on the other side of the world. Everywhere we go people approach, "May I practice my English with you?" I begin writing desperately to graduate theatre departments at NYU, Northwestern, and UCLA—places I hope will save us and give us a plan post-China. I can't eavesdrop here. I'm too big, too noticed and famous.

**I is for interesting.** My Chinese students, English majors, love the word "interesting." One student even names herself—"Interesting." Helen names herself after the brave girl, Helen Burns, from

*Jane Eyre*. Her best friend, Jenny, names herself after the brave girl from *Love Story*. They both say, "It would be *interesting* to create a student newspaper. We could fill it with *interesting* stories." And so, we do that too.

Ms. Xing often says, "It is very *interesting* how you teach the class." I regularly show films in the computer lab. We have exactly TWO FILMS that play all the way through: *Kramer Vs. Kramer* and *Amadeus*. Another colleague, Mr. Fang, says, "I do not find Mr. and Mrs. Kramer *interesting*. I prefer the mystery books."

Ms. Xing says, "Mrs. Kramer is *interesting* like all American women. Perhaps, Mrs. Kerry, you will get the divorce in five years like Mrs. Kramer. Do you think so?"

I do not appreciate Ms. Xing's prediction, but Kiffen finds it hilarious.

Everybody says, "Oh, perhaps China is very *interesting* for you."

When I began to hate the word I say, "How else could we say *interesting*?" and my students come up with all kinds of words: compelling, fascinating, intriguing . . . So we ban the word "interesting" from the classroom. We play vocabulary games. One game is called "Granny's Fat Cat" and we work our way alphabetically through the game—Granny's *astonishing* cat, Granny's *beautiful* cat, Granny's *courteous* cat, and so on. When it came to "I," they know to avoid "interesting," so one student cries out Granny's "intellectual" cat.

The students are my sister's age, and we make each other laugh. They are eager to learn everything—music, conversation, poetry, and theatre. They memorize Emily Dickinson's poem, "I'm Nobody," and they insist that it is perhaps better to BE a "nobody" than a "somebody" because a nobody attracts less attention. And then class is over. I move to the window and look out at the green rice fields and wonder how to fill the rest of the day. The water buffalo and farmer have jobs to do. The construction workers are doing their jobs. Am I doing enough? Have I run to China to avoid competing with playwrights and actors? So, I can say I've done something "interesting" all the way across the world? I hear my father, a football coach, in my ear—*Got a game plan yet? What's after China, Aunt Gertrude?* He nicknamed me Aunt Gertrude as a child because I was a nervous kid who fretted about tornadoes, the end of the world, and going blind like Helen Keller.

\* \* \* \* \*

**M is for Money.** As the school year ends, the administration asks us to stay—they like our teaching. But teach another year. What? They get us drunk on rice wine and we say yes and then we waffle once sober in the gray Ningbo light of day. *Another year? Are you kidding me?* They offer us more money, but we are paid in Chinese money, and they deny my request for FEC—Foreign Exchange Currency, which can be exchanged into dollars. Chinese money must be spent in China.

The two other foreign teachers are leaving too. We will be the only two foreigners in a city of one million Chinese. I've seen the other occasional Westerner pass through town, and I've skulked along behind them like we're somehow related. I'm going crazy. I listen to Laurie Anderson on my Walkman. What would Carson do here? What about Isak Dinesen? We've climbed three of the five holy mountains in China and rubbed the heads of Buddha and lit incense for good luck and tied rocks in trees. But I don't know how to live in the rice fields for another year.

And we'll be twenty-six soon. Impossibly old. "Should we go?" I ask Kiffen.

"We can stay or go. What do you want to do?"

"Maybe we should stay. The students are so sweet and good. But I can't take it."

"Then let's go. We'll have another adventure."

Round and round. How does he stand me? Finally, we decide to go home, which will be either to my parents' basement or his mother's farmhouse, because we will go home broke because of the Chinese money thing.

It's called Renmenbi—and we've been paid lots of it. We buy beautiful pieces of silk—red, gold, lime, purple—with roosters and rabbits and dragons. The rest we spend for tickets on the Trans-Siberian Railroad where we take a train from Beijing to Berlin where the train wheels get changed at each new border. I bring *A Member of the Wedding* and Isak Dinesen's *Letters from Africa* on the Trans-Siberian. They are my touchstones on the train across China, Russia, Poland, and Germany for ten days. I do not yet know that once upon a time Carson McCullers invited Isak Dinesen to lunch, along with Marilyn Monroe and Arthur Miller.

Something terrible and irreparable *almost* happens in West Berlin for it is still West Berlin then—on a train platform—and I wondered for decades to come if I made some kind of Faustian bargain during those dark and furious seconds.

Back in the United States we must get jobs fast, so we move into my parents' Atlanta basement where we lived pre-China. We give away the pieces of Chinese silk as gifts. I'm trying to be a playwright like Lillian Hellman or Beth Henley. I've read everything by Tennessee Williams, Eugene O'Neill, and Edward Albee, but I land a job as office assistant for architects who need their blueprints and coffee NOW.

I am invisible to them. The head secretary offers me hair and make-up tips. She makes me feel like Miss Amelia stomping around this boutique agency of glass brick and designer building plans. I think of hog-killing time and crossed eyes "exchanging one long and secret gaze of grief."

My football coach dad is a little lost too, but I don't see that. He has been fired by the Atlanta Falcons so he's now working with a commercial sports guy doing something that could lead to something, so sometimes he and I take MARTA together to our respective jobs downtown, so Kiffen can use his car to go to his temporary job at Gulf Oil or some other awful place.

Kiffen and I are also trying to decide whether to move to New York or LA or Chicago. I am determined not to stay in Atlanta. That equals failure for me. But the NYU and UCLA graduate programs won't save us. They tell us no.

Northwestern says to try again next year.

One morning while on MARTA with my dad, I complain to him about the monstrous egos of the men in the architecture firm where I'm sent to make coffee or get coffee or file while getting yelled at, which makes me drop the blueprints like a frazzled Vera in *Alice's Restaurant*. Dad is reading the sports page and says without looking up, "Well, honey, you gotta understand when men are at work, they don't have time to be polite or sensitive. They're getting the job done, my dear."

Could he or would he have said that very thing about women at work? *Well, honey, you gotta understand that when women are at work.* No, he would not have said that. My life is a time bomb, ticking away.

\* \* \* \* \*

**S is for Symposium.** And then I see it. A miracle! A Carson McCullers Symposium announcement in the newspaper to take place in her hometown of Columbus, Georgia—it's the first one of its kind! Edward Albee, the playwright, will be there. David Diamond, the composer, too! Leonard Cohen said, "There is a crack in everything. That's how the light gets in." That's how it feels seeing the announcement for the symposium.

There will be screenings of *The Heart Is a Lonely Hunter* and *The Member of the Wedding*. As if we are citizens of the literary world, this Carson McCullers Symposium is a gift. Carson's words saved me in the rice fields of Ningbo, and now she is beckoning us to her hometown a few hours south of Atlanta. I will call in sick the day of the symposium. The architects need their files and blueprints, but I have no blueprint for my life. Carson gave me one and made me pay attention to where I was living in Ningbo, China.

She also said ". . . we are homesick most for the places we have never known." We leave early on Friday morning for Columbus State University. I have never been to a symposium. I didn't even know such things exist. We may even meet Edward Albee. Kiffen and I performed the first scene from *Who's Afraid of Virginia Woolf?* at "All Night Theatre" in Knoxville a few years earlier, but I will not tell him this—I will do something even more annoying.

We drive the 108 miles south as the sun rises over the city. We slip into the darkened auditorium where Virginia Spencer Carr, David Diamond, and Edward Albee sit at a table on the stage discussing Carson McCullers. I see "The Twisted Trinity" in my program and I'm in awe that someone was so clever to think of that. Edward Albee is talking about the time Tennessee Williams and Carson McCullers both revised their plays at the kitchen table.

I love imagining that table where they wrote together in comfort, Carson and Tennessee. I think of how writers help each other along the road. I didn't know that Carson helped Truman Capote when he moved to New York and then ended up furious with him. Truman then helped his childhood best friend, Nelle Harper Lee, when she moved to New York. And he grew jealous of her success and floated the idiotic rumor that he wrote *Mockingbird*.

But I love all of them. Weren't they all in that lonely world together facing a blank page . . . the fear and loneliness?

This is what I remember of the Symposium.

The room is blue and quiet as the experts hold court on stage.

I buy *The Lonely Hunter,* and Virginia Spencer Carr signs it. I have never had a book signed by an author. She thanks me for the letter I sent her and says, "Yes, you're the one who went to China. How interesting."

On Saturday afternoon, Carr leads a tour through Columbus to Carson's home where a plaque is dedicated to her, but a family lives in the home so we don't go inside. Carr describes the time the town held a celebration for Carson's success, but when Carson came to the party, she didn't talk to anyone. I try to imagine being a famous writer and coming back to a tiny southern town not speaking to anyone.

But here is my moment of embarrassment. This is how I remember it.

I have my play with me. My first play—the one that sent my mother into a "how dare you missy" raging fit followed by silent treatment. It is my MFA thesis. It is a great Catholic snore of a play of living rooms and monologues and the friendly neighbor with a sunny outlook on life—its own terrible twisted trinity. Lessons learned, blech. But somehow, we figure out where Edward Albee will be on campus late on Saturday after the tour to Carson's home, and we wait for him.

Kiffen had said, "Give him your play. Maybe he'll say no, but we're here, and he's Edward Albee." We approach him, I ask, and Edward Albee is gracious.

He says, "I'd love to read your play. I'll read it on the plane tomorrow."

He could have said so many things like, "Are you kidding?" or "Go away."

But in that moment, Edward Albee is amused and kind. Did he read the play on the plane? I don't know. I never heard from him, but it was enough for him to say, "I would love to read your play" because he made me feel like a member of something in the world.

The next day is Sunday, and Atlanta and the architects loom, but I want to cross the river into Phenix City, Alabama to trace Carson's path. I am on high alert for Carson McCullers's characters. We find one. As we drive through a neighborhood, a woman is placing large ceramic pigs in her yard. There are probably thirty or so ceramic pigs on blankets. We stop to talk to her. She says, "I've loved pigs my whole life. So I've started a business, Dot's Pigs."

We admire the range of pigs lined up. They are artistic renderings of pigs of all shapes, pink, about the size of a newborn, painted with different flower designs.

"Here," she says, "Take my business card."

The card says, "Dot's Pigs. Lay-away plan available."

We thank Dot, who shouts, "Come back! Christmas is coming."

We promise to come back, but we never do. Instead, we save our money, get pregnant, move to Hollywood, teach and write and raise three kids. We name our first child— not Carson—but Flannery. I write my first novel about a coach's daughter. I write some Smoky Mountain novels for kids. I write a biography of Harper Lee, which brings me back to live in the South after twenty years on the West Coast.

Nowadays I wander the landscapes of Alabama and California, with Kiffen tenured on the West Coast, and me in the Deep South. Our three children grew up. One wanders the streets of Los Angeles, chasing pigeons and talking to the ghost of Jean Harlow. He tells me to write a play called "Lunch in Nyack" about the famous lunch with Carson McCullers, Isak Dinesen, Marilyn Monroe, and Arthur Miller—I tell him there was reported dancing on the table after lunch, which is what I want in my play whether there was or wasn't. Arthur Miller denied there was any dancing, but he would say that. My son and I have this conversation over pizza, because we are trying hard to talk about something creative, but we are both crying because he struggles with the darkness of addiction. I tell him about Isak's diet of champagne and oysters, and he tells me Marilyn wanted to make a movie about Jean Harlow. I foolishly plead and beg and bargain with him to go into treatment and he says, "You know nothing of my life," and he gets up and walks away.

Our middle child, Lucy, lives in Chicago, and paints pictures and studies art therapy in order to work with children and autism. The youngest, Norah, will begin college this year and study public health in Alabama.

But our three children almost never were—not any of them.

It is 1987 again on the train platform in Berlin when I make that Faustian bargain. We are with people we'd collected on the Trans-Siberian Railroad. We wear backpacks and carry our bulging net-bags from China. I hold a portable typewriter. Kiffen announces, "The train is coming! Hurry." We are a large slow-moving group, six or seven, and he gets on the train first. But the rest of us can't make it, so he gets off, or tries to; the door closes on his foot leaving it inside the train while the rest of his body is on the outside of the train. How funny to leave your foot behind along with a backpack, and the train begins to move forward. He, or rather his foot, is inside the first car moving toward the tunnel. He flips into the air like a rag doll, higher. I scream and throw my typewriter over my head and jump at the train. And in the moment of seeing my young husband suspended in a midair cartwheel, I plead and beg and bargain for him to live no matter what. Make me suffer anything else—I can take it. Give me any amount of pain but not this—don't let him die. The train miraculously shuts down, and he's on the ground. The conductors come over to yell at us in German—and Kiffen leaps up, foot still attached, no blood, not a scratch, laughing, "I'm fine, I'm fine, I'm fine."

Was it a Faustian bargain at the train in Berlin? Did some kind of evil spirit hear my scream to save my husband but make our beautiful boy a drug addict? Are there such things? Has my grief made me crazy? Will our lonely raging boy ever find peace or "the we of me?" I'm told not to ask those questions. I'm told not to ask why but just to live in the moment and find gratitude. I remember a young couple, who read to each other *The Member of the Wedding* at night under a mosquito net, made plans for a future, and a marriage began in the green rice fields of Ningbo long ago.

> *"The whole world was this symphony, and there was not enough of her to listen."* - The Heart Is a Lonely Hunter

# Works Cited

McCullers, Carson. *The Heart Is a Lonely Hunter.* 1940. *Carson McCullers: Complete Novels.* Edited by Carlos L. Dews. Library of Congress, 2001.

---. *The Member of the Wedding.* 1946. *The Collected Works of Carson McCullers.* Edited by Carlos L. Dews. Library of America, 2001.

# "Except For This Queer Marriage": Taboo Pairings and Gender Restrictions in *The Ballad of the Sad Café*

## James Mayo

For years, scholars have commented on the nature of homoerotic or "taboo" relationships in the stories and novels of Carson McCullers, with many pointing out that the true nature of these relationships is most often presented in an ambiguous manner. Whether this is due to social mores or censorship of the times or McCullers's desire to present readers with ambiguity is unclear, but it's common that these relationships fail, resulting in works that end with characters heartbroken, alone, and desolate. From the muted relationship between John Singer and Antonapoulos, to Biff Brannon's assuming of his dead wife's persona in *The Heart Is a Lonely Hunter,* and to Miss Amelia's assuming a masculine persona in *The Ballad of the Sad Café*, McCullers presents us with characters who are operating outside of the accepted moral code and social notions of gender roles and sexual identity.

And while it's true that, as many have pointed out, these relationships can be explained away as platonic and the gender-bending as either tomboyish or "prissy" behavior, it's McCullers's description of Miss Amelia's liquor in *The Ballad of the Sad Café* that gives us solid footing on which to advance as we explore this topic:

> It is known that if a message is written with lemon juice on a clean sheet of paper there will be no sign of it. But if the paper is held for a moment to the fire then the letters turn brown and the meaning becomes clear. Imagine that the whisky is fire and that the message is that which is known only in the soul of man—then the worth of Miss Amelia's liquor can be understood. Things that have gone unnoticed, thoughts that have been harbored far back in the dark mind, are suddenly recognized and comprehended. (McCullers 203)

McCullers goes on to point out that those common, working class Southerners who spin looms or weave all day can see beauty, whether it's found suddenly in a marsh lily or the "weird radiance of [the] midnight January sky." This description gives us a metaphor by which we can safely explore the gender bending and sexual identity issues that are prevalent in her works. McCullers gives us the words in lemon juice, and we hold them to the fire. And while the characters "may suffer [. . .] or be spent with joy," the "experience has shown the truth," and readers are warmed and see the "message hidden there" (203). In this case, the message we see is that the novella and thus the main characters follow a three-stage pattern of development, but they all end up in a world that is diminished and in which they have no place.

All three of the main characters of *Ballad* are described in a way that should immediately make us consider questions of gender identity. Miss Amelia is clearly presented as masculine, with her overalls and swamp boots, her "unnatural" size and strength, and her powerful position in the community. Cousin Lymon, on the other hand, with his "prissy" ways that remind the locals of Morris Finestein, his harlequin-like dress, and his constant sicknesses and physical weaknesses, evokes notions of femininity. Marvin Macy is presented as the stereotypical, overly-masculine Southern male. Though he is considered widely as the most handsome man around, he is in fact "an evil character" (217). He is the reason many young girls in the area have been ruined, and he tempts the weak with the marijuana he keeps in his pocket (217). Macy even changes the weather when he returns, bringing first a heat wave that destroys the slaughtered pork and later snow, which few in the town have ever seen before. It is only natural that he would end up in prison after his failed marriage to Amelia leads him to his worst behavior.

Before considering the effects that the taboo pairing (or pairings, in this case) have on Miss Amelia, we must consider a pattern that is seen consistently throughout the work. There is movement from bad, to good, and back to bad, a three-stage pattern that mirrors the triangulated relationship that is at the heart of the novella. The town begins as "dreary," becomes "cheerful" when the café is operating and returns to "dreary" in the end. The patrons of the café, no matter their sense of manners or propriety, begin as typical Southern uncouth or provincial types, instinctively have manners, and conduct themselves properly in the café, but return to their provincial ways when the café is closed. Cousin Lymon shows up sad and tattered, becomes a different person when taken in by Miss Amelia, and returns to his former self after the fight. Marvin Macy is evil before falling in love with Amelia, changes his ways, but returns to his former self, compared more than once to the devil, after the love goes sour. Miss Amelia herself goes through these changes from bad, to good, and back to bad. There are three rooms above her café, there have been three significant men in her life, and the three form a triangulated relationship once Macy moves in.

Just as Amelia's café and Lymon's presence change the town for the better, Marvin Macy's love for Amelia causes him to change his ways and reform "completely" (218). He is nicer to others and becomes a Christian, and after two years, he finally has the strength to declare himself to Miss Amelia. Thus the "queer marriage" takes place. To the delight of the townspeople, who are just as curious about this romance as the readers are, Miss Amelia leaves the marriage altar and walks right back to her store to conduct business, leaving a confused, lovesick husband to follow two paces behind her. Their wedding night, as readers learn, was a disaster, with Miss Amelia stomping down the stairs in what is considered traditional male clothing (breeches and khaki jacket), her face dark, to drink coffee and smoke her father's pipe by the fire. After three days, Marvin Macy, the groom in a "sorry fix" (220), presented Amelia with a paper that "signed over to her the whole of his worldly goods" (221). And finally, after days of sexual frustration, Macy comes home drunk and tries to force the issue of consummation, only to be hit in the face by the stronger Miss Amelia. Once the "queer marriage" ends, Macy leaves town to pursue a life of crime and eventual time in the penitentiary, while Miss Amelia never again mentions his name, only referring to him as "that loom-fixer I was married to" (222).

Amelia's relationship with Cousin Lymon is, in a fashion typical for McCullers, presented to readers in a very subtle manner. As mentioned earlier, the affection she shows him could be explained away as simple human compassion or platonic love, as is the case with many of McCullers's characters. When the hunchback sits crying on the edge of Miss Amelia's premises, she reaches over and touches his hump to comfort him. Even at this early stage of the novella, this action will seem out of character. But as their relationship and the café develop, they fall into the easy routine of a couple in love, though McCullers does omit the intimate, physical details of the relationship. Amelia begins wearing the red dress on Sundays, switching her gender identity to make herself more attractive. The two spend a great deal of time together, as tasks that Amelia had previously performed alone are now completed with his company. They hunt together, they manage her properties together, they chop sugar cane together, they journey through the swamp together, with Amelia even carrying Lymon on her back when the path leads through a bog (214-15). McCullers tells us an "explanation is due for all this behavior" (215). Maintaining that the change in Amelia can't be noticed from the outside, she is in love, perhaps for the first time. The physical nature of this love is only given to us as possible scenarios as seen through the eyes of the people in town. The subject of constant rumor, which is to be expected considering the nature of the relationship, they are considered by many as "living in sin" (215) by those who, at the same time, relish the gothic nature of this romance between a "powerful blunderbuss of a person" and a "weakly little hunchback" (215). The "good people" maintain that "if these two have found some satisfaction of the flesh between themselves, then it was a matter concerning them and God alone" (215). However, the general consensus is that the relationship is taboo, perhaps from a religious position, perhaps based on physical differences and gender roles, or perhaps because it's incestuous (or any combination of the three). It is at this point that McCullers offers readers her definition of love, one that maintains that "this lover can be a man, woman, child, or indeed any human creature on this earth" (216). In other words, any person, no matter how flawed or unusual, can become the lover or the beloved. This would include any pairing, no matter how the eyes of the outwardly world judged it.

Following the pattern McCullers has established, the relationship between Miss Amelia and Cousin Lymon must end and it cannot end well. This begins when Marvin Macy returns. The facts concerning Amelia's marriage to Macy have been kept from Lymon, and he is at once infatuated with and intrigued by Marvin Macy. Cousin Lymon follows Macy wherever he goes, even waiting outside of Mrs. Hale's house and serenading Macy before he wakes up. Cousin Lymon flirts overtly and publicly with Macy:

> Cousin Lymon had a very peculiar accomplishment, which he used whenever he wished to ingratiate himself with someone. He would stand very still, and with just a little concentration, he could wiggle his large pale ears with marvelous quickness and ease. This trick he always used when he wanted to get something special out of Miss Amelia, and to her it was irresistible. Now as he stood there the hunchback's ears were wiggling furiously on his head, but it was not Miss Amelia at whom he was looking this time. The hunchback was smiling at Marvin Macy with an entreaty that was near to desperation. (235)

But every attempt that Lymon makes to win the affection of Marvin Macy is met with violence, reminiscent of the way Amelia rebuffed Macy after their marriage. Miss Amelia is a witness to this flirtation and knows that she will lose Cousin Lymon to Macy and tries to keep him by wearing the ill-fitting red dress on a daily basis. However, the relationship between the three of them takes a dramatic turn when Cousin Lymon invites Macy to move into Miss Amelia's three rooms above the café. At this point, Amelia, afraid of losing Lymon completely, does nothing to get rid of the interloper, the man, according to Amelia, whose "split hoof" would never enter her premises.

The pairing of Miss Amelia and Lymon at some point merges into a trio after Marvin Macy settles in above the café, with McCullers playing with the number three once again (three men in her life, three rooms above her café, the three of them living there together), and the tension gradually increases, as everyone in town knows that Miss Amelia and Marvin Macy will eventually have to resort to physical violence to settle the matter. And while it may be easy to settle with the notion that Miss Amelia picks up her traditional feminine identity in order to save her relationship with Cousin Lymon and to see the fight between Amelia and Macy as just an act of physical violence over who will take possession of the hunchback, there is more than the suggestion that there is something larger at work, as we see McCullers's pattern of threes coming to fruition. The sexual nature of the fight, with the tension building for days or weeks, Marvin Macy's greasing himself and going shirtless, seems to relieve the tension built years before with the unconsummated marriage:

> For a few seconds after the first blows they merely shuffled their feet around on the bare floor, experimenting with various positions, and making mock fists. Then, like wildcats, they were suddenly on each other. There was the sound of knocks, panting, and thumpings on the floor. (249)

As the fight progresses, we see "their hipbones braced against each other" and their swaying "backward and forward, from side to side" (249). Who wins eventually and releases the pent up aggression and tension will be determined by the third lover as in an act of betrayal he attacks Amelia just as she has overpowered Macy, allowing Macy to recover just enough to win the fight. The fight offers the characters the opportunity to settle their sexual and physical differences once and for all. Both have the need for dominance and control over the other, and conventional thinking would tell us that the physically stronger (Miss Amelia in this case) should win the fight. But as the taboo pairings are established through bent gender norms, the fight will, in fact, have just the opposite effect. And it is only fitting that the climactic scene has the three of them entwined together on the floor of the café.

This dark story, I would argue, is not just presented to us as a parable or cautionary tale, but as a fairy tale that ends badly. It could only end with Amelia alone again, sitting by the window, ostensibly hoping for the return of Cousin Lymon or Marvin Macy (or perhaps both), as the track of her love has followed the pattern of three established within the novella. And these taboo relationships and the switching of traditional gender roles could only take place where it does, in an isolated place far from the outside (normal) world. We see this in the numerous references to Society City, the largest nearby town. There is no place for Miss Amelia's love for Cousin Lymon or, for that matter, Cousin Lymon's love for Marvin Macy.

# WORKS CITED

McCullers, Carson. *Collected Stories of Carson McCullers*. Mariner, 1998.

# "Some Unheard-of Thing": Performing Xenophobia and Gender Conformity in the Play *The Member of the Wedding*

## Liz Mayo

In her stage adaptation of *The Member of the Wedding*, Carson McCullers uses figurative incest to depict socio-economic barriers and a pervasive fear of foreign bodies. She explores how a young girl's infatuation with her older brother is the *least* taboo relation in the 1940s South. This is an era where so many other relationships—interracial, homosexual, and unwed—were far more socially unacceptable than the affection Frankie holds. At the heart of this time and region is the same irrational anxiety about outsiders or foreign bodies.

In *Everybody Lies,* Seth Stephens-Davidowitz writes about the data he uncovered on American sexual desires. He notes, "If you define being in the closet as picking partners based on what society wants rather than what you want, many people are in the closet" ("Proof"). In short, we fantasize often about one thing, but we choose to keep this desire hidden for fear of becoming a social outcast. McCullers's characters grapple with what they want versus what they know they *should* want. Frankie, like all of these contemporary humans lying about their desires, is someone who simply seeks acceptance within society. When she and other characters are shamed or punished for their wanting, they are forced into a figurative or literal death, ultimately conforming to what they feel culture desires them to be and to want.

Born to a middle-class family in 1917 Columbus, Georgia, McCullers, like many of the androgynous, young female protagonists in her work, had a sexually ambiguous identity. Even as a young girl, McCullers's friends and family found her quite unusual. Her time was divided between music and writing, with playwriting being one of her hobbies. As Lawrence Graver notes in his biography of McCullers, she was drawn to the "incest, lunacy, and murder" of Eugene O'Neill (5). Often favoring triangulated relationships in favor of traditional pairings (Adams 551), her unconventional sexual visioning reverberates throughout her writing. Known for writing about the outcasts of the traditional South, McCullers herself, in many ways, personified the very people she sought to portray: chronically ill and married to a bisexual man she later divorced, she died relatively young at the age of fifty. Her greatest successes came from her novels, in particular *The Heart Is a Lonely Hunter* and *The Member of the Wedding*, which McCullers later adapted into the play discussed here.

Francis Dedmond paraphrases a critic from *The New Yorker* who, after reading the novel version of *The Member of the Wedding*, proclaimed that McCullers's work had "many components of great writing but lacked a sense of drama" (47). Her novel, however, caught the eye of one man: southern playwright, Tennessee Williams. He immediately invited McCullers and her husband to spend the summer of 1946 with him, intending that McCullers transform her novel that lacked "drama" into a real drama (Dedmond 47). Without hesitation, the pair set forth to do just that. For obvious reasons, much of what transpires in the novel has been condensed or cut altogether, but McCullers remained true to her theme of the individual's need to find a place where he or she belongs in a violent region. This search takes place amidst the exploration of the connection between "sexual intolerance and racial bigotry" (Adams 553) in the South that remained firmly fixed to these debilitating labels. Unlike the private act of reading the inner thoughts of a precocious preteen, McCullers's play creates a forum that "demands a completely objective, third-person point of view, with no omniscience of character"—an act that must be achieved within the practical time constraints of a theatrical production (Dedmond 49).

After seeking the help of script doctors and experienced playwrights alike, suffering a stroke, and battling over legal issues concerning the production of the play, McCullers's final version debuted at New York's Empire Theatre on January 5, 1950, under the direction of Harold Clurman. The play garnered immediate critical acclaim and won the New York Dramatists Circle Award for best play, two Donaldson awards, and the Theatre Club Inc.'s gold medal for best playwright of the year before completing a successful 501 performances on Broadway. Several actors from the play, including

Ethel Waters as Berenice, Julie Harris as Frankie, and five-year-old Brandon De Wilde as John Henry, later starred in the 1952 film version adapted by Edna and Edward Anhalt and directed by Fred Zinnemann. For her work in the film, Julie Harris was nominated for an Academy Award for Best Actress in a Leading Role. The play was later revived by the Phoenix Theatre in 1975, by the Roundabout Theatre in 1989, and by the Young Vic Theatre in London in 2007. As Virginia Spencer Carr remarks, the stage adaptation of *The Member of the Wedding* gave McCullers "emotional release as well as extraordinary acclaim and financial security" (104).

Frankie's infatuation with her brother Jarvis and his fiancée Janice escalates when they announce their plans to marry. She fantasizes that they will take her with them and become a happy family. The opening scene shows Frankie gazing in adoration at the couple. She says to Janice, "It was such a surprise when Jarvis wrote home you are going to be married." Janice responds, "I hope it wasn't a bad surprise." Frankie says, "Oh, Heavens no! (*with great feeling*). As a matter of fact . . . (*She strokes Janice's shoes tenderly and Jarvis's army boot.*) If only you knew how I feel" (McCullers 3-4). She knows that something inside of her feels different when she sees the two of them together, but her innocence does not allow her to pinpoint her feelings. She says, "Oh I can't understand it! The way it all just suddenly happened . . . I have never been so puzzled . . . They are so beautiful" (12). Frankie even wishes to change her name to Jasmine to be in lilting consonantal harmony with their names (26). She eventually declares, "I know that the bride and my brother are the 'we' of me. So I'm going with them, and joining with the wedding . . . I love the two of them so much and we belong to be together" (52). Frankie does not realize at this point the unlikelihood of her own fantasy, nor does she understand how this improbable relationship will eventually relate to the unjust love laws that constrict everyone around her. McCullers rewrites Frankie, in this time before puberty, as the site for an ambiguous body where none of her "childhood" longings would be deemed depraved. This wishful thinking is made all the more open to interpretation, as Frankie herself does not fit into the part of traditional girlhood. Her admiration for Janice, a lesbian longing, is rendered harmless both for Frankie's age and neutered appearance. It is this version of Frankie who imagines a life where she is not only a "member" of this trio, but also traveling together and becoming "members of the whole world" (88). Her inability to find a place in her hot, southern town—in a home where her widowed father barely notices her existence—leads Frankie into her fantasies of membership and, ultimately, acceptance. For McKay Jenkins, McCullers's characters' androgyny symbolizes "a world beyond the 'horror' of sexuality, which to [McCullers] represented not only the violence of desire . . . but artistic and spiritual shackling as well" (181). Jenkins further comments about McCullers's characters' search for a "sexless innocence" where the possibilities of loving all types of people are endless (182). The sexed body does not have this luxury, as it is forced to couple only with an acceptable partner according to societal laws. It is in this staid climate of the 1940s South where Frankie's body cannot find membership for her unsexed self.

Berenice, Frankie's black maid and mother figure, attempts to teach Frankie about the taboo nature of her obsession with Jarvis and Janice. Berenice says, "If you start out falling in love with some unheard-of thing like that, what is going to happen to you? . . . So what will become of you?" (80). Because Berenice, as a black woman in the pre-Civil Rights Movement South, has had to confront the limitations of who she can and cannot love, she is better equipped to understand the implications of Frankie's actions. Like a mother, Berenice takes a tough love approach to make Frankie understand that her childhood longings will never work in the real world. Gary Richards remarks on the double nature of Frankie's fantasy. Not only is incest taboo, but also Frankie's by-proxy relationship with Janice is forbidden as an act of homosexuality; this threesome would, additionally, counteract the expected monogamy that accompanies traditional marriage laws (188). Frankie's obsession further intensifies until the reality of the situation is apparent at the same moment that everything else in the play begins to fall apart. Berenice, who herself is an anomaly as a black woman with one blue glass eye, becomes the blind seer, of sorts. She guides both Frankie and her cousin John Henry by the laws of social acceptance, proclaiming, "When folks are lonesome and left out, they turn so mean" (45). Though she recognizes the unrealistic nature of Frankie's obsession with Jarvis, she also remarks about the fact that everyone on this planet needs to love and be loved.

As Frankie's fantasy slowly dissipates in the wake of reality, McCullers depicts how Frankie's incestuous feelings are the *least* unnatural things about her situation. Though her longing to be a part of the couple, to attend their honeymoon, and live with them breaks social rules, it cannot compare to the inhumane actions of Frankie's surrounding environment in the 1940s American South. Racism, homophobia, and classism are all issues that Frankie strives to ignore until the reality of her brother and sister-in-law's departure after the wedding becomes wholly apparent. In many ways, the unusual nature of Frankie's longing is assuaged by the fact that she is still a child, and an audience or readers can forgive innocent childhood fantasies. Still, Rachel Adams views McCullers's depiction of Frankie's longing as the author's own challenge toward traditional marital roles, since Frankie does not wish to become a bride but instead longs to be a "member" (573). It is too simple, however, to posit this dramatic structuring as McCullers's personal anti-heteronormative fantasy. Instead, this link represents McCullers's post-Antebellum South that, under human atrocities like Jim Crow laws and the continued problematic sexist structuring of Southern families, highlighted the position of 1940s Southern society's freaks: a butch girl, a feminine boy, and a black, one-eyed maid living in the home of a widower shadow figure and creating their own safe space within the confines of the kitchen that houses their longing and imaginings.

Frankie breaks gender norms through her appearance and her actions, which render her a "freak" in Southern society. She is a lanky girl with a close-buzzed haircut. Even her name is gender neutral. Like McCullers, Frankie is androgynous, and she enjoys writing plays about crooks and cowboys. Janice asks, "Do you ever have romances?" Frankie responds, ". . . I had crook shows for the most part. You see I never believed in love until now. [*Her look lingers on Janice and Jarvis . . .* ]" (8-9). McCullers challenges traditional female norms that were especially stringent in the South. Unlike the older girls that form a club near Frankie's home—a group she is not invited to join—Frankie's dirty appearance, lanky form, and buzz-cut head set her apart as a grotesque deformity of womanhood. Sarah Gleeson-White writes, "The female adolescent is perhaps even more grotesque than her adult counterpart for not only is she female, but also she is in that liminal state between childhood and adulthood and, in the case of Mick [the female protagonist in *The Heart Is a Lonely Hunter*] and Frankie, between masculine and feminine gender identification" (111). She retreats into the company of her younger male cousin, John Henry, and the two of them are obsessed with the "freaks" that come to town with the carnival. Frankie says, "I doubt if they ever get married or go to a wedding." In response, John Henry remarks that the "little old pin-head at the fair" was the "cutest little girl I ever saw. I never saw anything so cute in my whole life" (28-9). This conversation follows the passing by of the girls in the club. Rachel Adams notes, "the awkward relationship between bodies and things highlights the limitations of an idealized femininity and facilitates the imagination of a new social order, one that would reject the normal in favor of the queer possibilities of the freak's extraordinary corporeal form" (553). The juxtaposition between the ideal and the "deformed" Southern female—the girls in dresses and the pin-head girl at the carnival—are flipped in their physical descriptions: while John Henry views the carnival girl as "cute," Frankie describes the newest member of the girls' club, Mary Littlejohn, as the "pasty fat girl with those tacky pigtails" (20).

Even Frankie's friend John Henry does not adhere to heteronormative male behavior. When Frankie gives John Henry a doll that she received from Jarvis instead of a prize from Alaska—a gift that brings great disappointment to Frankie, who would never be interested in playing with traditionally female gendered toys—John Henry says, "You serious when you give me this? [*He pulls up the doll's dress and pats her.*] I will name her Belle" (27). He plays "mommy" to the doll and "*holds out an imaginary skirt and begins to skip around the room with one finger resting on the top of his head*" (28-9). Neither of the children recognizes their own social idiosyncrasies, but they slowly become aware of the rules that dictate their ability to touch and be touched by certain others. Unlike the restrictive society around the children, they find beauty and awe in the other "foreign bodies" of their era, including the carnival freaks and Honey, Berenice's homosexual black relative.

Berenice tells the children about all of the other "unnatural" pairings she has known: handsome men who loved ugly women, good women who loved evil men, and men who loved other men. She tells the story of Lily Mae Jenkins, a transvestite who fell in love with a man and "changed into a girl" (56-7). Frankie is incredulous. She cannot believe that there ever was such a person. John Henry innocently asks, "How did that boy change into a girl? Did he kiss his elbow? [*He tries to kiss his elbow*]" (58). McKinnie and Dews describe Berenice's reasoning behind relaying this tale: "Berenice seems to associate what Frankie wants to do with what Lily Mae has done because both are considered unacceptable behavior by society" (65). Frankie later tells Berenice about an incident that happened while she was in town. She says:

> I was walking along and I passed two stores with a alley in between. The sun was frying hot. And just as I passed this alley, I caught a *glimpse* of something in the corner of my left eye. A dark double shape. And this glimpse brought to my mind—so sudden and clear—my brother and the bride that I just stood there and couldn't hardly bear to look and see what it was . . . Then I turn slowly and look. And you know what was there? . . . It was just two colored boys. That was all. But it gave me such a queer feeling. (72)

This account, though Frankie does not understand it, is something that Berenice immediately comprehends. Frankie has connected all of the events of the past weeks in her mind. She knows that her love for Jarvis is forbidden because it is an act of incest, as is her love for Janice because it would be akin to Lily Mae Jenkins becoming a girl—an act of homosexuality. It is no small leap to compare Jarvis and Janice to two black boys because the pairings are equally prescribed love laws to which Frankie must conform. Especially in a restrictive Southern culture, Frankie cannot love any of these people for fear of social repercussions.

As if Frankie intuits the danger of entering the socio-political sphere, it is only natural that she finds comfort in her love for her brother. Jarvis is from the same space as Frankie: the same home and the same womb so he is familiar. Her attachment to her brother is underscored by her near-orphan's existence in a home where her father is nearly always absent or at least insufficient as a nurturer, and her mother died giving birth to her; Frankie finds in Jarvis and Janice a love that will also mimic that of parental figures. Bertram

Wyatt-Brown examines brother-sister relationships that flourished under a complicated system of familial ethics. He states, "The system of honor or, to use the more familiar terms, patriarchy and womanly subordination, engendered these emotions as a way to cope with the process of maturing. Wherever fathers exercised their right to rule—and to be free—children were likely to see in each other idealizations that were a comfort to them both" (253).

Frankie's situation is unique, if not more problematic, because of the early death of her mother and her rarely present father. Frankie says, "Jarvis remembers mother . . . and I don't remember her at all" (36). Her father works incessantly and has little interaction with Frankie. She thinks aloud, "Sometimes I wonder if papa loves me or not?" (54). When the temporary security of this parental bond is removed—security brought on by Jarvis and Janice's presence due to the impending wedding—Frankie's environment collapses. Kathryn Lee Seidel's work corroborates this problematic father-daughter bond where the intimacy between the two can become heightened in a house where the mother has died in childhood or from some disease (430). The only difference in this play is that Jarvis has become the stand-in parent for the father, and he will, ultimately, "abandon" Frankie just like her mother and father did.

After the wedding, Frankie makes preparations to leave, giving away her costumes to John Henry and bidding adieu to various spaces in the house. As the bride and her brother move to leave, Frankie shouts, "*We!* When you say *we*, you only mean you and Jarvis. And I am not included" (100). She is determined to go away, and her next plan is to dress like a boy and join the Merchant Marines (103), another nod to her male-gendered proclivities. A storm escalates, and Frankie leaves with her father's pistol and a suitcase. When she returns, John Henry has taken ill and dies unexpectedly. Berenice's friend, Honey, who is featured more in the novel, has drawn a razor on a white man and eventually ends up hanging himself in prison. John Henry was too *abnormal* to exist in the normal world, and this leads to his death. Honey commits an act that is against all that has been ordained: he, twice, steps out of his socially dictated space. Patricia Yaeger comments, "The South itself is in crisis, anxious about the end of the war and the advent of racial catastrophe, and its children are caught within a racial, homosocial ideology that demands terrible conformity to its norms" (181). In short, neither John Henry nor Honey are welcome in a Southern white man's club, thus their incompatibility with Southern culture leads to their demise.

Lingering over all of this local tragedy is the worldwide news of the atom bomb, which sets the tone for the hostile world outside of Frankie's community. Frankie moves towards puberty as she becomes increasingly more aware of the inhumane ways in which humans—all members of the same planet—treat one another. She says, "There are so many things about the world I do not understand" (89). She reads in the newspaper more news about the bomb. She says, "The paper says this new atom bomb is worth twenty thousand tons of T.N.T. . . . The paper says the bomb is a very important science discovery" (90). All of these outside influences only enter the house when Frankie comes to terms with the limitations of her love. She cannot be with her brother, with other women, or with men of another color. McCullers's inclusion of incest makes this taboo seem less so in a world where everything else is so broken. Why would Frankie's obsession with Jarvis be harmful if people can die simply for their skin color or their sexual preference? How could her affection compare to a bomb that can kill millions of people? Incest here is juxtaposed against a socially and politically unjust system that harms from the outside. Loving her brother seems safe to Frankie. Why look further when things beyond the home can only destroy? More than love of a black male or for someone of the same sex, Frankie's adoration of her brother could be the most accepted love in her Southern world.

After Janice and Jarvis leave, Frankie runs away from home, but she returns, stating, "When I was running around the dark scary streets, I begun to realize that my plans for Hollywood and the Merchant Marines were child plans that would not work" (108). At the close of the scene—Frankie's move from prepubescent girlhood to socially and culturally aware young womanhood—Frankie states, "I realize that the world is certainly—a sudden place" (111). The start of the next scene shows the same house and yard, but all of the childish things are removed. Frankie no longer looks to Berenice for guidance, and as her idealized love for Jarvis and Janice was removed, in creeps something new: racism. She says to Berenice, "You could never possibly understand it. It's just not in you" (113), seemingly setting Berenice apart as an inferior race. We learn that nearly simultaneous with John Henry's and Honey's deaths, Frankie has befriended the very thing she once abhorred: Mary Littlejohn, a paragon of young, Southern femininity. Judith Giblin James notes, "... poignant is her [Frankie's] capitulation at the end when—symbolically discarding her childhood boyishness with the death of John Henry—she becomes a giddy girl preparing tea sandwiches in anticipation of the visit of her new friend, Mary Littlejohn. She has become a parody of the feminine role .... This is no happy ending" (55). When Frankie outgrows the possibilities of her unsexed self and learns that the outside world can infiltrate her home and kill the people she loves, she loses her admiration for the "freaks" with whom she was once so captivated. She conforms and retreats into the most readily available place for her in Southern culture; she performs, by acceptable Southern womanhood standards, her prescribed role. This girlish Frankie—who now goes by the more feminine Frances—underscores Sarah Gleeson-White's notion that McCullers's works "highlight the specific constraints of entering womanhood in Southern society" and the tales become "the story of female limits" (112). Frankie molds herself into an outwardly feminine girl who is placidly compliant yet assertive of her white supremacy. She learns what so many adults know: it is simply easier to perform conformity.

Frankie's move into adolescence—when a change in her body reflects a shift in her childhood innocence—highlights a greater fear of these transformations within a xenophobic Southern culture. Still, the play form, unlike novel depictions, creates a stage where this change and stasis—which replays again and again in a drama—can become a unique act upon each night of every new production. McCullers's play focuses on societies in which its members are confined by laws that dictate who they can love. The pervasive fear of foreign bodies that necessitates these "laws" is more critical in a contemporary post-9/11 world where an American population again rethinks its regulations for membership into this country. Dramatic interpretation of this fear creates an empathetic audience, as these "enemies," both internal and external, are now all the more near. We are offered the possibility of a female body attempting to break from the confines of her restrictive Southern home—Frankie wishing to see the world, for example, but instead dying a figurative death of socio-normative conformity.

McCullers's characters understand this: it is our painfully awkward adulthood that bends us into what the world intends for us. In Frankie, McCullers offers a glimpse at the young body's non-binary malleability—a revolt against constricting Southern life until adolescence demands one's allegiance to only one sex; in short, are we male or are we female? And like Frankie's South, even the contemporary South is not comfortable with the in-between. Frankie's inevitable transformation into Frances means she cannot exist in the same form once her desires are firmly closeted. In the end, it is a cautionary tale: the outsider transforms into an insider, trading authenticity for cognitive dissonance and club membership.

# WORKS CITED

Adams, Rachel. "A Mixture of Delicious and Freak." *American Literature*, vol. 71, no. 3, 1999, pp. 551-583.

Carr, Virginia Spencer. *Understanding Carson McCullers*. U of South Carolina P, 2005.

Dedmond, Francis B. "Doing Her Own Thing: Carson McCullers' Dramatization of *The Member of the Wedding*." *South Atlantic Bulletin*, vol. 40, no. 2, 1975, pp. 47-52.

Gleeson-White, Sarah. "Revisiting the Southern Grotesque: Mikhail Bakhtin and the Case of Carson McCullers." *Southern Literary Journal*, vol. 33, no. 2, 2001, pp. 108-123.

Graver, Lawrence. *Carson McCullers*. U of Minnesota P, 1969.

James, Judith Giblin. "Carson McCullers, Lillian Smith, and the Politics of Broadway." McDonald and Paige, pp. 42-60.

Jenkins, McKay. *The South in Black and White: Race, Sex, and Literature in the 1940s*. U of North Carolina P, 1999.

McCullers, Carson. *The Member of the Wedding: A Play*. New Directions, 1951.

McDonald, Robert L. and Linda Rohrer Paige, editors. *Southern Women Playwrights: New Essays in Literary History and Criticism*. U of Alabama P, 2002.

McKinnie, Betty E., and Carlos L. Dews. "The Delayed Entrance of Lily Mae Jenkins: Queer Identity, Gender Ambiguity, and Southern Ambivalence in Carson McCullers's *The Member of the Wedding.*" McDonald and Paige, pp. 61-72.

Richards, Gary. *Lovers and Beloveds: Sexual Otherness in Southern Fiction, 1936-1961.* Louisiana State UP, 2005.

Seidel, Kathryn Lee. "Myths of Southern Womanhood in Contemporary Southern Literature." *The History of Southern Women's Literature*, edited by Carolyn Perry and Mary Louise Weaks, Louisiana State UP, 2002, pp. 429-438.

Stephens-Davidowitz, Seth. "Proof that Americans are Lying about Their Sexual Desires." Interview by Sean Illing, *Vox*, Vox Media, 27 June 2017, www.vox.com.

Wyatt-Brown, Bertram. *Southern Honor: Ethics and Behavior in the Old South.* Oxford UP, 2007

Yaeger, Patricia. *Dirt and Desire: Reconstructing Southern Women's Writing, 1930-1990.* U of Chicago P, 2000.

# Angels, Tomboys, and Melancholy, Carson McCullers and the Swiss Writer Annemarie Schwarzenbach

Annette Runte

**Friendships and Influences**

In 1940, Carson McCullers and the Swiss journalist Annemarie Schwarzenbach, whose biographies show some astonishing affinities, met in New York City by chance (Savigneau 2001:68-70). Both published their first novels at a very young age and treated similar problems in their literary works: human loneliness and the impossibility of reciprocal love (cf. Bloom 1986). With the publication of *The Heart Is a Lonely Hunter*, the Georgian writer had become famous overnight. Searching for information about German Jews, she called upon Erika Mann, Thomas Mann's eldest daughter in American exile, who received her at the Bedford Hotel. Carson describes in her unfinished autobiography, how deeply impressed she was, when an elegant *garçonne* with a boyish look entered the room: "She had a face that I knew would haunt me to the end of my life" and "a look of suffering [...] that I could not define" (McCullers 1999:21). Carson fell madly in love with the Swiss heiress, scion of a wealthy family, and never surmounted that passion (Carr 1975:100). But Annemarie, infatuated with Erika Mann, whom she courted in vain for a decade, could not respond to Carson's demands (cf. Miermont 2004:63, 161). They became close friends, however, even if they were soon separated under dramatic circumstances, when, after a suicide attempt, Schwarzenbach was committed to a psychiatric hospital and then deported to Europe. The correspondence which lasted until Annemarie's early death in 1942, was partially destroyed (Miermont 2004:383-385; Alexis Schwarzenbach 2011:419).

The long forgotten Swiss author[1] was rediscovered in the 1980s and became a feminist 'cult figure' as well as an object of literary, cultural, and gender studies (cf. Fähnders/Tobler 2008). Already well known as a travelling reporter for her famous photo portraits in the European press, Annemarie Schwarzenbach became the icon of the 'inconsolable angel' (Roger Martin du Gard)[2] grieving over the European catastrophe. Today, she is seen, like Carson McCullers (cf. Gleeson-White 2003), as a forerunner of gender deconstruction (cf. Mayer 2005). I will examine their friendship in its historical and social context by a comparison of selected biographic and literary texts revealing a certain number of affinities and differences between two social outsiders, who saw themselves as 'kindred souls'.[3] As Carson did not understand German and Annemarie did not publish in English, it is difficult to evaluate mutual influences. Interested in the problematic of gender transgression, I focus on the figure of the tomboy in McCullers's novels and on the trope of the angel in Schwarzenbach's semi-fictional travel books regarding the interference of fact and fiction in modernist literature (Pfeiffer 2015:23). Both topics converge in the allegoric articulation of melancholy which is examined under the aspects of a significant paradox, concerning both authors: the absence of mother figures in their literary work (Savigneau 2001:39) and the importance of the mother-daughter relationship in their ego documents. Although literature does neither reflect nor express the author's life, because texts are often 'over-determined' by discursive processes and rhetoric operations, my thesis is that a 'symptomatic reading' (Louis Althusser) allows one to search for traces (e.g., contradictions, omissions, distortions, etc.) of specific textual idiosyncrasies marking the singularity of subjectivity as a signifying practice (cf. Julia Kristeva 1997).[4]

## 1. Androgynous Love and Travel Writing

In a recent web article on Annemarie Schwarzenbach, Laura Smith observes that "androgyny was nearly always what people mentioned first about her." Marianne Breslauer, Schwarzenbach's "photographer friend", whose "muse" she became (Smith 2017:2), once said that Annemarie was "neither a man nor a woman, but an [...] archangel" (qtd. in 2017:2). The Swiss ethnologist Ella Maillart, whom Schwarzenbach accompanied to Afghanistan in 1939, used the same topic and drew a portrait of her companion, which met the interpretative standards of traditional physiognomy the Swiss pastor Johann Caspar Lavater had set in the late 18th century. In his system, it is the face that expresses the soul. Maillart writes:

> Calm as usual, her colourless face was a symbol I was trying to read: devoid of all pretense, it was a 'simple' face in the sense of true, artless, not concerned with itself. Under the mass of close-cropped hair the head seemed too big [...] for so frail a neck. [...] The eyes set wide apart, changing shades of dark-blue grey, [...] belonged to a soul in love with beauty that would often wince away from a discordant world; they could shine with enthusiasm, with affection, [...] but I never saw them laugh. [...] Melancholy in the modelling of the pale, irregular mouth—lips that were inhaling smoke with silent voracity. [...] The small chin was particularly youthful, making one think of a puzzled child ready to ask for protection. [...] Writing was the only ritual of her life: she subordinated everything to it. (Maillart 1994:3)

While Maillart thought that Schwarzenbach's "subtle body" and "pensive face" "put forth a charm that acted powerfully on those who are attracted by the tragic greatness of androgyny" (1994:4), Smith remarks that "through her" entire "life, her androgyny would prove both inspiration and trap" (Smith 2017:2). Carson, too, was struck by Annemarie's outer appearance which she later described in "an unpublished essay" (Savigneau 2001:69): Her head like that of Donatello's David, "her blonde hair [...] smooth and cut like a boy's" (qtd. in 2001:69), with "sideswept bangs" (Smith 2017:2), her "blue eyes dark and slow moving; her mouth childish and soft with shily parted lips" (Savigneau 2001:70). Carson was "immediately conquered by Annemarie's androgynous beauty" (2001:68) and liked to imagine the ambiguous person as her double. For her part, Schwarzenbach "was used to being wooed" and "enjoyed [...] the adulation of the touching child that Carson seemed to be. But her own sights were firmly set on seducing Erika Mann" (2001:70).

At the time of meeting McCullers, Schwarzenbach lived together with Margot von Opel, the wife of the German industrial Fritz von Opel, who had just fled from fascist Germany to the USA. Thomas Mann, who later called Annemarie a 'devastated angel' (Miermont 2004:44), destroyed by drugs, once made her an embarrassing compliment during a dinner in Munich. "[L]ooking at her out of the corner of his eye with a mixture of uneasiness and pleasure, he finally observed: 'It's curious, if you were a *boy,* you would have to be considered *extraordinarily* handsome'" (qtd. in Savigneau 2001:69). Did the famous writer, trying to hide his homosexual inclinations, want to suggest that Annemarie looked like the androgynous Polish boy 'Tadzio' in his early novella *Death in Venice* (1911)?

Born in Zurich in 1908, Annemarie enjoyed a happy childhood, spending her time reading, riding horseback, and playing the piano. Even if she profited from a more privileged social environment than Carson, she equally strived for an artistic career. Both girls were idolized as a young genius ("Wunderkind")[5] by their mothers who tolerated their boyish behaviour. Renée Schwarzenbach, daughter of a general and amateur photographer (Alexis Schwarzenbach 2011:24), felt amused to see Annemarie impersonating a brave soldier or a handsome page, for she had been herself a tomboy in her youth. She even encouraged her daughter to pose in the role of the 'gallant with the rose', a breeches part from Richard Strauss's opera *Der Rosenkavalier* (1911), in which Renée's best friend, the Wagnerian singer Emmy Krüger, excelled. Although Renée lived in a secret lesbian partnership, tolerated by her husband, she did not support her daughter's crushes on women, particularly on Erika Mann, whose anti-fascist satirical cabaret *The Peppermill* was attacked by Swiss Nazis, mostly as a result of Renée's intrigue, which escalated in a public scandal during its Zurich guest performance, in November 1934 (2011:226-235). In his diary (12-11-1934), Thomas Mann called 'old mother Schwarzenbach' a hysterical woman, almost driven mad by her 'capitalist hatred' against socialist ideas (Alexis Schwarzenbach 2005:35). Whereas Annemarie did not hide her short-lived lesbian love affairs, for instance with Mopsa Sternheim, the playwright's daughter (cf. Rider 2004:88), Renée Schwarzenbach's stable longterm relationship with Emmy Krüger was concealed from the public, an opposite strategy of coping with so-called 'abnormal' behaviour, due to major discursive changes. What had still seemed a 'natural inclination' in the 19th century, became a medicalized 'perversion' (Alexis Schwarzenbach 2005:41), the psychiatrist Oscar Forel used to treat with electroshocks, also in Annemarie's case (Alexis Schwarzenbach 2008:397).[6]

When, in 1930, she met the Mann siblings who had already 'outed' themselves as homosexuals on the German stage, Annemarie finished her studies of history with a PhD degree and published her first novel, *Freunde um Bernhard* (*Bernhard's Circle*, 1931). It tackles a German-speaking 'Lost Generation' (Gertrude Stein), disorientated by the radical rupture with humanist traditions as a consequence of the First World War. In a contemporary newspaper article of the late 1920s, Schwarzenbach wrote: "Our parents are citizens in a homeland they have created for themselves, but we are total strangers in their country, completely insecure and with nothing to hold on to" (qtd. in Alexis Schwarzenbach2011:65, translated by A.R.).[7] Inspired by the invention around 1900 of youth and reform movements (like the German *Wandervogel*), criticising modern civilization and promoting a natural way of life, the increasingly popular adolescent novel—a new 'genre' which Schwarzenbach and McCullers adopted in a different way—treated conflicts between individual and society, often carried out within the family, from the young people's point of view (cf. Wucherpfennig 1980), for example, in Heimito von Doderer's novella *Jutta Bamberger* (1924-1926) about an odd girl's self-discovery as a woman loving women.

In the bohemian setting of student life in Paris, Schwarzenbach's novel *Bernard's Circle* presents a patchwork of interwoven male and female friendships with a pessimistic outlook. Rebelling against their bourgeois families, the youthful artists feel "boundlessly alone" in their search for meaning. Visiting a photo-exposition, the spoilt naïve title hero, a 'portrait of the (unknown) authoress as a young man' (even figuring as such on the book's cover), "does not know whether the pictures", he contemplates, "represent boys or girls", because they all look "alike": Their big eyes are "wide open, their faces express some painful tension" (Schwarzenbach 2011:78-79). The uncertainty of their sexual gender turns androgynous perfection[8] into narcissistic indifference. In her novel, girls only play a minor role as the young men's mirror images, so that Erika Mann reproved the absence of emancipated women in the literary production of her 'Swiss child', growing more and more dependent on her as a mother substitute, a part that Erika did not intend to play at all (Alexis Schwarzenbach 2011:165). Schwarzenbach's next book, *Lyrical Novella* (1933), written during a longer stay in Berlin (from 1931 to 1932), may be read as the 'camouflage' (cf. Detering 1994) of a masked lesbian subtext, in which the male narrator's unattainable idol, a Berlin cabaret singer, "intimate and distant" at the same time, seems to be "an incarnation of both Erika and Renée" (Perret 2011:131). Praising its 'lightness' à la Hemingway, Klaus Mann blamed the "thinly veiled confession" (qtd. in Perret 2011:88) not to take a clear political position.

In her subsequent 'travel books' (1936-1942), Schwarzenbach presented 'gender trouble' in a more indirect way, reducing it, for instance, to a para-textual device, by switching the narrator's identity from female to male in the revised version of *Death in Persia* (written in 1935 / 1936). In the preface of the original text, the author insinuates a melancholic narrating position which turns out to be a feminine one:

> This book will bring little joy to the reader. It [...] is about errant ways and its subject is despair. [...] Although we may be occasionally happy for no reason, it is unacceptable to be *unhappy* for no reason. [...] This is more or less the position of the girl who wrote these notes. (Schwarzenbach 2013:3-4)

In the second, more conventional and slightly optimistic version (*The Happy Valley*), published in 1940, the narrator is a man. At the same time, the concept of travelling is rather that of a psychological trip than of a geographical one: "Persia? - Foreign countries? [...] They are only detours for remembrance, secret paths of homesickness" (Schwarzenbach 2010:19).

> Did that mean the way to the Promised Land? Shouldn't I have [...] better returned home in time? Had I ventured forward too far? [...]—This horrible twilight, this fatal vastness! —I was not made for it, I had not chosen it, [...] when I was peacefully playing in the shadow of the trees, [...] reflected in a blue lake [...]. Oh, if I think of those past evenings at home, spent in a tender mood, [...] without pain and sorrow. Never more! [...] Now, far away from any comfort and consolation, totally alone. The strangeness of the foreign land touched me, I did not recognize myself anymore, [...] alienated from my very self. (58-60, translated by A. R.)

A few pages later, the puzzled *ego*, travelling for the sake of forgetting, is confronted with the 'return of the repressed' (68-69). The narrator's escapist flight from civilization turns out to be no liberation at all (75, 88). As a picaresque outsider, persecuted by normal people (97-99), the paranoid outlaw defends himself during a fantasized lawsuit (103). At the court trial, a widowed mother figure weeps for her son, who, in the end, is visited by 'his' angel (100). Biblical allusions (128-129), however, are presented from a distant, ironic point of view (185), signalling the anti-hero's disillusion (195). Although Schwarzenbach often focuses on social and political problems in her (unpublished) travel report about Afghanistan (*All the Roads are Open*, 1939-1940), for instance at the beginning of the Second World War (2011a:77), the forced domestication of nomadic tribes by the Soviet government (27, 32-33), or the segregation of sexes in Islamic countries (52-53, 56-60), the first person-narrator adopts a sententious master discourse, whenever she tackles personal crises or existential themes.

> 'Our life is like a journey...'—and so the journey seems to me less an adventure [...] than a concentrated likeness of our existence: residents of a city, citizens of a country, [...] member of a family and clan and entangled by [...] the habits of 'everyday life' [...], we often feel too secure, [...] easily induced to believe in a constancy that makes [...] each change in external circumstances a catastrophe [...]. We forget that [there is] constant motion [...] for our would-be peace of mind. (2011a:23-24)

In spite of such critical reflections, Schwarzenbach tends to neutralize sexual transgressions, in her later 'African writings' (1940-1942), by promoting an ascetic program which transforms polarization into mystic union (*unio mystica*). The typescript of her final prose work, *Das Wunder des Baums* (*The Miracle of the Tree*), written in 1941/1942 in the Congo, transmits the message that only the gift of spiritual love (2011b:229) leads to redemption (204) by (self-)abnegation (221), allowing a kind of 'second birth' (235).

## 2. Tomboys, Angels, and the Allegory of Melancholy

While literary criticism used to interpret the *tomboy figure* in McCullers's novels and novellas as a grotesque symbol of human isolation (cf. Bloom 1986, Clark/Friedman 1996) in the tradition of 'Southern Gothic' (Logan 1996:1), feminist thinking conceived of female 'masculinization' (cf. Runte 1996:352-360) as a revolt against oppression (Westling 1986:112-116). If the 'grotesque', as a principle of distortion and alienation, had influenced the Gothic Novel by means of the tension between horrible and comical elements, the resulting "incongruity between style and subject" (Thomsen 1974:107) gained an increasing importance in the 20$^{th}$ century. On the threshold between reality and fantasy (301), the grotesque became associated with psychopathology (Graham-Bertolini 2016:176-178), on the one hand, and with eccentricity (Thomsen 1974:291), on the other hand. But whereas the "gothic takes place outside of society in a nightmare setting, [...] the grotesque takes place within society in the daylight setting of ordinary communal activity" (Alan Spiegel, qtd. in Gleeson-White 2003:124-125). The question is how the social character of the tomboy, a specifically American stereotype of benign gender deviance, entered the 'magic realism' (cf. Scheffel 1990) of the burlesque and absurd configurations of modern literature?

In the history of the United States, the cultural phenomenon of tomboyism was closely linked to colonization, immigration, and women's emancipation since the 19$^{th}$ century. The Pioneer myth of the tough Puritan farmer's wife gave way to the patriotic heroine of the Civil War (1861-1865), before the struggle for women's rights opened access to male domains. In the 20$^{th}$ century, a "male identified" (Abate 2008:31) 'amazon', striving for independence, would not necessarily marry anymore. Although the "shift" in the social functions of "tomboyhood" transformed the "beneficial conduct" (49) of an 'all Americanizing' type of 'girl scout' into a stigmatizing pathology, making the 'New Woman' responsible for lower birth rates or sexual immorality. Even "while women [...] continued to infiltrate the public sphere", the "feminist-modernist vision" of the *New Woman* was "darken[ing]" during the 1930s (Gilbert/Gubar 1996:147-148). Nevertheless, the boom of tomboy icons in popular culture (film, comic strips, toys, etc.) during Depression and the Second World War, when millions of women engaged in the workforce, makes evident that the 'tomboy-spirit' was badly needed again.

In McCullers's prose of the 1940s, however, the tomboy "turns freakishly queer" (Abate 2008:145)—the meaning of both terms ('freak' resp. 'queer') overlapping in the Kinsey era (160)—so that the 'taming of the tomboy' remains an ambivalent narrative, highlighting collective "anxieties" (155) as well as gender norms (166). According to Mikhail Bakhtin's (1965) conception of the 'grotesque body', Sarah Gleeson-White defines the "female adolescent body" "as a liminal site of becoming" (2003:8), a somehow Deleuzian reformulation of the 'rites of passage' (Victor Turner). Therefore, the freak, a "trope" for "otherness" (23), undermines hierarchical dichotomies. But rebellion against "inferiority" (Matlock-Ziemann 2005:99) seems to be based on the unconscious "rejection of womanhood" (14) in the Freudian sense. Thus 'male bonding', acted out in McCullers's mythic constellations (*The Ballad of the Sad Café*), illustrates a defence against the fear of castration, a means of femininity (64), so that masculinization signifies empowerment. A complex character like Frankie, however, evokes a significant privation, insofar as phallic arrogance alludes to an irreparable lacking. The contemporary German trope of the *Knäbin* ('boyette') implicitly refers to that bedrock of melancholy, for instance in Georg Trakl's enigmatic poems[9] or in the phantasmatic Oriental realms of the expressionist writer Else Lasker-Schüler (cf. Schuller 1994). As a 'male virgin' in a weird fluid body, the tomboy does not only have a paradoxical status within the patriarchal order, but its literary configuration is closely connected with anti-classic traditions. While platonic aesthetics constitute the male body as the universal norm, and the female body as deviation[10] (cf. Johann Joachim Winckelmann in the 18th century), this gendered opposition is destabilized by various counter traditions, from mannerist via 'gothic' and decadent styles to experimental vanguards. Therefore, 'queering the tomboy' anticipates post-modern deconstruction, by means of quotation, distortion, hybridization, and irony.

Never describing herself as an *angel*, Annemarie Schwarzenbach gives a secularized transcendental meaning to that sublime emblem. Just as many other German speaking poets of the early 20th century, such as Rainer Maria Rilke, Franz Werfel or Nelly Sachs, Schwarzenbach returned to the angel topic in order to articulate psychic borderline states. Even Franz Kafka evokes the uncanny, dreamlike event of an archangel breaking through the ceiling of his apartment, in his diary of 25 June 1914:

> I paced up and down the room from early morning unto twilight. [...] My eyes had travelled over every wall [...]. Towards evening [...] I happened [...] to glance [...] at the ceiling. And finally, [...] this room [...] began to stir. [...] Little pieces of plaster broke off with a distinct thud, fell here and there [...]. The cracks [...] made no pattern yet, but it was already possible somehow to imagine one. But I put these games aside, when a bluish violet began to mix with the white; it spread out from the centre of the ceiling [...] where the shabby electric lamp was stuck. [...] things striving to break through seemed to be hovering above [...], an arm was thrust out, a silver sword swung to and fro. It was meant for me, there was no doubt of that; a vision intended for my liberation was being prepared. I sprang upon the table to make everything ready [...]. In the dim light, [...] an angel in bluish-violet robes girt with gold cords sank slowly down on great white silken-shining wings [...]. 'An angel then!' I thought, 'it has been flying towards me all the day and in my disbelief I did not know it. Now it will speak to me.' I lowered my eyes. When I raised them again, the angel was still there [...], hanging rather far off under the ceiling (which has closed again), but it was no living angel, only a painted wooden figurehead off the prop of some ship, one of the kind that hangs from the ceiling in sailors' taverns, nothing more. (Kafka 1976:390-392)

This long quotation from Kafka's diary does not only show the unmarked transition between his literary texts and his ego documents, serving as an experimental space for writing, but also the irruption of the fantastic into daily life, the hero taking it for granted, in his complete indifference with regard to the unreal dimension, as, for example, in the famous story *The Metamorphosis* (1915), in which a young man awakes, seeing his body transformed into a giant insect, but does not care about it at all, trying to continue his normal life. The impossible event, related in the most simple 'realist' manner, also sheds light upon the semantic complexity of Kafka's angel's trope, functioning as a religious metaphor of the "distance of God in a post-traditional world" (Powell 2009:20-22) as well as an allegory of aesthetic creation. In suspense between the living and the dead, the fantastic vision ends up in nothing but a piece of wood, thus materializing the limit of the 'real', which—in its Lacanian sense (cf. Lacan 1964:49-54, 152)—cannot be symbolized, like death or ecstasy, but constitutes the borderline, if not the transcendental condition of the symbolic order. The *ego*, mere observer of a spectacular phenomenon, might be read as a neurotic person whose petty obsessions open up the psychotic gap between the real and the symbolic, in order to fill the void with meaningful fantasies, imaginations, and conjectures.

On a meta-level, Kafka's parable deconstructs classic aesthetics in the sense of Goethe, whom he adored, because the fragmentation and self-reflectivity of modernist writing no longer maintain the 'organic' unity between form and content. Radical contingency, like the "cracks" in the ceiling, no longer shows a meaningful "pattern", because sense must be constructed by the reader. The Romantic conception of transcendental totality as the impossible project and endless procedure of representing the infinite through the finite, by means of paradox, fragmentation, and irony (cf. Friedrich Schlegel or Novalis), is equally shattered; and so is the mystic belief in angelic mediation between heaven and earth, leading to transparent signs and communication without misunderstanding (Swedenborg 1758).[11] According to Christian theology, angels might be considered as 'officers of the sky' (Agamben 2007:37, 50) with two central tasks, the adoration of God (rise of angels) and the administration of the world (descent of angels). As the equivocal nature of those semi-beings is compatible with hierarchical systems, they historically muted to secularized bureaucrats (57), who re-emerge in Kafka's recurrent figures of 'assistants' or 'messengers', for instance in his latest novel *The Castle*.

Although Schwarzenbach could not have known Kafka's text at the time of her writing *Death in Persia* (1935/1936), for his diaries were not published until 1937, her image of the dehumanized angel seems to be closer to the Prague author's allegory than to Klaus Mann's use of the traditional symbol, degrading it to a didactic device, namely the fairy-tale character of a beautiful young boy, who teaches the protagonist how to find his 'mission in life' (*The Volcano*, 1939). As a figure of style, the angel had already re-appeared in Stefan George's hermetic poetry, admired by Schwarzenbach. Leaving behind their Christian roles of messenger and guardian, Schwarzenbach's dreadful heavenly creatures rather approach Rilke's angels—abstract beings of uncertain status, fatal to mankind by their potential of empathy (Böttcher 2006:27-42). In her posthumously published travel book *Death in Persia*, the narrator's dialogue with 'The Angel' (title of the 8th chapter of the First Part) reminds more of Kafka's parabolic enigmas than of a biblical lesson. Suddenly appearing and vanishing again, the sexless extra-terrestrial is presented as grammatically masculine: "He stood there, but I don't know if he looked at me." (Schwarzenbach 2013:36) Contradicting himself, he finishes his annulled speech acts by cynical verdicts and pessimistic prophecies in a dialogue with the first person narrator, which also might be interpreted as soliloquy of a split *ego*.

> He leant towards me. 'For you are weak', he said, 'the weakest of them all, but you are sincere. And therefore I decided to fight for you, to lift your fear of death.' 'I was not afraid', I said softly. 'Your fear', said the angel, 'was so great that you wanted to hide your face, [...] in the deep water of death.' At this, I fell silent. 'Do not believe that I can relieve you of anything', said the angel, who was so near now that I could have easily touched him. 'I'm thinking', I said, 'that if only you would let me touch you then it would be easier for me. If only I were allowed to reach out my hand!' 'You cannot move', said the angel pleasantly, 'you are utterly helpless and exposed to the angels of this land, who are terrible creatures. Do not have false hope. Even my decision to fight for you means nothing so far.' [...]. 'I did not come here to relieve you of anything', said the angel. [...] I just wanted to see [...] if you could bear the bleakness and solitude of my country.' 'Your country?' I asked, doubtingly. 'Do not expect too much of me', he said harshly. 'We angels are also bound. There are thousands of angels in this country that you may meet and grasp for the sake of your salvation. But you have no guard-

ian angel like they told you back home. There is nothing that can remedy your solitude. Out here, you have to be content to be one in a thousand...' [...] It was dreadful how this feeling of vulnerability seeped through my limp body to my heart. 'I am afraid', I said and [...] tried to look at him. I hoped his gaze would rescue me again [...]. But he was standing in the shadows. And I realized with a sudden desperation that he was not a human being I could cling to or feel a common desperation with [...]. Exhausted to death, I said, 'I can't go on any more.' He simply said, 'You are sincere to the point of obstinacy. That does not help much when you have to deal with forces which are stronger than you – than all of you.'– And he left. [...] And then, no one was there. (36-41)

As a metaphor for the 'Other', the incommensurable foreign(er), the angel becomes the unreachable one[12] in all its phallic splendour. He does not only destroy the *ego*'s hope for shelter by human warmth and empathy but teaches his lonely 'partner' that desire can never meet reciprocal love. As an Eastern angel, he insinuates that individualism is nothing but a Western problem. Taking the role of a supreme judge, his somewhat Machiavellian speech culminates in a final verdict, the hopelessness of narcissistic demands. Contrary to Kafka's narrative, Schwarzenbach's angel configuration tends to a metaphysical 'master discourse', striving for Buddhist 'in-difference'. During his second emergence, the angel as a representative of the symbolic law, translating Islamic fatalism into Christian "humility" (109), repeatedly advises the *ego* to "give up" (109), not without a promise of hope: "You are at the end but that's when help is closest to hand" (110).[13] In Schwarzenbach's last novel, *The Miracle of the Tree* (written in 1941/1942), the authoritarian angelic 'super-ego' is transformed into a fraternal guide to sublimation, the voice of an *alter ego* stimulating the torn and forlorn post-romantic poet (Marc) to strive for his 'true self' by poetic creation. In the novel's versified, epic version (under the title *Marc*, written in 1942), which is still more optimistic, the angel even becomes the protagonist's 'brother', his 'sweet mirror image' so that the hero is finally enabled to 'love without fear' (Schwarzenbach 2012:257).

If Schwarzenbach's compulsive travelling were more of a search than a flight, her compulsive writing might have been a compensation for its senselessness. Thus the fantasy of the angel, as a symbol of androgyny, becomes a symptom of melancholy, the dark side of narcissism.

> The people in this country are so terribly solitary! One would have to wear seven-league boots to get from one village to the next, and what separates each place is [a] different kind of wilderness. [...] High mountain ranges cut them off from one another. On the plain are empty half-deserts, undulating moon landscapes, which, in the drifting light, are set in motion like the sea. And endlessly, endlessly straight, the road runs through it. [...] There is no [...] common consciousness. They are so alone that they are not even aware of their poverty and misery. [...] But much lonelier [...] still is the [Happy] Lar Valley; it is past humanity as it is past the tree line. [...] I have tried to live in Persia in every way. I haven't managed to. (Schwarzenbach 2013: 29-31, 61)

The narrator goes through a "disastrous" estrangement "in foreign surroundings which [are] impenetrable, [and] uncanny" (Henke 1998:135), so that a kind of de-humanization takes place: the Other is present, yet unattainable (146). *Death in Persia* depicts the "expedition" into an "apocalyptic scenery" (143), articulating the mutual projection between inner and outer worlds, opening up the allegoric split between the signifier and the signified in Walter Benjamin's and Paul de Man's (1979) sense. The melancholic atmosphere does not arise from the cultural differences between Orient and Occident, but it materializes in the heterotopic sites of the non-identical or the in-between (Decock/Schaffers 2008:14), and the mythical dimension of endless space incarnates the sublime ruin of sense.

> Oh, wonderful metamorphosis of this land – the evening colours leading to the majestic composure of the night [...]. Wideness, wideness, flowing down into the planes [...] and the glooming body of the huge mountain [Damavand] has become a hovering star [...]. And the river is a mirror of immeasurable depth. [...] We are sinking, sinking – or is it

mourning [...] filling me up [...] What do I call mourning? [...] What is gathering inside myself, is silence. (Schwarzenbach 2010:28-29, translated by A. R.)

Schwarzenbach's so-called 'impersonal diary' is an 'auto-graphy' in the first person, pronounced by a fragile subject who is about to lose itself. The narrative confusion does not offer any motivation, explanation or coherence, and the angel is the delirious hallucination of the ravaged *ego*'s 'desert-ion' into a deadly 'desert' of loss.

I have known [...] nights in Persia when everything lay in darkness and there was no way out. [...] The night dreams began [...], it didn't protect me from the clanging of the caravan bells, the cries of the drivers, [...] or the slow murmuring of the silver river. There was no protection against these things. Nothing could be done to stop them and I wept for my mother. As though a mortal soul could have heard me. Slowly I began to understand. This was the beginning of the fear. And I can never get over it, never forget it. (Schwarzenbach 2013:54, 60)

In strong contrast to Kafka's simple style and sober description without any psychological dimension, Schwarzenbach adopts the 'inner monologue' (cf. Arthur Schnitzler) in a more expressionist than symbolist manner. By means of a homodiegetic perspective, the modern subject's psychic labyrinth is deployed, with preconscious layers of feeling, thinking and associating. The 'stream-of-consciousness' technique leads to a meander of inward and outward impressions and sensations, often interrupted by reflections on certain atmospheres, emotions, or remembrances, thus producing a heterogeneous bulk of futile, yet loosely connected significations. The primacy of mood, memory and inner monologue over action, observation and commentary is intensified by the dense texture of fragmented narration, in which temporal levels are overlapping each other, dominated by elegiac tone. In the 'dialogue(s) with the dead', the apostrophe of the lost Other tends to abolish the limits between the self and the others (Decock/Schaffers 2008:63). The ambivalence of symbiotic union appears as a picture-puzzle, and its equivocation leads to an arabesque of never ending *'travelling writing'*, ultimately addressed to the 'object' as a fundamentally lost one, to the Mother as the 'first symbolic Other' (Lacan 1994:67-69).[14] The narrator, "a person at the end of her strength" (Schwarzenbach 2013:32), resigns to her fate after having legitimated herself with regard to her secular judge, maternal authority:

> It will continue like this, you think, always. Mother, you think (how the name makes you weep!)—I did something wrong. [...] But it wasn't me, it was life itself. All the paths—those I took, those I avoided—have ended here in this 'Happy Valley' from which there is no exit and so it is a place like death. (35)

## 3. Mothers' Daughters

In her autoanalysis of 1935, the psychiatrist Oscar Forel had asked for, Annemarie Schwarzenbach wrote:

> To write about my mother, is the beginning of all things, [...] but also the most difficult [...]. The future life, Erika Mann talks about, in order to spur my courage, [...] is nothing but a moral extortion. Who might convince me that it is exactly me who should participate in the political struggle? [...] The reason of all my suffering is that no one else has suffered more [...] than my mother. I am responsible for it. She is an extraordinary woman, and she knows it. [...] The essence of her character is love and kindness, but also striving for absolute power. [...] She is either totally good or totally bad. [...] She suffers for me, and that makes her helpless. [...] She [...] is a victim herself and awakens my pity [...]. She has ruined me with her love [...]. It is evident that her hatred against Erika Mann does not mean anything else but jealousy. [...] My mother isolated me, in order to keep me by her side. [...] But I could not leave her, because I loved her. (qtd. in Alexis Schwarzenbach 2011: 264-265, translated by A. R.)

In Schwarzenbach's psychoanalytically inspired confession, concerning the relationship with her mother, maternal desire is supposed to be the reason for her own difficulties. Insofar as Renée Schwarzenbach's contradictory attitude towards her daughter reproduces itself as a mirror image on Annemarie's side, both women remain mutually fixed upon each other. Although passionate love between mother and daughter implied negative consequences for both of them, they could not live without it. Aggressive complaints turn into feelings of guilt, but empathy seems to mask deeper identifications and wishes. Even if Erika remains a positive mother substitute in Annemarie's fantasies, as a political activist, she is about to lose her authority. Schwarzenbach's somewhat erratic mode of arguing leads to the conclusion that there is no escape from the resentment at maternal ambivalence. So the final result of Annemarie's self-diagnosis corresponds to the ultimate statement of her 'travel books': 'There is no way out'. Such a closure might have been a source for depression.

According to Sigmund Freud (1917), 'melancholy', the traditional term for depression, must be distinguished from normal mourning by the inability to overcome a traumatic loss. The depressed individual cannot transfer the libidinal investment onto a new object, because it is fixed on the old one which became part of the 'ego'. Freud explains the pathological inclusion as an effect of an 'introjection' instead of a normal 'identification', which always maintains a distance between the self and the other. Thus Annemarie's constant yearning for her dominant mother shows how impossible it was for the daughter to separate from her emotionally. McCullers, too, kept up the strong bond with her mother Marguerite, called 'Bébé', who accepted everything Carson did or wanted to do (Carr 1975:188), except becoming pregnant, that means: the daughter becoming a mother herself (cf. McCullers 1999:47,188). In contrast to Annemarie, Carson enjoyed a harmonious partnership with her mother. They slept in twin beds for years, and when Marguerite was dying, she even excused her daughter's absence with her last words: "Thank goodness, [Carson] isn't here", it "would be too much for her" (qtd. in: McCullers 1999:52). Nevertheless, Carson often gave a melancholic impression on others, and so did her writing. In July 1940, Klaus Mann recorded in his diary: "Reading [...] *The Heart is a Lonely Hunter*—the melancholy novel by that strange girl [...] that came to see us [...]. An abysmal sadness, but [...] devoid of sentimentality. Rather grim and concise" (qtd. in Carr 1975:100).

"Even though their life styles [...] were vastly different" (Carr 1975:102), both women writers, whom Alexandra Lavizarri (2008:41) conceives of as the tragi-comic circus couple of the lucky fellow (Carson) and the unlucky one (Annemarie), had much in common. They were both married, but often lived separated from their husbands; Schwarzenbach's fake marriage with the French diplomat Claude Clarac, a homosexual, turned into a lifelong friendship. Favourite children of "overprotective mother[s]" (Carr 1975:102), the two authors grew up as male identified 'loners', whose rather weak fathers would never counterbalance their wives' influence on their daughters. Annemarie's mother preferred her to her three brothers, as if the tomboy were superior to a real son. Carson, on her side, once proclaimed that she was "born a man" and defined herself as an "invert", according to Havelock Ellis's genetic theory of inborn inversion (qtd. in: Kenschaft 1996:221). The two writers had both suffered from traumatic experiences: Annemarie complained about her mother's as well as Erika Mann's ambivalence towards her and regretted the failure of her literary career (Miermont 2004:331); Carson could scarcely overcome the painful separation from her beloved piano teacher Mary Tucker, then suffered from her husband's infidelities, violence and suicide (in 1953), and was highly shocked by Annemarie's sudden death (in 1942), and by that of her mother (in 1955)—not to speak of her bad health and multiple handicaps. Sharing the taste for androgynous 'self-fashioning' (Stephen Greenblatt), which Marguerite Smith just tolerated (McCullers 1999:58), both girls did not correspond to the cultural stereotype of motherless tomboys, but rather falsify the mechanist assumption that female identification would automatically be the product of a maternal role model (Westling 1996:155).

Contrary to psychological reductionism, the French psychoanalyst Jacques Lacan thinks that it is not the mother's absence, but her tantalizing presence which causes the problem.[15] The two women writers remained fixed on the image of the mother as ultimate love object. While Annemarie destroyed herself in the struggle for a lesbian partnership, Carson seemed to survive in the frame of a bisexual trio, that means a couple, including another man or woman. According to Lacan, both daughters might be seen in the narcissistic position of the 'mother's phallus', unconsciously preventing them from accepting sexual difference. Whereas Annemarie was exclusively lesbian, trying to offer what she lacked (cf. Lacan 1982), Carson might be considered as hysterical (cf. Lacan 1994:17, 84, 138), in that she wanted to be the female exception, paradoxically sustaining male desire, by subtracting herself from the series of female objects. Thus the hysteric discourse demonstrates that desire is always the 'desire of the desire of the Other'. This Lacanian argument might be confirmed by Carson's bisexuality as well as her exhibitionist and eccentric tendencies, for instance her close friendships with Edith Sitwell or Isak Dinesen, and maybe also by her psychosomatic symptoms. Anyway, the structural distinction between the two female authors sheds a light on the specific difference of their respective mother-daughter-relationship. For the opposition between imaginary ambivalence (Schwarzenbach), on the one hand, and real union (McCullers)[16], on the other hand, cannot be explained by the popular 'mother blame theory', as Schwarzenbach's editor Roger Perret puts it: "All her life", Annemarie would have "offered up her pain [...] like roses to her mother." Finally, it was not the "role of the 'suffering cavalier'" (Perret 2011:96-97), but a women's friendship (cf. Faderman 1981, Yalom 2015) that prevailed: sublimation instead of female masochism.

## 4. Passionate Friendship and Triangularization

Though both writers had to endure similar blows of fate (rejection, loss, death, etc.), Carson seems to have been less traumatized than Annemarie who got addicted to morphine and tried to kill herself several times, even if she fought hard against desperation, mostly by working. Anticipating 'New Journalism', a mixture of objective report and subjective narration (Wichor 2013:92), Schwarzenbach wrote about two hundred articles on the rise of fascism in Europe and on social problems in the USA, indeed an "enormous amount" for a "notoriously depressed woman" (Neely 2001:11). Professional writing gave her some safety, but in her private correspondence, affective instability remained a constant feature. From the beginning, Schwarzenbach complained about McCullers's submission (qtd. in Augustin 2008:299) and about her inability to "admit certain fatalities" (qtd. in Lavizarri 2008:107). In July 1940, Annemarie "confided her uneasiness to Klaus Mann" (Savigneau 2001:74):

> It will be probably very difficult for you to understand that it is young Carson McCullers who has sparked such a violent crisis; she is seriously ill and lives in an imaginary world so bizarre, so remote from reality that it is absolutely impossible to get her to listen to reason. I thought that I had acted with all due caution and had treated her gently, but she is waiting for me to arrive from one day to the next, convinced that I am her destiny. And now her husband has left her because of it. Naturally, Margot [von Opel] is right to say that one is not entirely blameless in such matters. (qtd. in Savigneau 2001:74)

Annemarie seemed to regret her disdainful attitude, after having left the USA. When her plans to participate in the anti-fascist resistance of De Gaulle's *France Libre* (at *Radio Brazzaville*) had failed, because she was taken for a spy[17], she found herself in an isolated situation, living in the Belgian Congo and trying to write a novel (*The Miracle of the Tree*), inspired by mystical experience, which she considered to be her best literary production and a true message to the world. Contrary to Schwarzenbach, who often reminded Carson, the "fragile and tyrannical woman-child" (Savigneau 2001:87), of the "terrific obligation of work" (letter to Carson (10-04-1941), qtd. in McCullers 1999:36), McCullers, with a gesture of rivalry, gave vent to her pent-up frustration in her only preserved letter to Annemarie:

> The more I am glad you finished your book, the more I am furious about myself. [...] For my own writing does not proceed at all. [...] It is like working on a complicated small gem. What I'd like to do is smashing it, hitting it in a rage [...]. It is true, that, in the past, I asked for more than you could possibly give me. But that is over, thanks God. Don't you ever forget that I love you." (letter from Carson (February 1942), qtd. in Augustin 2008:312-313, translated by A. R.)

According to McCullers's 'philosophy of love' (McCullers 2001:

417-418), Schwarzenbach renounced the part of the unhappy 'lover' and took over the one of the paranoid 'beloved'. Thus she transformed the triangular structure[18], marking both writers' lives (Annemarie / Erika ['mother'] / lesbian lover, e.g., Margot von Opel); Carson / Reeves / David Diamond) as well as McCullers's literary work (*Reflections in a Golden Eye, Ballad of the Sad Café, Member of the Wedding*)[19], into a dualistic one (lover / beloved = daughter / mother). The ambivalence of the 'homo-gendered' mother-daughter relationship seems to be replaced by a hierarchical lesbian power-play, in which the lover takes over the 'feminine' part of subjection and the beloved one plays the 'masculine' part of the pasha (cf. Lacan 1977a). If the closed up maternal dyad of the "mirror stage", according to Lacan (1977b) is not broken open by a third element, namely the 'father', as representative of the law—then the access to the symbolic order, to difference as well as to limitation, will be blocked for the child, which will remain in the narcissistic position of the mother's phallus.

My thesis is that the 'oedipal triangularization' (cf. Weber 1991)[20] might be considered as supplemented by heterosexual as well as homosexual love triangles, because one of the elements of those trios, the excluded one who may change, subliminally usurps the 'paternal function', without being in the father's symbolic position. This kind of deferred action only leads to never ending imaginary 'duals', acted out as 'duels'. The virtual love triangle 'Carson / Annemarie / Margot [Erika]' might be read as an unhappy sequence, a kind of 'metonymy', such as in Racine's tragedies: 'Carson loves Annemarie who loves Erika who loves Therese [Giehse], etc.'

The fact that triangular constellations remained ambivalent to McCullers, has been highlighted by Carlos L. Dews's most interesting observation that her autobiographic "lack of mention" of the "intimate connection between Carson, Reeves, and Diamond" (in 1941) would be "particularly significant", because "the trio seemed destined for a triangular relationship like those later depicted" in her novels and novellas. "[R]ecalling the reasons for her divorce from Reeves", Carson "fails to mention the betrayal she felt when Reeves and Diamond moved to Rochester, leaving her out of the triangular relationship she desired" (Dews 1999:xx). Whereas Carson might have equally imagined a love triangle between Annemarie, Reeves, and herself, which was not realized, in fact, although her husband and the new Swiss friend got on "extremely well together" (Savigneau 2001:70), Schwarzenbach, however, never thought of it, preferring the dyadic mode. In 1940, she was completely absorbed by her stormy relationship to Margot von Opel whom she had even followed to North America (Miermont 2004:287). Annemarie was not only erotically dependent on the ex-cabaret singer but attacked her under the influence of alcohol and Benzedrine, trying to strangle Margot (299). Schwarzenbach explained her violence by her inability to build up and maintain a lasting emotional bond (300). Carson's masochist subservience, her persecution of the androgynous idol, must have bothered Annemarie to a high degree, for she could not return Carson's intense love. If Schwarzenbach reacted in a rather sadistic way, she only repeated the games she played with other women, who had fallen in love with her during psychiatric internment. Dr. Forel mentioned those erotic adventures in his medical report:

> Usually, she is keeping in suspense three or four different patients, like a real Don Juan. [...] Other people are only toys for her. The neurotic mouse turns—so to speak—into a neurotic cat, whenever she meets weaker women, who are highly attracted by her and do not understand her mystifications, until it is too late. (qtd. in Alexis Schwarzenbach 2011:259, translated by A.R.)

When Carson recalled their friendship in 1957, she said that, in her life, there had been no other person she had loved more than Annemarie (Lavizarri 2008:9). After Schwarzenbach's sudden death at age 34 (in November 1942), Carson had a terrible nervous breakdown, and the loss of her mother, thirteen years later (in June 1955), threw her into such a deep sadness that she needed psychotherapy, as she was no longer able to write.

In 1958, McCullers "sought help" from Dr. Mary Mercer, a child psychiatrist in her neighbourhood, "not only for relief from physical and emotional suffering, but also a block in her creative life". In the beginning of her treatment which lasted for about one year, "McCullers suggested" that "some of their therapy sessions" (Dews 2016:22) were recorded by Dictaphone. "These recording 'experiments'" (nine sessions between April and May 1958) "performed a dual role—they provided an opportunity for McCullers to free-associate in a traditional psychoanalytic mode and also for her to try to continue to write, speaking the text into the microphone [...] and using the transcripts of what she had spoken as a first draft of her work" (Dews 2016:23). Reconstructing in detail the astonishing history of McCullers's literary and personal estate, which had been finally "bequeathed to the Carson McCullers Center for Writers and Musicians at Columbus State University", "after Dr. Mercer's death in 2013" (2016:29), Carlos L. Dews, editor and authority on McCullers's works, has recently published for the first time "all the text from the transcripts of the recorded therapy sessions [...] that involve Annemarie Schwarzenbach" (2016:31)[21]. The fact that "five of the transcripts are almost entirely dedicated to her", "indicates that the deep emotional connections" Carson had "with Schwarzenbach remained of great significance to her", still "thirteen years after her death" (2016:30). This new material, "at once private and public" (Masterton Sherazi 2016:54), is of inestimable value for further research and will be partly considered in the end of this article. Its most explicit passages relate "to McCullers's sexuality and her feelings of unrequited love" for the "Swiss author" (Dews 2016:57). Obsessed with Annemarie, Carson "talked about" her "endlessly, every anecdote reminding her of something Schwarzenbach said or did" (Smith 2017:4).

The five published transcripts all refer to one decisive event, when Schwarzenbach was sent to Bellevue hospital (NYC) by the police, after having tried to commit suicide in her brother Freddy's apartment, at the beginning of January 1941[22]. The occasion of their father's unexpected death in November 1940 was an enormous shock for his daughter. His son Alfred, called 'Freddy', director of the Swiss silk company in the USA since 1934 (Alexis Schwarzenbach 2011:344), wrote to his younger brother Hans, called 'Hasi', that he was not willing to spend any more money on Annemarie's expensive medical therapies, for instance the long-term stay at a sanatorium in Kansas (at about 70,000 francs), the doctors had recommended. In his cynical letters (26-09-1940, 28-11-1940), he accuses his sister of uncontrollable drug abuse and makes fun of her lesbian preferences:

> Dame Opel and Annemarie often have a little fight but love

> each other ardently. [...] What shall I do? If you let her go on with it, she will go to the dogs more and more. It makes me sick [...]. You can never see her alone, always a broad at her side, disgusting. [...] She thinks that the sluts she's so crazy about will make a genius out of her. [...] I send you some of her poems, please, judge for yourself. (qtd. in Alexis Schwarzenbach 2011:344, translated by A. R.)

In late November 1940, Annemarie "was hospitalized in a Connecticut psychiatric clinic". McCullers wrote her regularly:

> but had no way of knowing whether her letters were passed on to her. Hospital visits, being absolutely prohibited, Carson let herself be persuaded to return to Columbus with her mother. She was there a few weeks later, early in 1941, when she learned that Annemarie had taken refuge at a friend's house in New York [in fact her brother's studio, A.R.] after escaping from the clinic. Carson took the first train north and went to join her. (Savigneau 2001:79)

McCullers's biographers describe the meeting between the two women in a sometimes erroneous way[23], and Alexis Schwarzenbach, her grand-nephew and latest biographer, does not mention it at all.

Although the psychotherapeutic Dictaphone sessions are based on oral speech, which is fragmented, often interrupts itself or changes temporal levels, leaping from one point to the other, the texts show a certain narrative coherence, nevertheless. In the first short transcript (14-04-1958), McCullers recalls Annemarie's situation in Freddy's flat at her arrival: "Freddy is a real angel. He had put a sheet to separate his studio to give her privacy and there was Annemarie playing Mozart on the gramophone, [...] endlessly", drinking 'gin.'" (qtd. in Dews 2016:31)

In the second transcript (21-04-1958), Carson reflects on the serial character of 'love triangles', before she depicts Annemarie's aggressive reaction to her surprise visit in detail.

> People who love one person, loves another person. [...] When I got there, Annemarie looked at me in a startled way [...]

and said, who are you? And I said, it's Carson. And she said, I want Dr. February. She had told me once [...] she was one of the first people to have insulin shock treatment. And she was analyzed by this Dr. February. Anyway, Dr. February fell in love with her. Annemarie seduced her. Dr. February would give her insulin shock treatments every morning and she would die, she said, and in the afternoon, she would make love, see? And so, I was kind of shocked. [...] She screamed, Dr. February. [...] And I had travelled all that way and Dr. February was all I got! (qtd. in Dews 2016: 32)

If Annemarie rejects Carson by offering her an imaginary 'love triangle', the identity of the third person is not clear. As someone with the last name of "February" never emerges in Schwarzenbach's ego documents, fictional texts or biographies, the medical doctor mentioned might have been the psychiatrist Dr. Gustava Favez whom Annemarie so deeply fell in love with, that she did not want to leave the clinic of Dr. Forel, in 1938 (cf. Miermont 2004:249). Even after her bicycle accident, in 1942, when she was transferred to that same hospital again, this time receiving electroshock therapy by Dr. Favez, she wrote in her very last letter to a friend, Annigna Goodly (15-10-1942): "I have just been liberated from the hell-like clinic 'Les Prangins', where only Dr. Favez was very kind to me, all the others were like hell" (qtd. in Alexis Schwarzenbach 2011:398, translated by A.R.). Was "Dr. February" a private code name for the beloved object whose identity Schwarzenbach did not want to reveal? The question about a possible psychoanalytic treatment, however, cannot be answered by lack of information. In the third transcript (25-04-1958), McCullers replies to Dr. Mercer's question, whether their relationship had been consummated, in a decisive, but rather contradictory way.

> I tried to tell you it was that I couldn't make love with her when she was in a different world. [...] Because I loved her. Because I respected her. Because I mean I could have slept with her but she also had that feeling. I slept with her. She was so tormented. Her moods were so...reality...and she also has...She was beyond my reach and I was beyond reach of her too, and she sensed it. (qtd. in Dews 2016:33)

In this passage, McCullers seems to indicate that she could only have a sexual relationship with someone on a level of equality and acceptance, that means reciprocal love. Does she thus rationalize her terrible defeat which she vividly describes at the end of the fourth transcript (28-04-1958)? After Schwarzenbach had forced McCullers to telephone her ex-lover Margot, who had just separated from her, Annemarie, in a sudden whim, nearly tried to rape Carson, but stopped her action as soon as she had started it.

> And then she said, you must call Margot. Freddy told me that she had hurled the telephone out of the window because [...] Margot hung up. [...] When I called Margot, she said [...] she will kill you! [...] she tried to kill me. She was sitting on my chest one night and strangling me. She's dangerous! [...] So I put down the receiver and Annemarie wanted to know what she said. And I said [...] she was having trouble with Fritz... and made up a story, [...] Annemarie was terribly jealous [...]. So then she said, take off your clothes. So I took off my clothes and she began to touch me. And I felt this flowering jazz passion, you know, and I felt I had her. I thought at last, I had Annemarie, at last, at last. And all the sacred fluids of my body were secreting, you know, sweat, tears, love juice [...]. So then, Annemarie just suddenly jumped out of the bed. (qtd. in Dews 2016:35-37)

Annemarie does not only suspect Carson of having an affair with the night club dancer Gypsy Rose Lee, also living in the house-sharing community of Brooklyn Heights, and often hanging around with McCullers at that time (Savigneau 2001:75-76), but she also wants to continue her love act with the striptease artist and would like Carson to assist.

> So then she began saying, I was Gypsy Rose Lee. That's the only reason I came to America because I wanted Gypsy Rose Lee. Yeah, yeah, when I was just...when I was...that flowering, that passion, Dr. Mercer, do you understand...when just suddenly I went Gypsy. I don't want you. You're too skinny. I was Gypsy Rose Lee and you, you've been seen in nightclubs

with her. I know. I've kept trace of you. You go around with her. Stay weekends with her. I know. You, you bring her to *be* [*me*?] right now. You get gypsy and bring her right here and I'll sleep with her and you can watch if you want to. [...] I ran out of the room, naked. (qtd. in Dews 2016:37)

Identities get confused, 'subjects' merge into 'objects', in the course of a reported dialogue that has muted into a delirious monologue. But in the end, it becomes imperatively clear that Carson is not Annemarie's object of desire. McCullers can 'have' her beloved idol Annemarie only as a dead one[24], in writing, in form of 'dead letters'[25], in the crypt of her memory, in the script of her books, as the effect of loss and desperation, by a never-ending process of mourning. Thus she recognizes at the end of the third transcript:

> I will tell you at one point I felt I had Annemarie, at last. I didn't know I never had Annemarie until C- [Klaus Mann, A.R.] wired me that she was dead. I knew I had her then. She would never leave me again. I saw her blessed face and rejoiced for she could never be hurt again…and that she was safe now in my heart. I lived for her in my work. (qtd. in Dews 2016:34)

Even if Carson confounded herself with her lost beloved lover again, sublimation had already begun.[26]

## 5. Writing as Sublimation

Failed triangularization, a blockade to the acknowledgement of Otherness, can be supplemented[27] by sublimation in Sigmund Freud's sense, which means: by deviating sexual drives towards non-sexual, cultural goals. As a determining force of the civilization process, sublimation takes on a disciplinary, repressive connotation. Julia Kristeva (1984), however, accentuates its pleasurable hedonistic implications.

Whenever there was no solution, Schwarzenbach and McCullers started writing (again). In her second novel, *Reflections in a Golden Eye* (1941), dedicated to Annemarie Clarac-Schwarzenbach, McCullers even invents 'bisexual' combinations of homosexual and heterosexual triangles (Captain Penderton / Leonora / Major Langdon; Captain Penderton / Private Williams / Leonora; Alice Langdon / Major Langdon / Anacleto), subtly hinting at patriarchal homo-social structures and their latent (male) homoeroticism (cf. Kosofsky Sedgwick 1985:21-28, 83-97). The latter also plays an important part in the triangle of the *Ballad of the Sad Café* (Marvin / Amelia / Cousin Lymon).

Shortly after their first meeting, Schwarzenbach included an enthusiastic review of *The Heart Is a Lonely Hunter*[28] into her portrait of Carson McCullers (Schwarzenbach 1995:263-264), published in the Swiss *National-Zeitung* (*National Newspaper*) in July 1940 (382). Stressing the typical American setting of the novel, Schwarzenbach praises its particular style that she judges neither realist nor romantic. What strikes her mostly, is the unmasking observation of the world seen through the eyes of a child. Identifying the author with the protagonist Mick Kelly, Schwarzenbach concludes: "a mixture of innocence and precocious resignation" (264). Later, both writers promised each other to translate their respective literary works into their own native language.[29]

Mutual appreciation does not exclude misunderstanding. Whereas Schwarzenbach thought McCullers's poem "The Twisted Trinity" (published in Klaus Mann's magazine *Decision*, in 1941) to be a perfect motto for her own novel from the Congo, *The Miracle of the Tree* (written in 1941-1942), aiming at the mystic union "between nature, human soul, and God's silence" (letter to McCullers (29-12-1941), qtd. in: Augustin 2008:306-307), Carson's verses suggest that only 'the Other', another person, might remedy the modern discrepancy between sign and meaning.

> Now all things fail, the trinity is twisted. Stone is not stone. And faces like the fractioned characters In dreams are incomplete. [...] The exiled intellect must add a new dimension: Something of you. (qtd. in: Augustin 2008:305)

Evidently, both authors had a quite different conception of writing. While McCullers was inspired by love, as her main theme, Schwarzenbach could only write under the condition of almost autistic isolation, which she finally considered her ultimate truth (Lavizarri 2008:309). Writing was not so much a therapy for her, 'exorcising the past' (cf. Maillart 1994:15), but most of all a search for spiritual, psychic freedom, based on the metaphysical condition of suffering, as her travel companion Ella Maillart underlines: "One thing is certain: she believed in suffering. She worshipped it as a source of greatness" (1994:73, cf. 197). Giving up journalism which she considered more and more as "a perpetual mirror of our unredeemed existence" (Schwarzenbach 2011:101)[30], Schwarzenbach transfigured the religious discourse into a mystic one. In the last lines of her epic poem "Marc" (1942), she paradoxically unites lover and beloved in angelic separation:

> [...] and if she leaves me and if she had only closed me in her arms
>
> For the sake of the angels' face announcing itself again and again,
> It would be more than enough. [...]
> But for you, my princess, [...] and for myself in the shadows
> Mercy has come too late. Nowhere but at your side,
> I fall into sleep. It is deep. [...]
> And we see him go away, the Prodigal Son.
> (Schwarzenbach 2012: 277-278, translated by A. R.)

Encouraging Carson to write, Annemarie finally returned to the angel topic (in a letter from the Congo, 29-12-1941), as a condensation of feminist resistance and platonic union:

> Carson, I talk so easily to you—about things which really are the subjects of my book. I think it deals with our *nun* heritage, our relation to men, to what we call [...] enemy—our bitter loving fight with the world first then with the angel who leads us back to the reborn calm of death. (qtd. in Savigneau 2001:96)

Annemarie's real death, driving Carson almost mad, was not enough. Renée Schwarzenbach and her own mother, Clara Wille, had to kill their dead (grand-)daughter a second time, symbolically, by destroying her personal estate, letters, diaries, manuscripts, etc. (cf. Miermont 2004: 383-385; Alexis Schwarzenbach 2011:419-423), yet were still unable to prevent her from being read.

*Notes*

[1] A Critical Edition of Annemarie Schwarzenbach's works is not yet available.

[2] In a letter (26-11-1938) to her Swiss friend, Anita Forrer, Annemarie Schwarzenbach tells her that the French writer Roger Martin Du Gard dedicated one of his books to her with the following words: "Pour lui remercier de promener sur terre son beau visage *d'ange inconsolable*" (qtd. in Alexis Schwarzenbach 2011:277, emphasis by A.R.), which means: "Whom I thank for meandering about this earth with the lovely face of an inconsolable angel" (qtd. in Savigneau 2001:69). Paul Valery's mistress, Catherine Pozzi, who made Annemarie's acquaintanceship in 1933, wrote to her son Claude Bourdet, a fighter in the French Resistance and a friend of Annemarie's: "Que de grace dans ce visage sérieux. Mais elle a un regard inquiet, comme sollicité par d'invisibles peines. [...] Elle vous donne *le mal d'Europe*" (qtd. in Miermont 2004:12-13, emphasis by A.R....) which means : "What a graceful serious face. But it has a worried look, as if alarmed by invisible pain, [...] giving you the impression of uneasiness about the state of Europe" (translated by A.R.).

[3] Tennessee Williams, who immediately remarked the "affinity" between Carson's "work and his own plays" (Kayser 2016:2), "at once" "recalled" that the both of them were "kindred souls". "There was something wounded in Carson, [...], as I was quick to discover" (qtd. in 2016:2), he said. Their close relationship "proved to be one of the most enduring friendships [...] she was ever to experience with a fellow artist" (qtd. Carr 1975, in 2016:3).

[4] Biographical information will concentrate on Annemarie Schwarzenbach, for many details of Carson McCullers's life history may be taken for granted in the context of this volume.

[5] "Wunderkind" is the title of one of McCullers early short stories, full of autobiographic allusions.

[6] Annemarie Schwarzenbach underwent several detoxication treatments in Switzerland and in the USA from the middle of the 1930s to the early 1940s, mostly because of her suffering from opiomania. In 1935, after a first suicide attempt, she stayed for two weeks at Dr. Oscar Forel's clinic in *Les Prangins*, near Geneva (Switzerland), where she had sexual relations with other female patients (Miermont 2004:193). In 1938, she was hospitalized five times in three different institutions, for instance, at Dr. Ruppaner's Clinic (Engadin), undergoing her first insulin therapy (2004: 241, 394), then at Ludwig Binswanger's well-known psychiatric hospital *Bellevue* (on Lake Constance), where she was diagnosed as 'schizophrenic'. In fall 1938, she returned to *Les Prangins*. Falling in love with her psychiatrist, Dr. Gustava Favez, Schwarzenbach did not want to leave the hospital (2004: 249). In 1940, however, she fled from a private sanatorium in Greenwich (NY), where she had been interned because of alcohol and speed abuse, and a short time afterwards, she was hospitalized in the public institution of *Bellevue* (NYC). Instead of being transferred to Kansas for a long-term stay in a psychiatric sanatorium, she was deported to Switzerland in February 1941 (Alexis Schwarzenbach 2011:337, 343-348). After her bicycle accident in September 1942, she was transferred from her home in Sils (Engadin) to Dr. Forel's clinic again and subjected to a series of electroshocks (2011:397).

[7] Translation by Annette Runte, as for all German and French quotations, if not indicated otherwise.

[8] Cf. the dominant Western tradition of thinking 'androgyny', from Neoplatonic to Romantic conceptions.

[9] Schwarzenbach wrote an essay on the poet "Georg Trakl" (1931) as part of her state examination in German at the University of Zurich. It is published (in the form of an annex) in Fähnders/Tobler (2004). In this text, she reads the melancholic traits of Trakl's lyrics with special regard to the poet's own depressive crises and considers him a 'tragic figure', such as the poets Friedrich Hölderlin or Arthur Rimbaud. Schwarzenbach's psychological thesis is that Trakl's vulnerability would have been the central reason for his loneliness.

[10] Cf. Ulrike Brunotte's article (2007), which links the Western

aesthetic evolution to the history of gendered power relations, for example 'male bonding' and modern 'masculinism'.

[11] According to Emanuel Swedenborg's semiotic conception from the middle of the 18th century, angels would communicate without any misunderstanding, that means without any loss of sense. Every signifier bi-univocally corresponds to a signified element, namely the one and only notion it signifies. In other words, there is total semantic transparency (cf. *De Caelo et Eius Mirabilibus et de inferno, ex Auditis et Visis*, 1758; *Heaven and Hell*).

[12] As unreachable as her death-bound lover Yalé, the daughter of the Turkish ambassador in Teheran, who knows that she will die from tuberculosis. "We had wanted to talk about happiness and didn't notice that we were thinking about death..." (Schwarzenbach 2013:81).

[13] This formula implicitly evokes Friedrich Hölderlin's verse from the hymn *Patmos* (1803, in *Vaterländische Gesänge*, i.e., *Songs of the Fatherland*): "Wo aber Gefahr ist, wächst das Rettende auch" ('In great danger, the saving power grows as well').

[14] Jacques Lacan's Seminar on Object Relations (IV, 1956-1957) has not yet been published in English.

[15] Savigneau seems to confirm such a view: "Carson was [...] suffering the consequences of some obscure kind of emotional deprivation, despite her mother's extreme (perhaps too extreme?) attention" (2001:15).

[16] "Relations between Carson and Marguerite Smith were highly complex and are poorly understood. Virginia Spencer Carr [...] comes up with only the most banal facts: "Marguerite was a mother proud of her daughter's success; Carson was a fragile daughter torn between her need to be protected and her wish to be free. Marguerite passed up no opportunity to tell people she met about her 'little prodigy' [...]." She "was both a source of assistance for Carson and an intrusion into her new life [...]. Most of the people who liked Carson, also liked her mother, Carr observes. Only a few of them, such as Janet Flanner, the famous *New Yorker* columnist, viewed her as harmful to the young woman; [...] as an abusive, catastrophic and 'abysmal' mother" (Savigneau 2001:78). Rita Smith, Carson's sister, mentioned that her mother wrote a letter to Carson "every day they were separated" (qtd. in 2001:79), but "that there remains no trace

of such a sustained correspondence" (2001:79).

[17] Married to Claude Clarac, who as a French diplomat was forced to work for the Vichy regime, Annemarie Clarac-Schwarzenbach had become French by marriage and lost her Swiss citizenship. As a daughter of a pro-Nazi family from Switzerland and German speaking, she was suspected of working for the enemy.

[18] It seems to be evident that the constellation of 'love triangles' plays an important part in the history of European literature, from its antique beginnings to the present. Trios are a constitutive element in comedy (cf. Shakespeare) and in prose 'genres', particularly in the sentimental novel of the 18$^{th}$ century (cf. Goethe's *Werther*, 1774) and the realist novels of the 19$^{th}$ century (cf. Balzac, George Sand, etc.), whereas in German (post)romanticism, 'triangularization' is produced by the 'splitting' of femininity ('mother / whore'), for instance in Joseph von Eichendorff's or Clemens Brentano's novellas.

[19] Biographic traces in the plot of McCullers's first drama *The Square Root of Wonderful* (1957) are equally organized in the form of interconnected trios (Molly / Philip Lovejoy / John Tucker; Molly / Lorena Lovejoy / Mother Lovejoy, etc.; cf. Kayser 2016:5).

[20] Its epistemological parallel would be the semiotic conception of 'triangularization', according to which the arbitrary correlation between signifier and signified (or reference) would be based either on the differential system (Saussure) or its pragmatic use (Peirce). The correlations between semiotics and Freudo-Lacanian psychoanalytic theory are analyzed by Samuel M. Weber (1991).

[21] The material relates to the following sessions: 14-04-1958, 25-04-1958, 28-04-1958, 09-05-1958, and 12-05-1958.

[22] The exact date of the event is neither given in the text of the session transcripts nor in the consulted biographies (cf. Alexis Schwarzenbach 2011:348).

[23] Miermont (2004:312-131) thinks that Annemarie lived in Alfred Wolkenberg's apartment, at that time, and that the medical doctor who dressed her wounds after the suicide attempt would have been Dr. Gumpert, Erika Mann's lover. She also writes that Annemarie would have thrown the telephone out the window in Carson's presence, but in reality, Carson arrived just after that incident (qtd. in Dews 2016:34). Savigneau resumes the whole scene without any further leading details: "in no time at all the police, accompanied by

a doctor, located the fugitive and had her hospitalized in Bellevue in White Plains" (2001:79).

[24] According to Elizabeth Bronfen (1992), the dead body of the female ideal (in literature or painting) was a condition of male authors' aesthetic sublimation.

[25] According to Georg Wilhelm Friedrich Hegel, the sign implies the 'death' of the thing it signifies. Signs make visible the invisible, but they are arbitrary and "ultimately inconclusive" (Jon Stewart. *The Unity of Hegel's 'Phenomenology of the Spirit'. A Systematic Interpretation*. Northwestern University Press, 2011, 219).

[26] I doubt whether Jean-Pierre Joecker is right, when he thinks that "for Carson love is not that of Eros", but only "friendship-love". The platonic tinge seems to be an effect of deception.

[27] In Jacques Derrida's sense of 'sublimation' within the frame of his logic of 'supplément', that means a replacement that never exactly reproduces something, but always alters and 'de-places' the replaced.

[28] Schwarzenbach relativized the literary value of McCullers's prize-winning novel *The Heart Is a Lonely Hunter* in a letter to Klaus Mann (21-06-1940): "ihr Buch ist aber doch in Grenzen nur gut zu nennen", that means: "her book is only good to a certain degree", or: "under certain aspects" (qtd. in*"Wir werden es schon zuwege bringen, das Leben"* 2001:177, translated by A.R.).

[29] In 1942, Schwarzenbach wrote to McCullers: "I [...] think that you will be the only one to translate my book" [*The Miracle of the Tree*] "which you will like—And I hope to translate yours [*Reflections in a Golden Eye*]" (qtd. in Savigneau 2001:97). Schwarzenbach does not think of the fact that Carson did not know the German language or at least not well enough for that task.

[30] Her travel companion Ella Maillart confirmed that: "Mentally we were very different. She was a poet moving among ideas shaped and enlivened by her imagination, her moods changing the world. Whereas I still believed in the reality of facts as such, thinking the external world responsible for my subjective life" (1994:75-76).

# WORKS CITED

Abate, Michelle Ann. *Tomboys. A Literary and Cultural History.* Temple UP, 2008.

Agamben, Giorgio. *Die Beamten des Himmels. Über Engel.* Translated from Italian into German by Andreas Hiepko. Leipzig: Verlag der Weltreligionen, 2007.

Augustin, Bettina. "Spiegelbild im Auge der Anderen. Annemarie Schwarzenbach und Carson McCullers—eine literarische Wahlverwandtschaft." *Inside out. Textorientierte Erkundungen des Werks von Annemarie Schwarzenbach.* Edited by Sofie Decock and Uta Schaffers. Bielefeld: Aisthesis, 2008, pp. 297-316.

Bloom, Harold, editor. *Carson McCullers: Blooms Modern Critical Views.* Chelsea House Publications, 1986.

Böttcher, Carina. *Engel in Literatur, Film und Werbung.* Heinrich-Heine-Universität Düsseldorf, 2006. Web.

Bronfen, Elizabeth. *Over Her Dead Body. Death, femininity, and aesthetic.* Manchester: Manchester UP, 1992.

Brunotte, Ulrike. "Die zwei Körper des Laokoon. Physiologie, Ästhetik und Politik hegemonialer Männlichkeit—Alexander von Humboldt, Winckelmann, Blüher." *Feminisierung der Kultur? Krisen der Männlichkeit und weibliche Avantgarden. / Féminisation de la civilisation? Crises de la masculinité et avant-gardes féminines.* Edited by Annette Runte and Eva Werth. Würzburg: Königshausen & Neumann, 2007, pp. 27-49.

Carr, Virginia Spencer. *The Lonely Hunter. A Biography of Carson McCullers.* Doubleday & Company, 1975.

Clark, Beverly Lyon and Melvin J. Friedman, editors. *Critical Essays on Carson McCullers.* G.L. Hall, 1996.

Decock, Sofie and Uta Schaffers, editors. "Einleitung. Neue Wege zu Annemarie Schwarzenbach." *Inside out. Textorientierte Erkundungen des Werks von Annemarie Schwarzenbach.* Bielefeld: Aisthesis, 2008(a), pp. 7-27.

---. "'Still—kein Wort über die Toten dieses Landes'. Gespräche mit den Toten in Annemarie Schwarzenbachs Roman *Das glückliche Tal.*" *Inside out. Textorientierte Erkundungen des Werks von Annemarie Schwarzenbach.* Bielefeld: Aisthesis, 2008(b), pp.

55-77.

De Man, Paul. *Allegories of Reading. Figural Language in Rousseau, Nietzsche, Rilke, and Proust.* Yale UP, 1979.

Detering, Heinrich. *Das offene Geheimnis. Zur literarischen Produktivität eines Tabus von Winckelmann bis Thomas Mann.* Göttingen. Wallstein, 1994.

Dews, Carlos L. "Introduction". *Illumination and Night Glare. The Unfinished Autobiography of Carson McCullers.* Edited by Carlos L. Dews. Madison, The University of Wisconsin Press, 1999, pp. xi-xxii.

Faderman, Lilian. *Surpassing the Love of Men. Romantic Friendship and Love between Women from the Renaissance to the Present.* London: The Women's Press, 1985.

Fähnders, Walter and Andreas Tobler. "Zum Erstdruck von Annemarie Schwarzenbachs 'Georg Trakl'". *Mitteilungen aus dem Brenner-Archiv*, vol. 23, 2004, pp. 47-59.

Fleischmann, Uta, editor. *"Wir werden es schon zuwege bringen, das Leben". Annemarie Schwarzenbach an Erika und Klaus Mann. Briefe 1930-1942.* Herbolzheim: Centaurus, 2001.

Freud, Sigmund. "Mourning and Melancholia." (1917). *The Standard Edition of the Complete Works of Sigmund Freud.* Translated from German under the General Editorship of James Strachey. In Collaboration with Anna Freud. Assisted by Alix Strachey and Alan Tyson. Volume XIV. London: The Hogarth Press and the Institute of Psychoanalysis, 1957, pp. 243-258.

Gilbert, Sandra M. and Susan Gubar. "Fighting for Life". *Critical Essays on Carson McCullers.* Edited by Beverly Lyon Clark and Melvin J. Friedman. G.L. Hall, 1996, pp. 147-154.

Gleeson-White, Sarah. *Strange Bodies. Gender and Identity in the Novels of Carson McCullers.* University of Alabama, 2003.

Graham-Bertolini, Alison. "'Nature is Not Abnormal; Only Lifelessness is Abnormal': Paradigms of the In-valid in *Reflections in a Golden Eye.*" *Carson McCullers in the Twenty-First Century.* Edited by Alison Graham-Bertolini and Casey Kayser. Palgrave Macmillan, 2016, pp. 175-189.

Henke, Silvia. "Schreibend, aus der Einsamkeit, in die Verwilderung, ins Schwarze. Zur Poetik von Annemarie Schwarzenbach, Adelheid Duvanel und Kristin T. Schnider".

Text und Kritik. Sonderband: Literatur in der Schweiz. Edited by Heinz Ludwig Arnold. Munich: Edition Text + Kritik, 1998, pp. 132-144.

Kafka, Franz. *The Diaries: 1910-1923*. Edited by Max Brod. Translated from German into English by Joseph Kresh. Schocken, 1976.

Kayser, Casey. "From Adaption to Influence: Carson McCullers on the Stage." *Carson McCullers in the Twenty-First Century*. Edited by Alison Graham-Bertolini and Casey Kayser. Palgrave Macmillan, 2016, pp. 1-20.

Kenschaft, Lori J. "Homoerotics and Human Connections: Reading Carson McCullers, As a Lesbian". *Critical Essays on Carson McCullers*. Edited by Beverly Lyon Clark and Melvin J. Friedman. G.L. Hall, 1996, pp. 220-233.

Kosofsky Sedgwick, Eve. *Between Men. English Literature and Male Homosocial Desire*. Columbia UP, 1985.

Kristeva, Julia. *Revolution in Poetic Language*. Introduction by Leon S. Roudiez. Columbia UP, 1984.

---. "The Semiotic and the Symbolic." *The Portable Kristeva*. Edited by Kelly Oliver. Columbia UP, 1997, pp. 32-70.

Lacan, Jacques. "The mirror stage as formative of the function of the I." (1949). Translated by Alan Sheridan. *Écrits. A Selection*. London: Tavistock, 1977(b), pp. 1-7.

---. "The signification of the phallus." (1958). Translated by Alan Sheridan. *Écrits. A Selection*. London: Tavistock, 1977(a), pp. 281-291.

---. "Guiding Remarks for a Congress on Feminine Sexuality" 1958 [Presented in Amsterdam, 5 September 1960]. Translated by Julia Evans (1958). *Jacques Lacan & the École Freudienne: Feminine Sexuality*. Edited by Juliet Mitchell and Jacqueline Rose. Macmillan, 1982, pp. 86-99.

---. *The Seminar Book XI. The Four Fundamental Concepts of Psychoanalysis*. Edited by Jacques-Alain Miller (Paris 1964). Translated by Alan Sheridan. London: Hogarth Press and the Institute of Psychoanalysis, 1977.

---. *Le Séminaire. Livre IV. La relation d'objet. 1956-1957*. Edited by Jacques-Alain Miller. Paris: Seuil, 1994.

Lavater, Johann Caspar. *Physiognomische Fragmente zur Beförderung der Menschenkenntnis und Menschenliebe*. Versuch

I-IV (1775-1778). Reprint. Hildesheim, 2002.

Lavizzari, Alexandra. *Fast eine Liebe. Annemarie Schwarzenbach und Carson McCullers*. Berlin: Edition Ebersbach, 2008.

Logan, Lisa. "Introduction." *Critical Essays on Carson McCullers*. Edited by Beverly Lyon Clark and Melvin J. Friedman. G.L. Hall, 1996, pp. 1-17.

Maillart, Ella K. *The Cruel Way*. (1947) New Introduction by Mary Russell. Beacon Press, 1994.

Masterton Sherazi, Melanie. "Collaborative Life Writing: The Dialogical Subject of Carson McCullers's Dictaphone 'Experiments' and Posthumous Autobiography, *Illumination and Night Glare*." *Carson McCullers in The Twenty-First Century*. Edited by Alison Graham-Bertolini and Casey Kayser. Palgrave Macmillan, 2016. pp. 49-66.

Matlock-Ziemann, Ellen. *Tomboys, Belles, and Other Ladies. The Female Body-Subject in Selected Works by Katherine Ann Porter and Carson McCullers*. Stockholm: Uppsala Universitet, 2005.

Mayer, Gesa. "Queere Freunde um Bernhard." *Annemarie Schwarzenbach. Analysen und Erstdrucke*. Edited by Walter Fähnders and Sabine Rohlf. Bielefeld: Aisthesis, 2005, pp. 63-79.

McCullers, Carson. *Illumination and Night Glare: The Unfinished Autobiography of Carson McCullers*. Edited by Carlos L. Dews. University of Wisconsin Press, 1999.

---. *The Ballad of the Sad Café. Complete Novels*. Edited by Carlos L. Dews. The Library of America, 2001, pp. 395-459.

---. "'Impromptu Journal of My Heart': Carson McCullers's Therapeutic Recordings, April-May 1958". *Carson McCullers in the Twenty-First Century*. Edited by Alison Graham-Bertolini and Casey Kayser. Palgrave Macmillan, 2016 pp. 21-48.

Neely, Jack. "Report from the Shadow Side". *Metro Pulse*, vol. 10, no. 49, 7 Dec. 2000. Web.

Perret, Roger. "Afterword." *Lyrical Novella*, by Annemarie Schwarzenbach. Translated by Lucy Renner Jones. Seagull Books, 2011, pp. 86-139.

Pfeiffer, K. Ludwig. *Fiktion und Tatsächlichkeit. Momente und Modelle funktionaler Textgeschichte*. Hamburg: Shoebox House, 2015.

Powell, Matthew T. "Kafka's Angel: The Distance of God in a Post-Traditional World". *Janus Head*, vol. no. 1. Trivium Publications, 2009, pp. 7-23.
Rieder, Ines. *Mopsa Sternheim. Ein Leben am Abgrund*. Vienna: Zaglossus, 2004.
Röttgers, Kurt and Monika Schmitz-Emans, editors. *Engel in der Literatur-, Philosophie- und Kulturgeschichte*. Essen/Ruhr: Die Blaue Eule, 2004.
Runte, Annette. *Biographische Operationen. Diskurse der Transsexualität*. Munich: Wilhelm Fink Verlag, 1996.
Savigneau, Josyane. *Carson McCullers. A Life*. Houghton Mifflin, 2001.
Scheffel, Michael. *Magischer Realismus. Die Geschichte eines Begriffes und ein Versuch seiner Bestimmung*. Tübingen: Stauffenburg, 1990.
Schuller, Marianne. "'Ich bin Wasser darum bin ich keine Frau'. Zur melancholischen Prosa Else Lasker-Schülers." *Fragmente. Schriftenreihe für Kultur-, Medien- und Psychoanalyse* 44/45. Kassel: Schriftenreihe der Gesamthochschule Kassel, 1994, pp. 11-24.
Schwarzenbach, Alexis. "'Der Anfang aller Dinge'. Annemarie Schwarzenbach und ihre Mutter Renée Wille-Schwarzenbach." *Annemarie Schwarzenbach. Analysen und Erstdrucke*. Edited by Walter Fähnders and Sabine Rohlf. Bielefeld: Aisthesis, 2005 pp. 21-45.
---. *Auf der Schwelle des Fremden. Das Leben der Annemarie Schwarzenbach*. Munich: Collection Rolf Heyne, 2011.
Schwarzenbach, Annemarie. "Carson McCullers." *Auf der Schattenseite. Reportagen und Fotografien*. Edited by Regina Dieterle and Roger Perret. Basel: Lenos, 1995, pp. 262-268.
---. *Freunde um Bernhard. Roman*. (1931). Basel: Lenos, 2008. Print.
---. *Lyric Novella*. (1933). Translated by Lucy Renner Jones. Seagull Books, 2001.
---. *Death in Persia*. (*1935/1936). Translated by Lucy Renner Jones. Seagull Books, 2013.
---. *All the Roads Are Open. An Afghan Journey 1939-1940*. Translated and introduced by Isabel Fargo Cole. Afterword by

Roger Perret. Seagull Books, 2011(a).

---. *Das glückliche Tal.* (1940). Basel: Lenos, 2010.

---. *Das Wunder des Baums. Roman.* (*1940/1941). Edited by Sofie Decock, Walter Fähnders, and Uta Schaffers. Zurich: Chronos, 2011.

---. "Marc". (1942) *Afrikanische Schriften. Reportagen —Lyrik— Autobiographisches.* Edited by Sofie Decock, Walter Fähnders, and Uta Schaffers. Zurich: Chronos, 2012, pp. 227-283.

Smith, Laura. "Androgyny was the power and the curse of the tragically glamorous writer Annemarie Schwarzenbach." Timeline.com (23-06-2017). Web.

Thomsen, Christian W. *Das Groteske im englischen Roman des 18. Jahrhunderts. Erscheinungsformen und Funktionen.* Darmstadt: Wissenschaftliche Buchgesellschaft, 1974.

Yalom, Marilyn and Theresa Donovan Brown. *The Social Sex. A History of Female Friendship.* Random House, 2015.

Weber, Samuel M. *Return to Freud: Jacques Lacan's Dislocation of Psychoanalysis.* Cambridge UP, 1991.

Westling, Louise. "Carson McCullers' Amazon Nightmare". *Carson McCullers. Modern Critical Views.* Edited by Harold Bloom. Chelsea House Publishers, 1986, pp. 109-116.

Wichor, Simone. *Zwishen Literatur und Journalismus. Die Reportagen und Feuilletons von Annemarie Schwarzenbach.* Bielefeld: Aisthesis, 2013.

Wucherpfennig, Wolf. *Kindheitskult und Irrationalismus in der Literatur um 1900. Friedrich Huch und seine Zeit.* Munich: Wilhelm Fink, 1980.

# Gothic Reverberations: Soundscapes in Ann Radcliff and Carson McCullers's *The Ballad of the Sad Café*

## Shannon Russell

Just before that "terrible character" Marvin Macy returns to wreak his revenge on his wife and community in *The Ballad of the Sad Café*, Miss Amelia, rather bizarrely, sits down to write "a story—a story in which there were foreigners, trap doors, and millions of dollars" (435). Currency differences aside, Miss Amelia's startling creative burst has some of the key ingredients of Ann Radcliffe's gothic novels—novels Jane Austen spoofs in *Northanger Abbey* when laughing at Catherine's Morland's romantic confusion of gothic and sexual longings—her musically alliterative musings on "broken promises and broken arches, phaetons and false hangings, Tilneys and trap doors" (103). In "Books I Remember," Carson McCullers offers her own sonic homage to Jane Austen's poetry when admiring her alluring "sharp charm" (467). She also counted the gothically influenced *Wuthering Heights* amongst her favourite books, and as a child read Edgar Allan Poe with "chill-blooded interest," thrilling to plots where "people got the best of other people in some unholy or scandalous way" (464-467). The influence of Isak Dinesen's *Seven Gothic Tales* has also long been the subject of critical debate (James 98, Westling 110). When considering the Gothic and its effects, critics often overlook the overheard. I want to tune into the reverberations between Ann Radcliffe's gothic novels and Carson McCullers's *The Ballad of the Sad Café* by turning away from trap doors to sound effects, to explore the synesthetic ways in which by reading both of these novelists, we hear through seeing. These writers choose particular soundscapes to dramatize their sense of the psychological mysteries of love, audibly exploring the boundaries between the rational and the irrational, which, in turn, allow these stories to reverberate in the particular way they do in the reader's imagination.

Radcliffe's novels have long been analyzed in relation to Edmund Burke's aesthetics of the sublime and the beautiful as well as eighteenth century theories of sensibility. Led by the precedence Burke gives to the eye in his writing, critics have focused on the visual landscapes of Radcliffe's novels—her famous "word painting"—and the ways in which her verbal pictures evoke emotional, psychological, moral, and spiritual responses in her characters and her readers. But Burke makes clear that "the eye is not the only organ of sensation by which a sublime passion may be produced. Sounds have a great power in these as in most other passions" (pt. II, sec. 18). He identifies "excessive loudness," as "sufficient to overpower the soul, to suspend its action, and to fill it with terror" while the strength of "shouting . . . amazes and confounds the imagination," "staggering" and hurrying the mind, so that even "the best-established tempers" are "borne down" (pt. II, sec. 18). Burke also recognized the dramatic importance of silence to the terror effects of sudden sounds, as well as the anxiety produced in humans by the cries of animals.

By contrast, the beautiful in music, with which the sublime is always in dialectic, "will not bear that loudness and strength of sound which may be used to raise other passions, nor notes which are shrill, or harsh or deep" (pt. III, sec. 25). The "passion excited by beauty," according to Burke, is "nearer to a species of melancholy, than to jollity and mirth" (pt. III, sec. 25). Pierre Dubois argues that Radcliffe complicates Burke's clear distinction between sublime and beautiful effects to invent a feminine sublime, demonstrating that in her novels, sublime responses to beautiful music could also be triggered in listeners by "soft sounds which swell gradually" ("Feminine Sublime" 457–469; *Georgian Novel*, 150, 175). This sublime effect is also articulated in the musical crescendo of McCullers's chain gang that closes her fictional ballad.

Melancholy affect and sound are also essential aspects of those pre-romantic heroes and heroines of sensibility who populate the sublime and beautiful landscapes of gothic fiction. They demonstrate their emotional sensitivity and ethical superiority, or, as John Mullan describes it, their ability to "thrum in tune" ("Sensibility," *In Our Time*) with others, by the sounds they make—weeping, moaning, and sighing, mainly—but also by creating and responding to soulful poetry and mournful music. As Frits Noske writes, in Radcliffe's novels, "music and melancholia have become almost synonymous concepts" with joyful music and comical loquaciousness expressed by servant characters who provide a "much-needed contrast" to the "noble sadness" of her heroines (166-167).

Sound is also implicit to the experience of reading gothic novels, for Radcliffe's sensitive readers expected her, quite literally, to play them, in an age where nerves were thought to be strings to be plucked like lutes or Aeolian harps (Trower, "Nerves"). Contemporary associationist philosophers like David Hartley argued that nerve vibrations created sensations that would then generate thought and feeling (*Observations*). To read Radcliffe was to experience a refining range of thrilling tremors, for if, as Robert Miles writes, "Radcliffe places the reader on the rack, so that the reader's nerves, tightly strung, vibrate, she will loosen them again through a comic interlude" (51). By stringing readers along to experience sublime and beautiful effects leading them to pity and terror, gothic novels were thought to cultivate elevated feeling and sympathy for others. Inspiring sublime terror was, therefore, desirable in fiction, according to Radcliffe's famous distinction, because terror "expands the soul, and awakens the faculties to a high degree of life" unlike horror which "contracts, freezes, and nearly annihilates them" ("Supernatural" 151).

Despite their clear importance to the acts of writing and reading gothic fiction, soundscapes have received limited critical attention. The dreamy quality of Radcliffe's imagined territories removed in time and space, yet strangely hovering between past and present, depend on a wide range of sound effects from the polyphonic mixing of poetry and prose, to her trademark manipulation of spooky sounds which suggest presence like mysterious echoes or disembodied sounds—overheard voices, sighs, and music. But "Radcliffe's sonic environments," according to Joan Passey, "are not merely audible language, or an accompaniment to visual landscape," they are "a means of expressing anxiety over the penetration and destabilization of self and society. Sound, in being a spectral force . . . [has] the ability to transcend, confuse and stimulate the imagination in a space where rationality and empiricism are being challenged" (202). Angela Archambault has argued that in the eighteenth-century, sound was recognized for its "potential to infiltrate, disturb and corrupt" and that gothic novels explore it as "an ungovernable force" to be reckoned with, suggestive of those novels' exploration of other forces of power and control.

Radcliffe also uses sound to structure her narratives (Noske 164), heightening tension and building suspense through dramatic contrasts of silence with sound, creating a dialectic between the awe-and terror-inspiring sonic sublime and a divinely soothing sonic beautiful. The "uncanny atmospheres and ghostliness" that inspire terror in Radcliffe's environments are usually preceded, as Isabella van Elferen writes, "by an unworldly silence", aided by meteorological predictors. Of course, Radcliffe famously explains away all supernatural possibilities by the end of her novels, a fact that left some contemporary readers disappointed, or even a little humiliated. Sir Walter Scott, for instance, described the readers of Radcliffe's fiction as "conscious listeners" whose imaginations can be influenced when their "nerves are tuned to a certain pitch," but who feel "angry with their senses for having been cheated" when the "stealthy step" they "hear" behind the arras curtain in Radcliffe's fiction turns out to be "only the noise made by the cat" (329). Despite the fact that her audible spectres disappointingly vanish in her novels, contemporary readers—or even fictional ones like Austen's Catherine Morland—thrilled to their sonically evoked presence throughout—a presence that reverberates in the imagination.

Perhaps, most suggestive in relation to McCullers's work, is Dubois's contention that Radcliffe has her characters use music to "fathom melancholy" rather than avoid it, and that her feminine sublime substitutes mystery for terror in terms of the ultimate effects of the audible on her characters and her readers (*Georgian Novel* 161–194). A case in point might be the character of Du Pont in *The Mysteries of Udolpho*. Not only is he a shadowy character who is responsible for many of the disembodied sounds and musical mysteries of the novel, but he appears to be a kind of offstage stalker who, unlike the hero Valancourt, is instrumental in Emily's protection and rescue from evil forces in the novel. Du Pont's odd and steadfast devotion is unrequited and, sadly, hopeless. He makes his chivalric and melancholic exit at the end of the novel when he is defeated by the romantic return of his rival Valancourt, in a dramatically staged scene when Emily's mournful lute playing in the gathering gloom of dusk is repeatedly interrupted by the sound of her lover's rapidly approaching footsteps. Though produced materially, from vibrations in bodies or instruments, sound is disembodied and ultimately suggestive of those human experiences that emotionally vibrate, though often escape our rational grasp, like love and its loss (Trower, *Senses* 2). As such, a writer's choice to invoke the presence of sound in fiction can allow them and the reader to access the mysterious and irrational nature of love, famously expressed by McCullers in the narrator's reflections on the "different countries" of the lover and beloved in *The Ballad of the Sad Café*.

\* \* \* \* \*

In her essay "The Russian Realists and Southern Literature" McCullers claims that the disturbing effects of the Southern Gothic school do not come from "the romantic or supernatural" as in gothic fiction, but from a "peculiar and intense realism" (469). But I would argue that she creates that realism not only through a philosophical affinity with Russian writers, nor simply through "a reconfiguration" of Radcliffe's works, as Dara Downey argues, to include things "peculiar" to McCullers's vision like the legacy of slavery, the queer, and the grotesque (366). Rather, the unsettling intensity of her writing can be seen to emerge, in part, through her recognition of the importance of sound and its effects. The disembodied nature of sound allows McCullers another sensory avenue to query the rigidity of boundaries in her society, particularly her demonstration, as Gleeson-White argues, that femininity can be "unsettling" in her work, and that gender is fluid, ambiguous, or "nomadic" ("A 'Calculable Woman'" 47, *Strange Bodies* 68). Sound is also employed, as in Radcliffe's fiction, to express the drama of injustice and to query the particular power dynamics in her society. Through soundscapes, McCullers evokes the "horror, beauty, and emotional ambivalence" (469) she identifies as effects shared by both Gothic and Southern Gothic writing.

In *The Ballad of the Sad Café*, McCullers creates her peculiar environment, like Radcliffe, (influenced by Burke), does hers, through the careful orchestration of sound and silence. "Lonesome, sad, and like a place that is far off and estranged from other places in the world," this "dreary" town is characterized by a deadly silence, where "talk" is heard only on Saturdays and where "there is nothing whatsoever to do" (397). The uncanny nature of that silence is intensified by the description of a nameless creature who haunts the ruined house she has locked herself into—her face appearing eerily "sexless" and ghostly white, "like the terrible dim faces known in dreams" (397). In this depressingly mute town, all that is left to do after one's shift at the mill is to walk out of it to "listen to the chain gang" (397), but the sound of that music is deferred until its description at the end of the novella, when, as Margaret Whitt observes, it will uncannily "haunt the heart"—teasingly reverberating (122).

Analysis of the ballad form, and McCullers's use of music to structure Miss Amelia's horror story has been often discussed (Barlow, Dazey, Edmonds, Millichap), but McCullers also relies, like Radcliffe, on a range of other sound effects. Linguistic refrains provide bass notes to convey the rhythms of this town. The silence or hum of the looms repeatedly registers the community's rising and falling employment, while the gossiping voices of the townsfolk operate like a Greek chorus—the narrator tells us to "think of them as a whole" as all have "wept and suffered" (399, 412). These "good people" feel a kind of "pity" towards Miss Amelia, compounded by "a mixture of exasperation, a ridiculous little inside tickle, and a deep unnamable sadness" (407). Their voices are often leavening agents on the tragic theatre of the principal actors, rather like Ann Radcliffe's chatty but devoted and down-to-earth servant characters provide comic relief from the heroine's sadness, as well as the fear and melancholy generated by those disembodied sounds in her novels.

Like Radcliffe, too, McCullers relies on Burkean dynamics of silence and sound to create dramatic tension and to outline her characters' emotional landscapes, often linking these to nature—the changeableness of the moon, the seasons, and unusual weather. The arrival of the trickster figure, Cousin Lymon, with his unstable romantic possibilities, occurs in a seductively dreamy soundscape "on a soft quiet evening" in spring, where one is lulled by the "faint, steady hum of the loom"—on such a "night when it is good to hear from faraway across dark fields, the slow song of a Negro on his way to make love" or "when it is pleasant to sit quietly and pick a guitar" (399). But there is a jarring warning note that audibly predicts the revolutions Lymon will bring to the town, in the "wild, hoarse howl" of a dog that precedes his appearance (400). Lymon's desperate crying, too, punctuates the tense silence of his arrival and plucks the heartstrings of Miss Amelia, seducing her to share her magical whiskey and invite him in. Three days later, the townspeople "act in unison," to assemble silently in the ominous and gathering "tension" at Miss Amelia's house, having imagined a gothic scenario where she has murdered "the pitiful and dirty little chatterer" and buried him in the swamp (410). Their expectations are confounded first by sound—"a noise at the head of the stair"—as a transformed Lymon appears to inaugurate the café while they stand by amazed and "still as death" (410). Meanwhile, the "low sound of Miss Amelia whistling to herself" audibly conveys her emotional contentment (411). Love for Lymon has released this happy sound, as he is the physical "stimulus for all the stored-up love which has lain quiet within the lover" (417).

As "a great mischief-maker" subject to lying and boasting enough to "shrivel the ears," Lymon has almost magical abilities to confuse the senses and distort perception through his manipulation of sound and silence, as he can miraculously cause "tension" and "trouble" between townspeople "without saying a word" (429–430). His power over Amelia is registered sonically, in the jingling tunes of the "fine mechanical piano" he cajoles her into buying for the café and will destroy when he leaves, and the "loud jingle" of money in his pocket which she is charmed into giving him despite her stinginess (415). The sonic dissonance in their conversation vocalizes the lopsided nature of their relationship, too, as Lymon is a "great chatterer" while Amelia speaks to him in a "low, thoughtful voice . . . getting nowhere" (426). McCullers dramatizes their clashing emotional soundtracks, as the romantic flow of Amelia's nostalgic memories of mornings with her father is insensitively interrupted by Lymon's irritable and tone-deaf complaint that "the grits we had this morning was poor" (427).

Miss Amelia's devotion leaves *her* deaf to the insult and "the conversation would go on endlessly", though the spectre of Marvin Macy, her "broken bridegroom . . . trapped in his cell in the penitentiary, was like a troubling undertone beneath the happy love of Miss Amelia and the gaiety of the café" (424, 427). When Henry Macy quietly and nervously warns her that his "split hoofed" brother with a heart "turned tough as the horns of satan" (420) has been released from prison, the soundscape turns mesmerizingly eerie:

> The drowzy buzz of swamp Mosquitos was like an echo of the silent night. . . . Somewhere in the darkness a woman sang in a high wild voice and the tune had no start and no finish and

was made up of only three notes which went on and on. (431)

Despite these uncanny sonic signals, or perhaps in tune with the narrative anxiety McCullers creates in us through them, the town enters a deceptively "happy time" where crops are good and the autumn moon hangs "round and orange" in the sky while Miss Amelia busily brews, stews, and prepares to barbeque (434). The quiet is ominous. If "there is no stillness like the quiet of the first cold nights of fall", McCullers interrupts the intensity of this silence with yet another unsettling alarm in the "thin, wild, whistle of the train" (434). All notice the unusual almost defiant noisiness of Miss Amelia's happiness in this season, for "she laughed often, with a deep ringing laugh, and her whistling had a sassy, tuneful trickery" while "the undertone of love" "lingered in her voice" when she spoke Lymon's name (434). These sonic contrasts aurally prepare readers for the unholy harvest or "fall" that will come with Macy's return—that remembered but suppressed "undertone"—symbolically vocalized when Lymon "heard the shifting of gears" in the car that drops him off in the centre of town (436). As Amelia regards Lymon's love for Macy with "sick amazement," atmospheric conditions go wild, the changeable weather ruining the pork slaughter and killing off a local family, while a surprise snowfall confounds everyone (438). It is a time of "waste and confusion" (440).

Macy causes this social dissonance, and his disruptive power is registered sonically His devilish, serpent-like charm over Lymon is expressed through music as "the tunes he sang glided slowly from his throat like eels" (449). Lymon's desperate love leaves him groaning, crying, and calling softly for Macy every morning in a voice "sad, luring and resigned" (444), while he futilely tries to charm him by wiggling his ears. Macy's ubiquitous guitar, and the manipulation of its strings make him a parody of the hero of sensibility. If his early love for Miss Amelia "reversed his character" to soften a heart "turned tough as the horns of satan" (420), her rejection of him excites his audible revenge. He, maddeningly, manipulates his guitar strings to mock her and to play on her nerves, echoing Burke's claim that sound can "amaze and confound" its hearer, as she disastrously "began following several courses at once, all of them contrary to each other" (442). Macy's vocal and musical reverberations elicit disorienting and unsettling responses:

> His strong fingers picked the strings with dainty skill, and everything he sang both lured and exasperated. This was usually more than Amelia could stand.
>
> 'Bust a gut!' She would repeat, in a shout.
>
> But always Marvin Macy had the answer ready for her. He would cover the strings to silence the quivering leftover tones, and reply with slow, sure insolence.
>
> 'Everything you holler at me bounces back on yourself. Yah! Yah!'
>
> Miss Amelia would have to stand there helpless, as no one has ever invented a way out of this trap. She could not shout out abuse that would bounce back on herself. He had the best of her, there was nothing she could do. (449)

At this moment, Miss Amelia is emotionally and sonically trapped; her silent powerlessness foreshadowing the gathering quiet leading up to the fight she will lose by sound—overpowered by Lymon's tricky and terrible cry "that caused a shrill bright shiver to run down the spine" (454). That shocking sound again confounds the senses, for what happened "has been a mystery ever since. The whole town was there to testify what happened, but there were those who doubted their eyesight" though all hear Miss Amelia's emotional defeat in her "sobbing with the last of her grating, winded breath" (454-455). The emotional violence done to her comes in the form of another sonic assault in the pounding anaphora which describes the desolation that follows. We are told that:

> "They unlocked the private cabinet of curios and took everything in it.
>
> They broke the mechanical piano.

They carved . . . They found . . . They poured . . . They went . . . They fixed . . . They did everything ruinous they could think of . . . [and] Then they went off together, the two of them" (455).

The violent destruction of the café is followed by that of Amelia's voice, which "lost its old vigor; there was none of the ring of vengeance in it . . . her voice was broken, soft, and sad as the wheezy whine of the Church pump-organ" (456). Lymon's betraying "cry" has left her "alone and silent"—the sonic victim not of Radcliffe's soul-expanding terror, but of a freezing, annihilating horror—or "the terror of living alone" (448).

But the novella ends mysteriously with a performance of Radcliffe's sonic sublime and beautiful. The Twelve Mortal Men coda to this story has long challenged readers to consider the meaning of its sound—the mental vibrations between it and the story that precedes it. Aurally, the rising and falling dynamics of the voices of the chain gang are in tune with the story that precedes the coda, as both articulate a movement from isolation to communal harmony back to isolation. Rising out of the steady beat of the picks, this is a work song to hypnotize and allay the shared pain of imprisonment, as Lawrence Levine has argued, whether in a chain gang, a love triangle, or a mill town—as voices become "intricately blended, both somber and joyful" (458). The racial mix of the singers deepens and expands the historical scope of the story, to include the local horrors of a South haunted by slavery, but these united voices also importantly suggest a timeless and universal application of sound to human suffering (Barlow 74–85)—like Burke's beautiful and melancholic music. Listeners experience a sublime reaction that "can cause the heart to broaden and the listener to grow cold with ecstasy and fright" (458). The song achieves music's potential for "boundary crossing transcendence" (von Elferen 32) when it swells beyond the twelve mortal singers and seems to come from "the earth itself, or the wide sky" (458)—nature's sublimely divine forces so celebrated in Radcliffe's fiction. As the music ends and there is only the ring of the picks and "a great hoarse breath" there is a clear echo with the preceding story, as the reader recalls the "deep hoarse breaths" of Amelia and Macy that were "the only sound in the café" during their fight (454, 458).

In this blended breathing is both a confirmation and a challenge to individual loneliness, for in its rhythm is the shared struggle of being human, with its pleasure and its pain.

Sounds throughout *The Ballad of the Sad Café* resonate, like they do in Radcliffe's fiction, with intense melancholy and mystery as both writers use them to explore the nature of love, self, and society. Though their source is not supernatural, the sounds we see through reading these writers linger and unsettle. What is gothic about the work of Radcliffe and McCullers is their shared sensibility that sound is a peculiarly stimulating force that can be used to haunt the reader's imagination.

# Works Cited

Austen, Jane. *Northanger Abbey*. Edited by Claire Grogan, Broadview Press, 2002.

Archambault, Angela. "The Function of Sound in the Gothic Novels of Ann Radcliffe, Matthew Lewis and Charles Maturin." *Etudes Epistémè: Noise and Sound in Eighteenth-Century Britain*, vol. 29, 2016. episteme.revues.org/965.

Barlow, Daniel Patrick. "And every day there is music": Folksong Roots and the Highway Chain Gang in "The Ballad of the Sad Café." *The Southern Literary Journal*, vol. 44, no. 1 (Fall 2011), pp. 74–85.

Burke, Edmund. *A Philosophical Enquiry into the Origin of Our Ideas of The Sublime and Beautiful, with Several Other Additions. The Harvard Classics*, edited by Charles W. Eliot, vol. 24, part 2. P.F. Collier & Son, 1909–14; Bartleby.com, 2001. www.bartleby.com/24/2/.

Dazey, Mary Ann. "Two Voices of the Single Narrator in *The Ballad of the Sad Café*." *The Southern Literary Journal*, vol. 17, no. 2 (spring 1985): 33-40.

Downey, Dara. "The Gothic and the Grotesque in the Novels of Carson McCullers." *The Palgrave Handbook of Southern Goth-*

ic. Edited by S.C. Street and C.L. Crow, Palgrave McMillan, 2016.

Dubois, Pierre. "Music and the Feminine Sublime in Ann Radcliffe's *Mysteries of Udolpho*." *Ètudes anglaises,* vol. 67, no. 4, 2014, pp.457–469.www.cairn.info/revue-etudes-anglaises-2014-4-p-457.htm

---. *Music in the Georgian Novel*. Cambridge UP, 2015.

Edmonds, Dale. *Carson McCullers*. Southern Writers Series, vol. 6. Steck-Vaughn, 1969.

Gleeson-White, Sarah. *Strange Bodies: Gender and Identity in the Novels of Carson McCullers*. University of Alabama Press, 2003.

---. "A 'Calculable Woman' and a 'Jittery Ninny': Performing Femininity in *The Heart Is a Lonely Hunter* and *The Ballad of the Sad Café*." *Reflections in a Critical Eye*. Edited by Jan Whitt, University Press of America, 2008, pp. 47–59.

Hartley, David. *Observations on Man, His Frame, His Duty, and His Expectations*, vol. 1. Joseph Johnson, 1791.

James, Judith Giblin. *Wunderkind: The Reputation of Carson McCullers, 1940-1990*. Camden House, 1995.

Levine, Lawrence. *Black Culture and Black Consciousness*. Oxford UP, 1977.

McCullers, Carson. *The Ballad of the Sad Café,* in *Carson McCullers: Complete Novels,* edited by Carlos Dews, *Library* of America, 2017, pp. 397–458.

---. "Books I Remember," *Stories, Plays, and Other Writings*, edited by Carlos Dews, *Library* of America, 2017, pp. 464-468.

Miles, Robert. *Anne Radcliffe: The Great Enchantress*. Manchester UP, 1995.

Millichap, Joseph R. "Carson McCullers' Literary Ballad." *Georgia Review*, vol. 27, 1973, pp. 329–339.

Noske, Frits. "Sound and Sentiment: The Function of Music in the Gothic Novel." *Music and Letters*, vol. 62, no. 2 (April 1981), pp. 162–175.

Passey, Joan. "Sound and Silence: the Aesthetics of the Auditory." *Horror Studies*, vol. 7, no. 2, 2016, pp. 189–204.

Radcliffe, Ann. *The Mysteries of Udolpho*.1794. Edited by Bonamy Dobrée, Oxford UP, 2008.

---. "On the Supernatural in Poetry by the Late Mrs. Radcliffe." *The New Monthly Magazine and Literary Journal*, vol. 16, no. 1, 1826, pp. 145-152.

Scott, Walter. "Mrs. Ann Radcliffe." *Lives of the Novelists*. Henry Frowde, Oxford UP, 1906, pp. 302–342.

"Sensibility." *In Our Time*. BBC Radio 4, 3 Jan. 2002.

Trower, Shelley. "Nerves, Vibration and the Aeolian Harp." *Romanticism and Victorianism on the Net*, no. 54, May 2009.

---. *Senses of Vibration: A History of the Pleasure and Pain of Sound*. The Continuum International Publishing Group, 2012.

van Elferen, Isabella. *Gothic Music: The Sounds of the Uncanny*. U of Wales Press, 2012.

Walsh, Margaret. "Carson McCullers' Anti-Fairy Tale: The Ballad of the Sad Café." *Pembroke Magazine*, vol. 20, 1988, pp. 24-29.

Westling, Louise. *Modern Critical Views: Carson McCullers*. Edited by Harold Bloom, Chelsea House Publishers, 1986, pp. 109–116.

Whitt, Margaret. "From Eros to Agape: Reconsidering the Chain Gang's Song in McCullers's "Ballad of the Sad Café." *Studies in Short Fiction*, vol. 33, 1996, pp. 119–122.

# The "Malady" Dr Copeland Was Unable to Treat

## Emilia Salomone

As an *Italy Reads* teacher, I had the chance to share my experience of the programme with the participants in the Centenary Conference on "Carson McCullers in the World" held at John Cabot University in Rome in July 2017.

In 2010, I was strongly encouraged to take part in *Italy Reads* by a friend of mine. I immediately decided to sign up because I was sure I was going to be involved in a valuable experience, and now I am pleased to state I was right.

I have since participated in several programmes which enhanced my abilities as a teacher and gave my students the chance to benefit from the study of important American authors and from activities (such as the visits of John Cabot University students to our school, the attendance of conferences, and the production of videos) associated with the programme.

Each year the *Italy Reads* book has been a precious source of inspiration for my students. The themes have been motivating, e.g., ordinary lives and the importance of enjoying human existence in *Our Time* by Thornton Wilder; loneliness and the pain of being different in *The Heart Is a Lonely Hunter* by Carson McCullers; memory, dreams and their failure in *The Great Gatsby* by F. Scott Fitzgerald; and identity and cross-culturalism in *The Namesake* by Jhumpa Lahiri, have been debated in a lively way.

This is why, as a teacher, in my short talk, I focused on one of the characters in *The Heart Is a Lonely Hunter*, Doctor Benedict Mady Copeland, since he, like me, believes in the relevance of education for future generations, their moral progress and personal fulfillment. Doctor Copeland, though, like the other protagonists of the novel, symbolizes the themes of the novel—isolation and social issues such as racism—as he experiences solitude, without being able to cope with it and being unable to treat the American malady—loneliness—despite his studies and his occupation.

In a Learning Unit on cultural differences, inclusion, and the issue of racism, I included some pages from this novel, which I noted for my students. When Carson McCullers started writing "The Mute" (later entitled *The Heart Is a Lonely Hunter*) in 1936, she had spent nearly two years in New York and was aware of the "American malady" that she decided to be the theme of her novel: loneliness. In this paper, I discuss how one of the five protagonists of *The Heart Is a Lonely Hunter*, Doctor Benedict Mady Copeland, experiences isolation without being able to cope with it because of his studies and occupation.

In one of the articles contained in *The Mortgaged Heart* McCullers wrote:

> This city, New York—consider the people in it, the eight million of us. An English friend of mine, when asked why he lived in New York City, said that he liked it here because he could be so alone. While it was my friend's desire to be alone, the aloneness of many Americans who live in cities is an involuntary and fearful thing. It has been said that loneliness is the great American malady. What is the nature of this loneliness? It would seem essentially to be a quest for identity . . . . The loneliness of Americans does not have its source in xenophobia; as a nation we are an outgoing people, reaching always for immediate contacts, further experience. But we tend to seek out things as individuals, alone. The Europeans, secure in family ties and rigid class loyalties, know little of the moral loneliness that is native to us Americans. (McCullers, "Loneliness" 259-60)

McCullers, who considered herself an American artist and "eternal maverick" (McCullers, "Loneliness" 266) was determined to deal exactly with the themes of isolation and loneliness in all her literary production; *The Heart Is a Lonely Hunter* is her first great example. In her outline of "The Mute" she wrote:

> The broad principal theme of this book is indicated in the first dozen pages. This is the theme of man's revolt against his own inner isolation and his urge to express himself as

fully as possible .... The general outline of this work can be expressed very simply. It is the story of five isolated, lonely people in their search for expression and spiritual integration with something greater than themselves. (McCullers, "Author's Outline" 136-37)

Singer, Biff, Mick, Jake and Dr Copeland are all lonely hunters, who are unable to express their anguished solitude, to find anyone who could really sympathize with them, helping them cope with their problems: absence of love, sexual identity, adolescence, class-consciousness, racism.

Unlike Jan Whitt who believes John Singer to be the most spiritually isolated character in the novel, I think Dr Copeland is the loneliest hunter of the group. As we start reading the fifth chapter of the first of the three parts of the novel, McCullers makes it immediately clear how the reader must perceive him: "Far from the main street, in one of the Negro sections of the town, Doctor Benedict Mady Copeland sat in the dark kitchen alone" (*Heart* 61). Like Singer, who "had been left in an alien land. Alone" (*Heart* 194), Dr. Copeland is:

> an alien in a strange land. Born in the South but educated in the North, he has returned to Georgia to rear his family and to lead people out of sickness and servitude. He dreams day and night of racial equality, but blames his own race for most of its problems .... A disciple of Marx and Spinoza, Copeland has named his children for them and planned their lives according to his dreams, but they are grown when the novel begins, and not one has followed the career he dictated .... At the family reunion, he sits alone, angry and frustrated .... Copeland is plagued by an inability to communicate and to cope with his moral isolation and estrangement from society. (Carr 30-31)

Dr Copeland is isolated both as a single individual and as a member of his social group; he is unable to communicate with his family and the people of his race, but McCullers intriguingly—and quite paradoxically—has him realize the only person he can really communicate with is Singer, a white deaf mute.

I will analyse these ideas more in detail, focusing first on the relationship between Dr Copeland and John Singer, since this relationship is what the novel is centred on. In *Heart*, McCullers describes the unique sympathy between Dr Copeland and Singer several times:

> [Mick Kelly and Jake Blount and] Doctor Copeland would come and talk in the silent room—for they felt that the mute would always understand whatever they wanted to say to him. And maybe even more than that (82) . . . . Many times Doctor Copeland talked to Mr Singer. Truly he was not like other white men. He was a wise man, and he understood the strong, true purpose in a way that other white men could not. He listened, and in his face there was something gentle and Jewish, the knowledge of one who belongs to a race that is oppressed (115). He watched the words shape on their lips. We Negroes want a chance to be free at last. And freedom is only the right to contribute. We want to serve and to share, to labor and in turn consume that which is due to us. But you are the only white man I have ever encountered who realizes this terrible need of my people (175). . . . But truly with the death of that white man a dark sorrow had lain down in his heart. He had talked to him as to no other white man and had trusted him and the mystery of his suicide left him baffled and without support. There was neither beginning nor end to this sorrow. Nor understanding. Always he would return in his thoughts to this white man who was not insolent or scornful but who was just. (284)

Jan Whitt tries to explain the attraction Dr Copeland feels for Singer by stating "Copeland believes Singer a Jew; he longs for identification with the members of oppressed races and cannot justify a friendship with a white man without casting him as a Jew" (*Heart* 30).

Furthermore, Dr Copeland is even ready to virtually impair himself, similar to Singer, in the most atrocious moment of the novel— when his daughter Portia informs him about the cruel punishment inflicted on her brother William, transformed into what Laurie

Champion describes as a black Christ (47-52):

> Portia spoke in a low voice, and she neither paused between words nor did the grief in her face soften. It was like a long song. She spoke and he could not understand. The sounds were distinct in his ear but they had no shape or meaning . . . . ". . . and their feets swolled up and they lay there and struggle on the floor and holler out. And nobody come. They hollered there for three days and three nights and nobody came." "I am deaf," said Doctor Copeland. "I cannot understand". (*Heart* 217-18)

As for Doctor Copeland's unsatisfactory relationship with his family and with the people of his own race, McCullers seems to imply that they are closely interrelated:

> He married and made a home. He went endlessly from house to house and spoke the mission and the truth. The hopeless suffering of his people made in him a madness, a wild and evil feeling of destruction. At times he drank strong liquor and beat his head against the floor. In his heart there was a savage violence, and once he grasped the poker from the hearth and struck down his wife. She took Hamilton, Karl Marx, William, and Portia with her to her father's home. He wrestled in his spirit and fought down the evil blackness. But Daisy did not come back to him. And eight years later when she died his sons were not children any more and they did not return to him. He was left an old man in an empty house. (122-23)

Despite his education, or perhaps exactly for this reason, Doctor Copeland makes his life a failure. He argues with Portia; he does not see William for a long period of time and at the family reunion, he feels just isolation, anger and frustration; moreover, he is disappointed by the resignation and passiveness of his people, for whom, more than a doctor he meant to be a teacher:

> All of his life he knew that there was a reason for his working.

> He always knew that he was meant to teach his people. All day he would go with his bag from house to house and on all things he would talk to them (65) . . . . "The Negro race of its own accord climbs up on the cross on every Friday," said Doctor Copeland . . . "I mean that I am always looking. I mean that if I could just find ten Negroes—ten of my own people—with spine and brains and courage who are willing to give all that they have—" (67) . . . "We will save ourselves. But not by prayers of mourning. Not by indolence or strong drink. Not by the pleasures of the body or by ignorance. Not by submission and humbleness. But by pride. By dignity. By becoming hard and strong. We must build strength for our real true purpose. (166)

The way Doctor Copeland organizes his speech at his annual party on Christmas Day, his use of repetition and contrast, reveals his education as well as his mastery of language, two qualities which, paradoxically, make him an alien. In a novel based on (the failure of) communication, the characters' use of language plays a pivotal role. As L.G. Giròn Echevarrìa noted:

> Carson McCullers was a master in the use of dialect to establish character and setting and to reinforce the key ideas of her fiction. Her ability to use variations in dialect to strengthen her fiction is nowhere more obvious than in her best two novels, *The Heart Is a Lonely Hunter* (1940) and *The Member of the Wedding* (1946). (103)

Biff, Mick, Jake and Dr Copeland speak in their own style, while for Singer, McCullers adopts an objective legendary style. McCullers chooses for Doctor Copeland:

> flawless standard English even with his children, who speak the dialect of the uneducated Southerner in a small town in Georgia, thus symbolizing his refusal to bend to the injustices he and the other members of his race suffer . . . . Dr Copeland's perfect English is a sign of education and of sophistication, but it also clearly identifies him as an outsider—someone

who remains out of touch with his immediate world and is regarded with suspicion by those around him. (Giròn Echevarrìa 103)

Copeland's absolute command of the English language, as well as his oratory skills, differentiate him from his family and his people, thus creating the conditions for his isolation and estrangement. It is as if Doctor Copeland was considered by them too similar to a white man, as it is clear from the sad but resolute reproach of his daughter Portia, whose language deviates most from the norm:

> "You all the time using that word—Negro," said Portia. "And that word has a way of hurting peoples' feelings. Even old plain nigger is better than that word. But polite peoples—no matter what shade they is—always says colored." Doctor Copeland did not answer. . . . "Hamilton or Buddy or Willie or me—none of us ever cares to talk like you. Us talk like our own Mama and her peoples and their peoples before them. You think out everything in your brain. While us rather talk from something in our hearts that has been there for a long time. That's one of them differences." "Yes," said Doctor Copeland. (67-8)

This is the moral lesson Portia—the unlearned, simple human being who, thanks to her human qualities, succeeds in bringing people together—teaches her father: the reason why he was unable to treat his own malady—loneliness—was his intellectual refusal of his own identity, his lack of warmth, his inability to use the language of his heart instead of the language of his reason, his incapacity to feel and show real sympathy, affection and understanding of his own people.

# Works Cited

Carr, Virginia Spencer. *Understanding Carson McCullers*. University of South Carolina P, 2005, pp. 30-31.

Champion, Laurie. "Black and White Christs in Carson McCullers's *The Heart Is a Lonely Hunter*." *The Southern Literary Journal*, vol. 24, no. 1, fall 1991, pp. 47-52.

Giròn Echevarrìa, Luis Gustavo."Dialect Variation in *The Heart Is a Lonely Hunter* and *The Member of the Wedding*." *Atlantis*, vol. XIII, nos.1-2, November 1991, p. 103.

McCullers, Carson. *The Heart Is a Lonely Hunter, Complete novels / Carson McCullers*. Edited by Carlos L. Dews, Library of America, 2001.

McCullers, Carson. "Loneliness . . .an American malady." *The Mortgaged Heart*. Edited by Margarita G. Smith. Houghton Mifflin, 1971, pp. 259-261.

---. "Author's Outline of *The Mute*." *The Mortgaged Heart*. Edited by Margarita G. Smith. Houghton Mifflin, 1971, pp. 124-149.

Whitt, Jan. "The Loneliest Hunter." *The Southern Literary Journal*, vol. 24, no. 2, spring 1992, pp. 26-35.

# READING CARSON IN ITALY
## "CARSON MCCULLERS AT SCAMPIA":
## AN EXPERIENCE WITH *ITALY READS*

### Mariarosaria Savino

Participating in "McCullers in the World: A Centenary Conference" at John Cabot University in July 2017 was a great honour for me. When I was offered this opportunity, I immediately accepted the proposal with enthusiasm, despite the anxiety of feeling not at ease in the role of lecturer, since I usually sit among attendees at conferences. Yet, I was glad to be there as a witness of how much reading and studying literature can contribute to making our world a better place. This is something I strongly believe in, and this is the main reason why I chose, so many years ago, to become a teacher. I believe in education.

As a teacher, the aim of my contribution to the conference was to share my experience teaching Carson McCullers at an Italian high school in Scampia, a suburb of Naples, as part of John Cabot University's *Italy Reads* English Language Reading and Cultural Exchange Program. Indeed, apart from anything else, this project helped me, as a teacher of English Language and Literature, to integrate character education into the classroom, by focusing on a variety of ways of drawing instructive insights from fictional life narratives.

In order to more fully understand the impact of Carson McCullers's *The Heart Is a Lonely Hunter* on the students from Liceo Elsa Morante in Scampia, I think it is fundamental to take into account the social, economic and cultural background of these students. Scampia is a suburban area in the north of Naples entirely made up of public housing that is subject to renewal projects aimed at transforming it from a dormitory quarter into a normal city neighbourhood. (Scampia has a bad reputation that is known not only to residents and all Neapolitans, but all over the world as well. Especially after the successful Italian television crime drama series called *Gomorrah*, based on the book *Gomorrah* by Roberto Saviano and the film *Gomorrah* directed by Matteo Garrone. The well-known "Sails" of Scampia are huge twenty-story housing blocks which turned out to be uninhabitable. Two of them have already been demolished. The local community has abandoned the common areas. Organized crime, the Camorra, has become deeply rooted in this area and opposes any kind of social-economic development, since this would cause it to lose its grip on the population.

It is clear what an impact Carson McCullers's novel might have had on these students at Liceo Elsa Morante. Their only weapon of hope for social redemption is education. Their attendance at school, their engagement in studying has made these students stronger and more aware of the choices they've made through a series of refusals, of No's they have been able to say. By choosing to go to school and study, in an area of Naples which is more challenging than others, they have been able to build their own identity. Having this awareness is what makes them more mature and responsible, more sensitive towards others. For this reason, they are a cut above the rest.

On November 11, 2011, when Professor Dews and Gina Spinelli, Executive Coordinator of John Cabot University's Reading and Cultural Exchange Program, together with three JCU student *Italy Reads* Volunteers (from Michigan USA, Jamaica and Russia), travelled to Scampia for a visit with our students, I am sure we all shared, first-hand, this desire for change. This visit took place within the context of *Italy Reads* 2011 and focused on the novel *The Heart Is a Lonely Hunter*, by Carson McCullers.

Six days prior to this visit, our students, several colleagues, and I had visited John Cabot University in Rome, where we attended a performance of the theatrical adaptation of the book produced by Gaby Ford's The English Theatre of Rome. The English Theatre of Rome generously provided for the cost of our transportation to JCU. During the day's visit, we met with the producer, Gaby Ford, the director, members of the cast, JCU *Italy Reads* Volunteers, faculty and staff. The activities at JCU provided opportunities for students to ask questions and share impressions about all aspects of the play. Our visit was a real experience of cultural exchange. I remember especially when one of our students, who played as an amateur actor at the community theatre in Scampia, asked to perform briefly in Neapolitan at the end of the performance. He wanted to share a bit of their culture with the American students. The students also enjoyed the professional performance of the theatrical production. The producer, cast and crew of The English Theatre of Rome were very approachable. Despite it being quite difficult for our students to understand the dialogues, they were very interested in the activities and participated in an enthusiastic way. Through theatre, the message of the work reached the audience in a variety of ways. Students discussed the choice of having a woman performing the role of Biff Brannon, which they didn't like very much because in the performance, she was quite an active character and not so contemplative as the character in the novel.

In terms of language teaching, this experience offered the students an opportunity of effecting a positive change in their attitude toward studying and learning a foreign language, contributing to their acquisition of skills and self-confidence. For the majority of the students, this cultural exchange program offered them the benefit of being exposed to the language outside of school. They experienced first-hand how learning English is so much more than just performing and mastering boring exercises in the textbook. I saw them trying to discuss the differences between the film version of the novel and the book. It gave me a feeling of success when some of them admitted that the experience of reading the novel was deeper and more enjoyable that just watching the film.

Despite their fears of making mistakes and their lack of fluency in communicating in English, when they met the student *Italy Reads* Volunteers, both at our school and at John Cabot University, they made great efforts to overcome language barriers. They wanted to express themselves and share their ideas. It was a challenge for them to read the novel, in terms of language, themes and situations. Still, they embarked upon this adventure with enthusiasm and eagerness. They were also very motivated by the will to win the video contest. Indeed, competing seems to have been for them the most attractive part of the activities. In preparing their video submissions in groups, they developed a variety of points of view, and they tried to express these views in a very creative way.

What surprised me the most was that the discussions went beyond the novel. Students were anxious to link their own sense of isolation as individuals and as a community within an image of their neighbourhood that reflected a reality they would like to change or to escape. They tried to understand Carson McCullers's ideas and to interpret them on the basis of their own life experience. Her novel has international appeal, but it acquired a relevant significance for them in that particular context.

All the characters in McCullers's novel long to leave their small-town lives and become a "member of the whole world". As we know, in *The Heart Is a Lonely Hunter*, the principal theme is that of man's revolt against his own inner isolation and his urge to express himself as fully as he can. As specific as the setting is, this novel is timeless; everyone in this novel is lonely and searching for who they are. Part one of the novel introduces this broad theme.

> The town was a fairly large one. On the main street there were several blocks of two- and three-story shops and business offices. But the largest buildings in the town were the factories, which employed a large percentage of the population. These cotton mills were big and flourishing and most of the workers in the town were very poor. Often in the faces along the streets there was the desperate look of hunger and of loneliness. (McCullers, *Heart* 5)

When I taught in Scampia, I had the impression that it is a place where good people are faced with a particular challenge to overcome threats along their paths towards happiness and serenity. This central theme of the book—"the desperate look of hunger and of loneliness"—preoccupied McCullers throughout her life and is a theme that interested my students most.

In addition, some characters in the novel offered good opportunities for interesting discussions about such topics as the need for communicating to the collective mind when you try to effect change by awakening the consciousness of people. The character of Jake Blount, for example, is one of extremes (physical, mental, and emotional). He helps to emphasize the precarious, or unstable, nature of life for all the characters in the novel, as we can understand from this quote taken from Part two in which Jake Blount is talking to John Singer about the evils of capitalism because he thinks that Singer is someone who shares his passion for socialism. However, unlike Dr Copeland, Blount thinks that the way to remedy all of these problems is to hold strikes to get pay raises and to raise people's awareness of the injustice under which they live. A worker's resistance to or fear of revolt baffles Jake, who assumes that any worker who would deliberately reject active social protest is also necessarily rejecting his own means of salvation.

> But say a man does know. He sees the world as it is and he looks back thousands of years to see how it all come about. He watches the slow agglutination of capital and power and he sees its pinnacle today. He sees America as a crazy house... He sees a whole damn army of unemployed and billions of dollars and thousands of miles of land wasted... He sees how when people suffer just so much they get mean and ugly and something dies in them. But the main thing he sees is that the whole system of the world is built on a lie. And although it's as plain as the shining sun—the don't-knows have lived with that lie so long they just can't see it. (McCullers, *Heart* 129-130)

In Part two of the novel, chapter 4, we read that, on his way home Jake walks through an alley and sees an inscription—"Ye shall eat the flesh of the mighty, and drink the blood of the princes of the earth"— written in red chalk on a wall (136). He writes beneath this message that whoever wrote those words should meet him there the next day at noon, or even the day after. Jake waits for two days but nobody appears. On the third day a rainstorm begins, and the words wash away. The Biblical words written on the wall interest Blount because he thinks that the person who would write such words might also aid him in his search for other people who are interested in riot or revolt.

The need to write messages on walls in the hope that others would understand "the truth" is very near to the reality of Scampia and of so many people who work hard to change things, especially when the aim is to awaken peoples' awareness of the need for a change in attitude.

This was a stimulating topic in classroom discussions. When you get off at the Scampia Subway Station, you are greeted by a big sign on the walls opposite the exit. On these signs, it is written both in

Italian and in English: WELCOME TO SCAMPIA, "If you believe in Scampia, you'll find a sea of love". And on one of the famous "Sails" of Scampia, you can find written: "Once the wind of abuses is finished, our 'Sails' will unfold towards happiness". But every wall and building of Scampia is full of writings expressing the need to overcome the limitations of this environment.

The students engaged in interesting discussions about this topic, especially in relation to the character of Mick Kelly. They liked her very much because of her adolescent dreams as well as her ambitions and efforts to overcome the limits of her social background, her rebellious and courageous spirit as she moves from childhood into adolescence. Like Mick, McCullers had serious ambitions of becoming a concert pianist when she grew up. Mick's attachment to music is important not only as a defining character trait but also because McCullers's musical sensibility shapes the entire structure of *The Heart Is a Lonely Hunter*; indeed, she once referred to the book as a fugue (McCullers, "Author's Outline" 508). Throughout the novel, music symbolizes Mick's energy and her pursuit of beauty.

> This was her, Mick Kelly, walking in the daytime and by herself at night. In the hot sun and in the dark with all the plans and feelings. This music was her—the real plain her. . . . This . . . music did not take a long time or a short time. It did not have anything to do with time going by at all. She sat with her arms around her legs, biting her salty knee very hard. The whole world was this symphony, and there was not enough of her to listen . . . . Now that it was over there was only her heart beating like a rabbit and this terrible hurt. (101-102)

This is what every student at Liceo Elsa Morante, in Scampia, is trying to do. With the help of their school, they're learning about their own experience and reaching out toward the future and toward the chance of finding their own way in life. What struck them the most in McCullers's novel was the power of friendship to cope with challenges. We can see this in the thoughts about friendship they wanted to express, despite their difficulties in managing the language.

I see education and teachers as a particularly important part of the effort to bring young people closer to opportunities and empower them to effect positive changes in their lives. I strongly believe that teaching / learning a foreign language is not only a question of using the right techniques or methodologies. It is above all, learning about and meeting the cultures where these languages are spoken.

In our case, English, as a global language, offers the opportunity to connect people from all over the world. John Cabot University's *Italy Reads* Program, centering on modern American literature, represents a pleasant way to help students, as well as teachers, to appreciate and benefit from the richness and diversity of other cultures. The *Italy Reads* Program creates a learning community where it is possible to share ideas and opinions where students and teachers can grow and shape their future.

Culture holds an important place in foreign language education. Teaching Carson McCullers to high school students in Scampia certainly contributed to arousing their passion for literature. It provided them with a universal link to a work of literature that opened the floor to the discussion of themes, ideas and beliefs that are often mirrored in the students' own time and place.

I'd like to end by quoting a couple of comments from Ann and Diedre, two JCU students who visited Liceo Elsa Morante in 2011, as this is representative of our world of global bridges: two students from two different countries, studying at an American university in another country, discussing literature and cultural similarities and differences in English, helping students who are learning and perfecting their skills in that language.

". . . there are some questions that people will not stop asking, regardless of country, age, or ability to express their thoughts in a foreign language. And this understanding makes this project an invaluable experience both for Italian and JCU students." *Anna, a JCU student from Russia*

"I watched and listened as students shared their life stories as it related to the book. They spoke earnestly about how they wanted to express their understanding of the story through media as well as share experiences of cultural and personal importance." *Diedré, a JCU student from Jamaica*

# WORKS CITED

McCullers, Carson. "Author's Outline of 'The Mute'." *Carson McCullers: Stories, Plays & Other Writings*. Edited by Carlos L. Dews. Library of America, 2017, pp. 486-509.

---. *The Heart Is a Lonely Hunter. Carson McCullers: Complete Novels*. Edited by Carlos L. Dews. Library of America, 2001, pp. 3-306.

---. *The Member of the Wedding. Carson McCullers: Stories, Plays & Other Writings*. Edited by Carlos L. Dews. Library of America, 2017, pp. 223-99.

# Privileged Isolation: Narrative Interiority and Prejudice in The Novels of Carson McCullers

## Glenn Willis

In an untitled short story, published after her death, Carson McCullers writes of a group of children shaped by the experience of building and crashing a homemade glider. In their responses, the children display a range of attitudes towards disillusionment and thwarted expectation:

> I don't care. I'm glad anyway even if it didn't work. I'd rather for it to be like it is now than not to have tried to build it. I don't care . . . . It ought to have worked though. It ought to have flown. I just can't see why it didn't. (McCullers, "Untitled Piece" 103)

While the story was eventually abandoned, with elements reworked into *The Heart Is a Lonely Hunter* (1940), the incident with the glider is a succinct example of a dynamic which is central to much of McCullers's fiction; the psychological experience of an imagined potential and the subsequent need to confront disillusionment. When approaching McCullers's novels, we are met with a dual response to the perceived stagnation of Southern life, roughly in line with the children's reactions to their crashed glider in the untitled piece. That is, a celebration of individualistic striving, which accepts the worth of an "imagined potential" despite its eventual failure to overcome prescriptive realities, alongside a bitter and outraged grieving for this failure. Often, this dynamic is used by critics to explore repressed queer and gender-questioning identities in McCullers's works, with queer or non-conforming characters frequently experiencing a similar trajectory of expectation and eventual disappointment. In a highly influential article, Rachel Adams suggests that McCullers's opposition to normative gender and racial roles was dependent on an historical and regional localising of her texts firmly within the confines of the modern Southern United States (552). Having suggested McCullers's outcast characters should be seen as embodiments of an explicitly regional form of non-conformity, Adams makes the newly conceived queer hopefulness of McCullers's texts dependent upon the very narrative interiority of this resistance:

> While resistance often remains at the level of imagined potential for her characters, the reader, open to the queer suggestions of McCullers's fiction is left to consider the possibilities of a world free from the tyranny of the normal. (553)

McCullers's works were no longer to be seen as simplistic metaphors of isolation or the "human condition". Rather, a focus on interiority and uncommunicable thought became an assertion of queer rebellion which, while remaining potential for McCullers's characters, was made available to the reader through her narratives.

If readings such as that of Adams, or the work of Sarah Gleeson-White, go too far in asserting the focus on this "potential" in McCullers's work, it is at the expense of the second child's reaction, the refusal to be comforted by the distance between imagined interior freedoms and crushing realities. That is not to say, however, that McCullers simply devalues individualistic imaginings in favour of stoic realities. Rather than solely celebrating the imaginative or solitary mind above the cruel social conditions it reacts against, I suggest that McCullers enacts a form of textual interiority, in which isolation is deemed a "privileged" narrative state and in doing so, she aestheticizes ideas of social marginalisation. In this regard, she cannot be said to seek an escape from Southern social paradigms, as the aesthetic privileging of her imaginative characters is independent from their ability (or inability) to enact their alternative states of being in a social or political sense. To make this clear, I suggest a comparison with the works of modernist author Katherine Mansfield, who implemented a similar form of textual interiority, and who was, I argue, a key influence on McCullers's early work.

## Mansfield, Modernism and the Subjectivity of Symbolism

McCullers's interest in Mansfield is well documented but largely understudied. In her unfinished and posthumously released autobiography, *Illumination and Night Glare*, McCullers discusses her experiences reading Mansfield early in life, stating:

> When I was about eleven my mother sent me to the grocery store and I carried a book, of course. It was by Katherine Mansfield. On the way I began reading and was so fascinated that I read under the street light and kept on reading as I asked for the supper groceries ( . . . ) as I grew older my love for Katherine Mansfield somehow was lost, and I seldom read her now". (*Illumination* 58-59)

While McCullers's fading interest in Mansfield may account for a relative lack of critical attention to any intertextual relationship between the two authors (at least after the publication of McCullers's fragmentary autobiography), it is unclear quite what age McCullers is referring to when she discusses "growing older", and it is therefore difficult to judge if Mansfield could have been a conscious influence on her early novels from this statement alone. Furthermore, this account was written shortly before her death at the age of fifty, and decades after the publication of her most widely discussed texts. Virginia Spencer Carr's expansive and highly influential biography, *The Lonely Hunter*, published in 1975, also referred to McCullers's early love for Mansfield, stating, "Virginia Johnson Storey, Carson's cousin-librarian, said that she once had had to buy a new Mansfield book of short stories for the library because Carson had literally 'read the pages to pieces'" (51). Carr's landmark work laid the foundation for much future discussion of McCullers's literary influences, in that it refers to McCullers's longstanding interest in canonical modernist authors, while suggesting a greater degree of commonality between McCullers and her Southern contemporaries. Certain similarities between the careers and styles of McCullers and Mansfield are, however, striking.

Mansfield, like McCullers, experienced a degree of critical dismissal in her lifetime. Her position as a well-connected female author, operating in the male-dominated English literary establishment of the early twentieth century left her open to personal attack, and also allowed her writing to be occasionally dismissed as unserious. T. S. Eliot put this particularly bluntly, stating:

> We are given neither comment nor suggestion of any moral issue of good or evil ( . . . ) As the material is limited in this way—and indeed our satisfaction recognises the skills with which the author has handled perfectly the minimum material—it is what I believe would be called feminine. (343)

While Eliot was explicit in his attempt to neatly package Mansfield's writing as "feminine", devaluing both her texts and any serious critical engagement with such seemingly insubstantial material, D. H. Lawrence, with whom Mansfield shared a passionate and often strained friendship, went as far as to parody Mansfield's art in his own texts.[1] As Kate Fullbrook points out, the character of Gudrun in *Women in Love* (1920), one of Lawrence's recurrent and thinly veiled depictions of Mansfield, is portrayed as an artist who does "small things 'marvellously' well while being afraid to make the grand gesture, implying, ultimately, a fear of greatness, a refusal of 'seriousness', an acquiescence to minor status" (3). The blatantly misogynist characterisation of Mansfield as a practitioner of "feminine" modernism saw her often belittled, with Virginia Woolf apparently satisfying the need for a "serious" female writer amongst the Bloomsbury Group and their contemporaries. Or, as Clare Hanson suggests in a comparison of the early reputations of Woolf and Mansfield, Mansfield was dismissed as overtly feminine while, "Woolf had become almost an honorary male modernist, the only female modernist to be considered 'great'" (304). Similarly, McCullers has occasionally been seen as an inferior Southern talent, with Louis Rubin comparing her unfavourably to Faulkner and Welty (260), and Pearl A. McHaney making only scathing mention of her in an overview of "Southern women writers", stating that, "in humour, the grotesque, place, and truth, Carson McCullers touches both Welty and O'Connor in kind if not in degree" (136-137).

More recent scholarship on Mansfield, however, has focused on the potential for her characters to reformulate "femininity" as a mode of discourse and to explore the nature of gendered representation, both on a personal and spatial level. Ruth Parkin-Gounelas goes as far as to suggest that, "Mansfield seems, fleetingly, to capture ( . . . ) moments of female relatedness and to grope toward the kind of specifically female discourse that feminists like Hélène Cixous have recently celebrated" (51). The similar trajectory of (relative) critical dismissal and subsequent reappraisal of both Mansfield and McCullers is more than coincidence. Rather, it speaks to the ability of their texts to engage with "alternative" states of being. That is, a resurgent interest in the potentially subversive discourses embedded in the ostensibly "feminine" interiorities of Mansfield's characters occurred alongside a newfound critical focus on the queer "potentials" of McCullers's writing. Hence Mansfield's narratives are readily brought into conversation with the more openly "transgressive" interiorities of McCullers's outcast characters. I therefore propose a reading of Mansfield's short fiction which emphasises the fraught nature of any potentially liberating interiority and suggest that this provides a framework to reinterpret the interior and psychological "potentials" of McCullers's characters as primarily aesthetic states.

In Mansfield's fiction, the emancipatory potential of interiority is frequently enacted through the re-codifying of exterior space into highly subjective symbols of the self. The fraught individuality of interiority is perhaps most explicitly explored in "Bliss" (1918). Before turning directly to the text, however, it is worth noting that "Bliss", perhaps more than any of Mansfield's other stories or collections, drew particular critical rebuke, with Virginia Woolf stating in a 1918 diary entry:

> I threw down *Bliss* with the exclamation, 'She's done for!' Indeed I don't see how much faith in her as a woman or writer can survive that sort of story. I shall have to accept the fact, I'm afraid, that her mind is a very thin soil, laid an inch or two deep upon very barren rock. For *Bliss* is long enough to give her a chance of going deeper. Instead she is content with superficial smartness; and the whole conception is poor, cheap, not the vision, however imperfect, of an interesting mind. She writes badly too. (2)

Woolf's accusations once again emphasise the perceived frivolity of Mansfield's writing, as well as reinforcing her status as a purposefully "minor" writer.[2] Such criticism perhaps stems from the supposed simplicity of Mansfield's central character, Bertha Young, and the "superficiality" of her position in relation to the text itself. Certainly, the exploration of narrative dynamics of interiority is the story's central concern. As a focalising presence, Bertha displays a fractured and uncertain interiority which is forced to confront its own lack of stability through its very representation on the page:

> "How idiotic civilisation is! Why be given a body if you have to keep it shut up in a case like a rare, rare fiddle?
>
> 'No, that about the fiddle is not quite what I mean,' she thought". (Mansfield, "Bliss" 92)

This fractured narration has led to Bertha being described, in the words of Saralyn R. Daly, as "a treacherously fallible narrator" (82). Bertha's narration is, however, more than simply "fallible" or unreliable. Rather, it is a conflicted representation of a constrained interior existence. For example, while hosting her guests at a dinner party, Bertha simultaneously mocks them and defends them from this mockery. Focalised through her, their mannerisms are rendered ridiculous. One guest states, "I *think* I've come across the *same* idea in a little French review, *quite* unknown in England" (Mansfield, "Bliss" 100). Bertha, however, is initially unwilling to accept this narratively imposed mockery. She attempts in vain to convince us that, "they were dears-dears-and she loved having them there, at her table, and giving them delicious food and wine" (Mansfield, "Bliss" 100). Hence the relationship between Bertha's focalising mind, the text and the reader is a conflicted one. Readers, through their very access to Bertha's interiority, are more equipped to get to the truth which she is unable or unwilling to accept. Her guests are not truly the pleasant company Bertha desires them to be. It is worth noting that Mansfield, for her part, saw this aspect of the story as comical and relatively good natured, writing to her husband, John Middleton Murry on the day she completed "Bliss": "You will 'recognise' some of the people. *Eddie* of course is a fish out of the ---- pond (which gave me joy)" (*Letters to John Middleton Murry* 189). The apparently light-hearted attitude of Mansfield, and her story, towards the foibles of her characters stands in contrast to the initial seriousness of Bertha, further emphasising the discrepancies between Bertha's interiorly focalised narration and the overall impression of the text as experienced by the reader.

Mansfield therefore characterises mentally interior space, both in a personal and a narrative sense, as potentially deceptive. Nowhere in her writing is this more apparent than in the story's central image, the pear tree at the bottom of Bertha's garden. The powerfully subjective nature of this image is gradually revealed to the reader, with the symbolic workings of Bertha's mind demonstrating what Polly Dickson describes as "the lure of a liberating disembodiment, ecstasy's sense of having been put outside oneself" (13). This takes the form of a projection of Bertha's unspoken queer desires for Miss Fulton, one of her guests, onto the textual space of the narrative through the symbol of the pear tree itself:

> And the two women stood side by side looking at the slender, flowering tree. Although it was still it seemed, like the flame of a candle, to stretch up, to point, to quiver in the bright air, to grow taller and taller as they gazed—almost to touch the rim of the round, silver moon.
>
> How long did they stand there? Both as it were, caught in that circle of unearthly light, understanding each other perfectly, creatures of another world. (Mansfield, "Bliss" 102)

The projection of Bertha's interior desires onto the wider text therefore represents the attempted reification of that interiority. This perceived sense of symbolic female unity is, however, shown to be a wishful conjuration. Recent work on Mansfield, notably that of Allan Pero suggests the image of the pear tree creates an expectation that Bertha's interior self will find legitimacy through identification with an exterior object and that while "the story seems to move toward the possibility that the unnameable bliss of the title is lesbian desire, the possibility becomes lost in the series of objects that Bertha comes upon in search of a symbolic knowledge that will accommodate her bliss but not snuff it out" (110). I would suggest that Mansfield's character seeks an exterior sign only to be confronted with the realisation that symbolism is itself an extension of an interior state, as opposed to an element of exterior reality. After discovering that it is her husband, and not herself who is the object of Pearl Fulton's desire, Bertha is confronted with the existence of the pear tree, now devoid of its symbolic value:

> Bertha simply ran over to the long windows.
>
> 'Oh what is going to happen now?' she cried.
>
> But the pear tree was as lovely as ever and as full of flower and as still. (Mansfield, "Bliss" 105).

While the pear tree is "as lovely as ever", it is nevertheless stripped of its queer illumination, the implication being that this mundane, non-symbolic form of existence has been embedded in, and masked by the focalising power of Bertha's interior presence in the text. The pear tree is therefore given the textual presence and potency of a symbol, while being stripped of any absolute value. Rather, it becomes an object upon which the process of symbolisation, through the presence of Bertha's focalising interiority can be enacted for the reader.

Such a reading may tempt us to simply devalue Bertha's initial experience of "bliss" as an illusion. However, the beauty of Mansfield's texts lies in the ephemerality of these moments of (perceived) reification of the interior self. Value is not placed primarily in the potential for a character's inner state to be reflected in the "external" positivistic reality of objective symbolism. Nor is the text concerned primarily with reifying an "imagined potential". Rather, the value of Bertha's interiority and imagined "bliss" is first and foremost aesthetic. The presence of Bertha's focalising mind allows not merely for the tree to become a vessel for the projection of queer potential, but rather for the aesthetic privileging of that mind and that queerness itself. That the "imagined potential" of Bertha's relationship with Miss Fulton is eventually thwarted does not devalue the aesthetic focalising of the world through her subjective interiority. Rather, we are made aware of her privileged position in the text, mirroring the creative function of the author herself by providing an interior basis for the construction of subjective symbolism and representation. We are nevertheless also reminded of the limitations of this privileged position, which is fundamentally incapable of enacting change beyond a symbolic or aesthetic level.

Such a reading places Mansfield's writing in close conversation with McCullers's early novels. The privileged yet fraught relationship between the active, imaginative mind and the "external" world is a central dynamic of *The Heart Is a Lonely Hunter*. Like the pear tree in Mansfield's story, central character John Singer serves as an object for the subjective projection of other characters' interior states, while also existing as an isolated character in his own right. McCullers makes clear his special status in the narrative in her outline of what would eventually become *The Heart Is a Lonely Hunter* but was initially dubbed "The Mute". She states:

> Singer is the first character in the book only in the sense that he is the symbol of isolation and thwarted expression and because the story pivots around him. In reality each one of his satellites is of far more importance than himself. The book will take all of its body and strength in the development of the four people who revolve about the mute. ("Outline of The Mute" 165)

In this sense, like Mansfield, McCullers privileges the subjective act of creativity, even if it stands in contrast to Singer's "reality". That is to say, her characters are given a privileged position in the narrative insofar as they are able to project a subjective symbolic interpretation of Singer, even when this stands in contrast to McCullers's own conception of Singer as a symbol of "isolation and thwarted expression". Furthermore, McCullers makes it clear that the privileged narrative position of her other characters reflects a deeper connection between their interior selves and the narrative itself, stating:

> The parts concerning Singer are never treated in a subjective manner. The style is oblique. ( . . . ) Except when he is understood through the eyes of other people the style is for the

main part simple and declarative. No attempt will be made to enter intimately into his subconscious. ("Outline" 165)

Singer's relative narrative exclusion is hence reflective of a marginalised interiority, which stands in contrast to that of the other characters. Furthermore, the linking of the narrative with the interior states of its characters carries a certain aesthetic weight, freeing them from the "simple and declarative" descriptions which accompany Singer in the text when he is not in the presence of his imaginative "satellites".

The subjective, creative function of McCullers's characters, like Bertha's subjective symbolisation of the pear tree in "Bliss" is, however, fraught and at times destructive. As prolific McCullers scholar, Jan Whitt, states, "by making Singer divine, the townspeople depersonalize and, in effect, murder him" (28). I suggest that McCullers not only emphasises the possibility for the "reality" of the symbolic object to be lost in any subjective interpretation (in this case, the "reality" of Singer in the eyes of the other characters), but also for the supposedly "privileged" state of creative interiority to become a factor in the societal marginalisation of her characters. That her characters are both explicitly creative and socially isolated in their interiority is made apparent in their frequent moments of characteristically modernist Flânerie. Nowhere is this clearer than in the case of the drunken outcast, and serial wanderer, Jake Blount. Blount's walks become a medium through which he can project his radical conception of the melancholic evils of unrestricted capitalism onto both the urban landscape itself and the townsfolk inhabiting it:

> The two-room shacks, each one like the other, were rotten and unpainted. The stink of food and sewage mingled with the dust in the air. The falls up the river made a faint rushing sound. People stood silently in the doorways or lounged on steps. They looked at Jake with yellow, expressionless faces. (McCullers, *Heart* 58)

In Blount's own conception, his creative vision distinguishes him from the other townspeople with their "yellow expressionless faces". While the "imagined potential" of other central characters takes the form of queer utopic imagining, Blount is driven instead by an imagined manifestation of collective social action. Crucially, this takes the form of an invitation to Flânerie itself, or rather, a plea for others to share in his own conception of the world. Surrounded by onlookers, he questions them, "So when you walk around the streets and think about it and see hungry, worn-out people and ricket-legged young'uns, don't it make you mad? Don't it?" (McCullers, *Heart* 62). This invitation to share in Blount's view of the world, and hence to share in the reality of his focalising interiority, is thwarted by a normalised view in which this outburst is intolerable. We are told that, "as he walked stiffly down the street the sound of their laughter and catcalls still followed him" (McCullers, *Heart* 62). Noah Mass highlights that scenes such as this in McCullers's fiction, in which states of "otherness" come into conflict with more accepted outlooks are used to delineate not only conditions of aberration but also simultaneously to explore the nature of these normative Southern identities (235). Blount's "otherness", here visible in his capacity to construct alternative representations of the town itself, while affording him a privileged position, narratively speaking, is faced with the "reality" of more normative views. That is to say, the privilege of narrative agency, derived from a state of focalising interiority is both partially emancipatory and deeply isolating. Blount therefore recognises his own privileged imaginative position, imploring others to enter into the interior space he has conceived of, and hence to limit his narratively reinforced isolation. Furthermore, just as Mansfield does not seek to overtly delegitimise a non-symbolic depiction of the pear tree in "Bliss", McCullers does not intervene to lend legitimacy to the subjective "potential" imaginings of her central characters, as the presence of the "normal" is insurmountable.

 Similar to Mansfield's story, McCullers's novels portray symbolic and interior valuations as aesthetically powerful, creating an expectation of reification and self-affirmation, only to leave these expectations open to eventual disillusionment. While characters whose interiorities are explored by McCullers's texts find themselves in a position of creative power, with a degree of agency far beyond that of mentally "inactive" characters such as Singer, this position is itself shown to be a factor in their experience of societal marginalisation. This creates a narrative formulation in which aesthetic value is independent from the ability of these interior and individualistic states to find affirmation in "exterior" reality, either through social acceptance or in any external or "objective" symbolism provided by the author.

## Narrative Privilege, Narrative Prejudice

While McCullers may be determined to undermine any perceived utopic potential of creative activity or individualistic thought, states of interiority are nevertheless, as I have argued, privileged in her narratives as spaces of aesthetic value. While it is also clear that McCullers was dedicated to challenging Jim Crow era prejudice, in engaging in a form of expression which did not attempt to sever ties with the realities of Southern social conditions, she can be seen to recreate social prejudices in the processes of narrative "privileging" as this paper has thus far discussed. In an oft-quoted 1940 review for *The New Republic*, fellow novelist and Southerner, Richard Wright, praised McCullers's ability to write African American and white characters with the same skill, stating:

> To me the most impressive aspect of *The Heart Is a Lonely Hunter* is the astonishing humanity that enables a white writer, for the first time in Southern fiction, to handle Negro characters with as much ease and justice as those of her own race. ("Inner Landscape" 18)

I suggest however, that although this ran contrary to McCullers's intentions, she nevertheless failed at times to challenge the very social prejudices she ostensibly stood against. In particular, early works such as *The Heart Is a Lonely Hunter* and *The Member of the Wedding* can be seen to exclude African American characters from the degrees of narrative interiority which other characters are afforded. However, when looking at McCullers's final novel, *Clock Without Hands*, we see a shift towards the narrative privileging of African American characters, alongside their white counterparts, and a focus on the psychological processes which accompany Southern racist beliefs, which can be seen to both acknowledge and rework the partial failings of her earlier texts.

Before discussing the relationship between race and narrative interiority in her works, it is important to consider the literary contexts McCullers saw herself in and consider the nature of racial representation in contemporary work she admired. Amongst other "Southern" novelists, McCullers reserved some of her most frank praise for Wright himself, stating:

> Another writer who was particularly dear to me is Richard Wright. ( . . . ) Dick and I often discussed the South, and his book [*Black Boy*,] is one of the finest books by a Southern [Negro.] He said of my work that I was the one Southern writer who was able to treat [Negroes] and white people with the same ease. I was so appalled by the humiliation that being a [Negro] in the South automatically entailed that I lost sight of the gradations of respectability and prestige within the [Negro] race. (*Illumination* 63-64)

In her non-fiction writing, McCullers frequently used ostensibly self-deprecating comments to mask a form of subtle boasting and hence it can be difficult to assign clear motivation to her moments of self-criticism. Here, however, writing shortly before her death, McCullers implies that Wright's glowing review of her first published novel was at least partially undeserved, and if she slyly intends to highlight her more evolved view of racial representation later in life, it is at the expense of her younger self. While it would be unfair to suggest that Wright, as a writer, excluded African American characters from ideas of narrative interiority, works such as *Native Son* (1940) are at least concerned with the difficulties of African American characters in finding forms of expression, even within Wright's narratives, which are given equal weight to those of their white counterparts. Critics such as Julieann Veronica Ulin are right to point out the shared concerns of McCullers's and Wright's novels, notably discriminatory employment and housing legislation and the intersections of political and personal discrimination in Southern racism (197). Ulin's comparison of *Native Son* and *Clock Without Hands*, perhaps partially delegitimises the common claim that McCullers was "ahead of her time" in terms of racial representation (fuelled in no small part by Wright's own early championing of her writing). *Clock Without Hands* was released in the early 1960s, over twenty years after *Native Son*, a period in which the Civil Rights Movement had emerged as a central political, social, and discursive force in the United States. While Wright, and to a lesser extent McCullers, were undoubtedly important figures in discussions of fictional representation of race, both before and during the most prominent era of the Civil Rights Movement, Wright's early work has been open to criticism, most notably by James Baldwin, for supposedly legitimising African American stereotypes and creating a binary of the "common" and the "intelligent Negro", to use Baldwin's terminology (37). I want to use a discussion of narrative interiority and its relationship to social prejudice to suggest that McCullers is open to similar criticism. Hence, I seek to partially temper Wright's praise, placing her early work firmly in the context of early and pre-Civil Rights Movement modes of representing race while suggesting narrative interiority played a key role in McCullers's efforts to rectify her own previous prejudices.

Apart from Wright, McCullers's most glowing praise for a contemporary writer was for Karen Blixen, in particular her autobiographical work *Out of Africa* (1937). McCullers was frank in her admiration of Blixen, stating, "I started *Out of Africa* ( ... ) and read until sundown. Never had I felt such enchantment. After years of reading this book, and I have read it many times, I still have a sense of both solace and freedom whenever I start it again" (*Illumination* 62). In a 1963 article for *Saturday Review*, McCullers states that her compulsive love for Blixen's writing coincided with the writing of *The Heart Is a Lonely Hunter* ("Isak Dinesen: In Praise of Radiance" 267). While McCullers primarily praises the richness of the African countryside in Blixen's descriptive prose, she nevertheless admires Blixen's literary handling of, "the natives for whom she had such great affection" ("Isak Dinesen: In Praise of Radiance" 270). McCullers shares with Blixen a tendency to portray interiority as having racially defined characteristics. Blixen's literary enterprise in *Out of Africa* is itself dependent upon her colonial position, from which she catalogues "Native" behaviours:

> It was not easy to get to know the Natives. They were quick of hearing, and evanescent; if you frightened them they could withdraw into a world of their own, in a second, like the wild

animals which at an abrupt movement from you are gone—simply are not there. (19)

The suggestion of a racially defined outlook or set of behaviours is characteristic of Blixen's writing. Often, she goes as far as to suggest that thought processes themselves are racially determined, frequently making claims such as "the Somali have a very different mentality from the Kikuyu" (Blixen 110). We can see shades of this in McCullers's handling of Doctor Copeland in *The Heart Is a Lonely Hunter*. In a particularly egregious moment, we are told that "the feeling that would come on him was a black, terrible Negro feeling" (McCullers, *Heart* 75). It is unclear to what extent this represents the focalising presence of Copeland himself (who feels the injustice of his own social exclusion) as opposed to a suggestion that his isolation is somehow distinct from that of other characters (beyond simply facing different social exclusions). What is clear, is that while Copeland occupies a similar position of textual "privilege" to other central characters, he is at times singled out for distinct narrative treatment.

Copeland, much more than McCullers's other focalising characters, is recurrently described in physical terms, as McCullers often emphasises the racial nature of her descriptions. For example, we are told that "the red glow from the chinks of the stove shone on his face—in this light his heavy lips looked almost purple against his black skin, and his grey hair, tight against his skull like a cap of lamb's wool, took on a bluish colour also" (McCullers, *Heart* 65-66). While McCullers may be excused for emphasising physical characteristics when introducing the lone African American focaliser in the text, this physical fixation is recurrent. Copeland speaks "so carefully that each syllable seemed to be filtered through his sullen, heavy lips," while we are also told that his daughter, Portia "spread out her lips and blew into her saucer of coffee" (McCullers, *Heart* 67, 70). Much more than simply demonstrating a fixation on the physical characteristics of her African American characters, McCullers's handling of Doctor Copeland creates an uncomfortable prejudice within her own system of interiority as a narrative privilege. While neither Copeland nor Portia can easily be dismissed as a racial caricature, there are parallels between Copeland and Wright's Bigger Thomas, protagonist of *Native Son*.[3] Copeland, like Bigger, while an adherent of Marxian Communism is portrayed as having only an emotional understanding of philosophical systems:

> Tonight he read Spinoza. He did not wholly understand the intricate play of ideas and the complex phrases, but as he read he sensed a strong, true purpose behind the words and he felt that he almost understood. (McCullers, *Heart* 66)

If we are to take the view, which critics such as Eileen Barrett have, that Copeland embodies a form of race and class struggle which is defiant of the widespread rhetoric of Black Nationalism or Christianity (219-220), we must consider that the difficulties facing this interior self-definition, which are present for all of McCullers's characters, are compounded by the narrative itself along racial lines. While he desires to express himself to Singer, as do all of the text's central characters, Copeland is also compelled to expound his beliefs to members of his own race. We are told that "if once he could tell it all to them, from the far away beginning until this very night, the telling would ease the sharp ache in his heart. But they would not listen or understand" (McCullers, *Heart* 132). While other characters fail to maintain their utopic interior conceptions due to the difficulties of acting upon them in a socially restrictive setting, Copeland is limited by McCullers's portrayals of African Americans in the South as content in their suffering and limited in their imagination. While Copeland attempts to share his passion for Marxian Socialism with his family and the town's African American population, he is met with both ignorance and a desire for normalised discussion at every turn. While he refers to his son as "Karl Marx", for example, Portia uses the normalised name "Buddy". Copeland is therefore isolated, not only as an imaginative focaliser unable to enact real world change, but as the lone African American intellectual in a rural town. McCullers makes this explicit, stating that "sometimes he thought that he had talked so much in the years before to his children and they had understood so little that now there was nothing at all to say" (*Heart* 76). McCullers is at times happy to conceive of African American intelligence, which she "privileges" with narrative interiority, as a state which is inherently isolating. In this respect, her narrative implicitly accepts ideas of a DuBoisian "talented tenth" of African Americans.

Copeland's isolated narrative position is therefore a reflection of his role not only as an African American, but more specifically as an educated African American. When McCullers, particularly in her early works, portrayed the imaginative powers or interiorities of poorly-educated African American characters, they frequently serve to reinforce normative conceptions of social position and gender. Along with Portia, we may include Berenice of *The Member of the Wedding* and Verily of *Clock Without Hands* in this category. Unlike the imagined spaces of her protagonists, the imaginings of these characters serve to purposefully reinforce a white heteronormative social order. In *The Heart Is a Lonely Hunter*, a religious reinforcement of racial inequality is made literal in the imagination of a poor black townsperson, known as "Grandpapa":

> I say to Him, 'Jesus Christ, us is all sad colored peoples.' And then he will place His holy hand upon our heads and straightaway us will be white as cotton. That the plan and reasoning that been in my heart a many a time. (McCullers, *Heart* 131)

Similarly, in an often-discussed scene in *The Member of the Wedding*, Berenice discusses a man who had "become a woman" by falling in love with another man, stating:

> He prisses around with a pink satin blouse and one arm akimbo. Now this Lily Mae fell in love with a man name Juney Jones. A man, mind you. And Lily Mae turned into a girl. He changed his nature and his sex and turned into a girl. (McCullers, *Member* 96)

Rachel Adams discusses the dual nature of Berenice's conception of gender roles, believing that Frankie cannot adopt "femininity" by dressing more maturely, while reinforcing "the idea of sexuality as a continuum by suggesting that a man who desires another man can voluntarily change from one sex to the other" (561). While Berenice is a richly drawn character, not entirely excluded from creativity or interiority (she is a skilled story teller), it is possible to suggest that McCullers excludes her from queer imaginings and alternative states of interiority for the same reason she excludes other uneducated

African American characters—that African Americans were frequently portrayed as fundamentally less capable of interiority in her works (although it must be stressed that McCullers clearly saw this as primarily resulting from poor education as opposed to a perceived racial inferiority). It is worth noting that critics such as Melissa Free have argued that to McCullers, homosexuality does represent a form of "inversion", in which the queer character is aligned with the opposing sex to the object of their desire (430). While Berenice may, as Adams suggests, imply a belief in the mutability of gender, it is to decry queerness and impose a form of gendered normality on Lily Mae's queer desire, as opposed to an attempt to align herself with the notions of "inverse" queer desire McCullers may have personally identified with. Furthermore, while McCullers may have considered herself to be what she described as an "invert" (Carr 167), the suggestion that a queer man is in fact a woman is a familiar form of prejudice that does not necessarily carry the same connotations of subversive freedom as McCullers's own gender identification. Even when conceiving of "alternative" states of being, outside of normalised social roles, Berenice and other poor or uneducated African American characters are excluded from enacting these states on a transgressive interior level, a privilege which is available to some of McCullers's poor or uneducated white characters.

While it is unclear to what extent McCullers saw these elements of her earlier novels as problematic (her discussion of Wright's praise suggests at least some form of perceived intellectual growth in relation to racial issues), it is apparent that in her final novel, *Clock Without Hands*, issues of creeping, subtle prejudice are discussed more centrally, and, I suggest, made dependent on now-familiar concepts of narrative interiority. Moments of racial prejudice in *The Heart Is a Lonely Hunter* are explicit and external rather than a result of subtle thought processes. However, Copeland is aware of the insipid nature of prejudice, thinking to himself "when he was younger it was 'Boy'—but now it was 'Uncle.' 'Uncle, run down to that filling station on the corner and send me a mechanic'" (McCullers, *Heart* 78). While other characters enact forms of banal prejudice, with Jake Blount refusing to incorporate rhetoric of racial equality into his grand social schemes, and Mick referring to Copeland as "Uncle", their motivations for these actions are left mysterious. Prejudice is therefore only interiorised by the victim—Copeland himself. *Clock Without Hands*, on the contrary, portrays the interior processes behind the enactment of racial discrimination from the perspective of the prejudiced figure. J. T. Malone, the dying pharmacist and otherwise upstanding Southern citizen, is both a sympathetic and deeply prejudiced central character. As when he rails against the "Jew grinds" who he believes unfairly kept him from graduating medical school (McCullers, *Clock* 12), Malone's focalised narration engages closely with the language and formation of prejudice. For example, on considering the blue eyes of Sherman Pew:

> Except for his eyes, he looked like any other colored boy. But his eyes were bluish-grey, and set in the dark face they had a bleak, violent look. The arms were too long, the chest too broad—and the expression alternated from emotional sensitivity to deliberate sullenness. The impression on Malone was such that he did not think of him in harmless terms as a colored boy—his mind automatically used the harsh term "bad n-----". (McCullers, *Clock* 15)

Malone's intolerance of miscegenation is unstated, rather McCullers emphasises the underlying and apparently instantaneous subconscious processes of signification which lie behind his prejudicial behaviours. While earlier works emphasise the aesthetic value of interior states, which is itself independent of their ability to enact social change or find outward expression, *Clock Without Hands* affirms the possible co-existence of this narrative privilege with social prejudice.

Indeed, *Clock Without Hands* is largely concerned with the issue of problematic imaginings. While McCullers's central characters' interior states typically involve a desired expression of queer otherness, the characters of Malone, and to a greater extent Judge Clane, enact a form of interiority which is itself socially conservative and normative. While these positions are largely dismissed by the text, their power and the allure of their interior imagining are nevertheless made clear. It is possible to conceive of Judge Clane's dreams of Civil War reparations for former slave states as possessing a similar "imagined potential" as the interiorities of McCullers's early queer characters, although again, she emphasises the potential for tragedy in this position. Craig Slaven suggests that while the Judge is out of touch with social and political realities, the text nevertheless questions conceptions of inevitable progress, as well as demonstrating the powerful allure of such "Lost Cause" narratives (253). While the Judge's fantastical desire for a form of revived Confederacy is eventually thwarted, it is nevertheless placed alongside Sherman Pew's equally unrealised dreams of social equality:

> That winter the Judge made a grave mistake about Sherman and Sherman made a still graver mistake about the Judge. Since both mistakes were fantasies which flowered as richly in the senile brain of the old man as they did in the heart of the thwarted boy, their human relationship was going very much amiss, choked as it were with the rank luxuriance of their separate dreams. (McCullers, *Clock* 139)

The Judge is treated with a similar narrative privileging as is Sherman, not due to any legitimacy of his vision, but as Slaven suggests, because this competing narrative has a resonance that, in opposing, McCullers does not seek to simply erase. Rather, similar to her portrayal of Malone's racial prejudice, McCullers is concerned with the interior states and processes which feed such beliefs.

While I have suggested that McCullers at times portrayed the imaginations of African American characters as inherently normative, her final novel undercuts these expectations by portraying a belief in the lack of African American interiority as an element of prejudicial normativity itself. In an exchange between Malone and the Judge, in which they discuss Sherman's oration of Dickens, we see a suggestion that Sherman does not truly engage with the book:

> 'Sherman reads Dickens with such pathos. Sometimes I cry and cry.'
>
> 'Does that boy ever cry?'
>
> 'No, but often he smiles at the humorous places.' (McCullers, *Clock* 112-13)

The reader however, provided access to the interior mind of Sherman himself, is given the real reason for his emotionless oration, "he hated reading Dickens, there were so many orphans in Dickens, and Sherman loathed books about orphans, feeling in them a reflection on himself" (McCullers, *Clock* 119). McCullers moves the prejudice of her earlier texts to the minds of her characters, where the processes of prejudicial thought are made visible to the reader. This includes making clear the psychological motivations of both black and white characters who enforce normativity. For example, if we are to place the Judge's servant, Verily in a similar category as Portia and other uneducated African American characters, telling Sherman he, "ought to be eating collards and cornpones in the kitchen like anybody else," (McCullers, *Clock* 144) she is at least motivated by a bitter awareness of Sherman's privileged ability to (temporally) transcend racially defined behaviour while she cannot. McCullers seems to suggest that African American characters are motivated by fear in their lack of interiority and resulting enforcement of normativity. While earlier novels simply recreated these prejudiced social conditions by limiting the interiority of their African American characters, *Clock Without Hands* explicitly attempts to portray such restrictions to creative individualism as a response to prejudice rather than an implicit justification for it.

The sympathetic narrative "privileging" of social outcasts of earlier texts is replaced by a process of interiority that attempts to problematise any suggestion that to be socially or textually isolated is an indication of ethical or intellectual superiority. The central characters of *The Clock Without Hands* are not all selected from the unfairly marginalised. Indeed, Malone experiences a form of isolation arising from the very natural process of death. Upon hearing the news of his late-stage leukaemia, Malone is transformed into a roaming flâneur, "In spite of the weakness of his disease, Malone was restless. Often he would walk aimlessly around the streets of the town—down through the shambling, crowded slums around the cotton mill, or through the Negro sections (McCullers, *Clock* 13). Malone, like Sherman, or any of McCullers's imaginative protagonists, is subject to the pressures of an external consensus, and McCullers is concerned with illuminating the mental processes which accompany an acquiescence to these forces. For example, "If Malone ever had misgivings about the ideas of the old Judge, he smothered them immediately" (McCullers, *Clock* 18). While typically McCullers's focalising characters engage with subversive conceptions of selfhood, Malone rather enacts processes of self-normalisation. Craig Slaven warns that McCullers's text at times reaffirms white innocence, by substituting responsibility for guilt (254). This same danger arises again from the almost banal descriptions of prejudicial interiority. While the reader may safely dismiss the imagined potential of the Judge's neo-Confederacy as horrifying, through Malone, McCullers attempts to walk a fine line between condemnation and understanding of the perceived interior preconditions for Southern normativity and racial segregation. In reappraising McCullers's handling of race, we must ensure that we do not decontextualize or overstate her progressive ideals. While I suggest McCullers acknowledges and attempts to atone for previous prejudicial discussions of race within the narrative structures of her texts, her later work fails to entirely escape a tendency to reinforce the very racial oppression she sought to oppose.

In limiting the effectiveness of an interior "imagined potential", I suggest McCullers seeks to ward off social complacency. In conceiving distinct valuations of aesthetic and socially emancipatory potentials, like Mansfield, she allows her texts to be at once powerful and hopeless. If there is a political call to action in her texts, it is in the failure of her marginalised characters to find acceptance or a platform for radical ideas. McCullers does not simply attempt to provide such a platform, as her characters, even in a state of narratively aligned interiority are beholden to normative social forces. Neither does she attempt to delegitimise imaginative interior expression. Rather, we are reminded that the aesthetic privilege of narrative interiority carries with it both the possibility for partial freedom, as well as the burden of potential failure. I suggest that McCullers's fiction is not utopic or triumphant, but rather that it represents an acceptance of the tireless struggle required for social change. In her assertion that interior or individualistic expression can have value regardless of its ability to find immediate acceptance, and in warning against the possibility for conflicting ideologies to employ narratives of wishful isolation and marginalised selfhood, McCullers celebrates the power of individualistic aestheticism and discourse while warning against their misuse. McCullers therefore charges her characters and her readers with enacting the social change implicitly demanded by her texts, rather than simply allowing marginalised forms of selfhood to find free expression in her narratives themselves. While I am resistant to a critical focus on the "imagined potentials" of McCullers's characters, I am sympathetic to a suggestion that she does not write from a position of total social despair. Rather, by creating a dual valuation of aesthetic and individualistic acts, she asserts that to be imaginative can be powerful despite its limitations and that failure is not the same as defeat. Furthermore, the changing dynamics of racial representation in her works creates a career spanning discussion of the potential misuse of aesthetic privilege and rhetorical power. By stripping the narrative interiority of her texts of any utopic function, McCullers holds her own creative acts up to greater scrutiny and suggests that the fight against social prejudice begins with a look inward.

*Notes*

[1] Lawrence's dismissal of Mansfield's writing as frivolous is particularly biting when we consider the ostensibly deep feelings Lawrence held for her. Mansfield states: "I remember once talking it over with Lawrence and he said 'We must swear a solemn pact of friendship. Friendship is as binding, as solemn as marriage. We take each other for life, through everything—for ever'" (*Letters and Journals* 250).

[2] While she could not have read Woolf's diary entry, it is apparent that Mansfield took such criticisms to heart, later writing that, "Such a prolonged exercise ought to have produced something a great deal better than *Bliss*; I hope the book on which I am now engaged will be more worthy of the interest of the public" ("Autobiography" 363).

[3] In drawing this parallel, I suggest only that these characters are similarly treated by their respective narratives. As each text was originally published in the same year and both McCullers and Wright were launched to fame only after the release of these novels, McCullers could not have been consciously influenced by Wright's novel.

# WORKS CITED

Adams, Rachel. "'A Mixture of Delicious and Freak': The Queer Fiction of Carson McCullers." *American Literature*, vol. 71, no. 3, 1999, pp. 551-583. *Jstor*, www.jstor.org/stable/2902739.

Baldwin, James. "Many Thousands Gone." *Notes of a Native Son*, Pluto Press Limited, 1985, pp. 24-45.

Barrett, Eileen. "The 'Astonishing Humanity' of Carson McCullers' *The Heart Is a Lonely Hunter* and James Baldwin's *Another Country*". *ANQ: A Quarterly Journal of Short Articles, Notes and Reviews*, vol. 24, no. 4, 2011, pp. 217-226. *Taylor & Francis Online*, doi: 10.1080/0895769X.2011.614882

Daly, Saralyn R. *Katherine Mansfield*. Twayne Publishers, 1965.

Dickson, Polly. "Interior Matters: Secrecy and Hunger in Katherine Mansfield's 'Bliss'." *Katherine Mansfield and Psychology*. Edited by Clare Hanson, Gerri Kimber and Todd Martin, Edinburgh University Press, 2016, pp. 11-23.

Eliot, T. S. *After Strange Gods*. Faber and Faber, 1934.

Free, Melissa. "Relegation and Rebellion: The Queer, the Grotesque and the Silent in the Fiction of Carson McCullers." *Studies in the Novel*, vol. 40, no. 4, 2008, pp. 426-446. *Jstor*, www.jstor.org/stable/29533895.

Fullbrook, Kate. *Katherine Mansfield*. The Harvest Press, 1986.

Gleeson-White, Sarah. "A Peculiarly Southern Form of Ugliness: Eudora Welty, Carson McCullers and Flannery O'Connor." *The Southern Literary Journal*, vol. 36, no. 1, 2003, pp. 46-57. *Project Muse*, doi: 10.1353/slj.2003.0032.

---. *Strange Bodies: Gender and Identity in the Novels of Carson McCullers*. The University of Alabama Press, 2003.

Hanson, Clare. "Katherine Mansfield." *The Gender of Modernism: A Critical Anthology*. Edited by Bonnie Kime Scott, Indiana University Press, 1990, pp. 298-305.

Lawrence, D. H. *Women in Love*. Penguin, 1996.

Mansfield, Katherine. "Autobiography." *The Diaries of Katherine Mansfield*. Edited by Gerri Kimber and Claire Davison, Edinburgh University Press, 2016, pp. 362-363.

---. "Bliss." *The Collected Stories of Katherine Mansfield*, Penguin Books, 1981, pp. 91-105.

---. "Letter to John Middleton Murry." February 28, 1918. *Letters of Katherine Mansfield to John Middleton Murry 1913-1922*. Edited by John Middleton Murry, Constable & Co, 1951, p. 189.

---. "Letter to Sydney Schiff." January 1922. *Letters and Journals of Katherine Mansfield*. Edited by C. K. Stead, Penguin, 1977, p. 250.

Mass, Noah. "'Caught and Loose': Southern Cosmopolitanism in Carson McCullers's *The Ballad of the Sad Café* and *The Member of the Wedding*." *Studies in American Fiction*, vol. 37, no. 2, 2010, pp. 225-246. *Project Muse*, doi: 10.1353/saf.2010.0008.

McCullers, Carson. *Clock Without Hands*. Penguin, 1987.

---. *Illumination and Night Glare: The Unfinished Autobiography of Carson McCullers*, edited by Carlos Dews, The University of Wisconsin Press, 1999.

---. "Isak Dinesen: In Praise of Radiance." *The Mortgaged Heart*, edited by Margarita G. Smith, Barrie & Jenkins, 1972, pp. 269-73.

---. "Outline of 'The Mute'." *Illumination and Night Glare: The Unfinished Autobiography of Carson McCullers*, edited by Carlos Dews, The University of Wisconsin Press, 1999, pp. 163-184.

---. *The Heart Is a Lonely Hunter*. Penguin, 1961.

---. *The Member of the Wedding*. Penguin, 1980.

---. "Untitled Piece." *The Mortgaged Heart*, edited by Margarita G. Smith, Barrie & Jenkins, 1972, pp. 98-123.

Parkin-Gounelas, Ruth. "Katherine Mansfield Reading Other Women: The Personality of the Text." *Katherine Mansfield*. Edited by Roger Robinson. Louisiana UP, 1994, pp. 36-52.

Pero, Allan. "'Jigging away into nothingness': Knowledge, Language and Feminine *Jouissance* in 'Bliss' and 'Psychology'." *Katherine Mansfield and Psychology*. Edited by Clare Hanson, Gerri Kimber and Todd Martin, Edinburgh University Press, 2016, pp. 100-113.

Rubin, Louis D. "Carson McCullers: The Aesthetic of Pain." *The Virginia Quarterly Review*, vol. 52, no. 2, 1977, pp. 265-284. *VQR Online*, www.tinyurl.com/ycpwfccj.

Slaven, Craig. "Jester's Mercurial Nature and the Hermeneutics of Time in McCullers' *Clock Without Hands*." *Carson McCullers in the Twenty-First Century*. Edited by Alison Graham-Bertolini and Casey Kayser, Palgrave Macmillan, 2016, pp. 251-267.

Ulin, Julieann V. "'The Astonishing Humanity': Domestic Discourses in the Friendship and Fiction of Richard Wright and Carson McCullers." *Richard Wright: New Readings in the 21$^{st}$ Century*. Edited by Alice Mikal Craven and William E. Dow, Palgrave Macmillan, 2011, pp. 193-214.

Whitt, Jan. "The Loneliest Hunter." *The Southern Literary Journal*, vol. 24, no. 2, 1992, pp. 26-35. *Proquest*, www.jstor.org/stable/20078042.

Woolf, Virginia. *A Writer's Diary: Being Extracts from the Diary of Virginia Woolf*. Edited by Leonard Woolf. The Hogarth Press, 1972.

Wright, Richard. "Inner Landscape." *Critical Essays on Carson McCullers*, edited by Beverley Lyon Clark and Melvin J. Friedman, MacMillan, 1996, pp. 17-18.

---. *Native Son*. Harper Perennial, 1998.

# CONTRIBUTORS

**Will Brantley** is a Professor of English at Middle Tennessee State University, where he teaches modern American literature, Southern literature, professional writing, and film studies. Brantley has published widely on Southern women writers including Carson McCullers; his *Feminine Sense in Southern Memoir: Smith, Glasgow, Welty, Hellman, Porter, and Hurston* (1993) received the Eudora Welty Award for an interpretive work of scholarship in modern letters. Brantley is also the editor of *Conversations with Pauline Kael* (1996) and the co-editor of *Conversations with Edmund White* (2017).

**Keith Byerman** is a Professor of English, African American Studies, and Gender Studies at Indiana State University. He is the author of eight books and numerous articles on African American and Southern literature and culture. He is currently writing a book on narratives of Hurricane Katrina. He teaches courses on Southern women writers, the Southern Gothic, and film and race, in addition to Southern and African American literature surveys.

**Sun Danping** is a PhD. candidate, Department of English Language and Culture, Guangdong University of Foreign Studies, P.R. China. She is an Assistant Professor of English who researches and writes about the twentieth-century modern and contemporary American literature. Her doctoral dissertation is on Carson McCullers. She has published two essays on Chinese comparative studies of Carson McCullers: "From 'Seeking Similarities' to 'Reserving Differences': A Review of Comparative Study between Carson McCullers and Chinese Writers" (2017) and "A Comparative Study on the Uglitic Appreciation of Carson McCullers and Mo Yan" (2017).

**Carlos Dews** is an authority on the life and work of Carson McCullers. He edited McCullers's unfinished biography, *Illumination and Night Glare*, published by the University of Wisconsin Press in 1997, and edited The Library of America's two volume *Complete Works* *of Carson McCullers*. He was the Founding Director of the Carson McCullers Center for Writers and Musicians at Columbus State University, in McCullers's hometown of Columbus, Georgia, and the Founding President of the Carson McCullers Society, an organization of scholars dedicated to research on McCullers's life and work. He is currently under contract with Houghton Mifflin Harcourt to edit the letters of Carson McCullers. Dews is the Dean of Academic Affairs and Professor of English at John Cabot University in Rome, Italy, where he also directs the Institute for Creative Writing and Literary Translation.

**Saundra Scribner Grace** spent much of her career working and traveling for the United Nations (UNIDO, UNRWA, UNEP, UNESCO, UNICEF, IFAD, FAO) in Europe, Africa, the Middle East, and in New York as an editor, writer, researcher, and producer of many international events, particularly in the field of the Advancement of Women. She has worked in English, Danish, French, Italian, and German, with undergraduate degrees in English and History, a Master's in Management and Organizational Development, and doctoral work in Ancient History (Pre-Christian Religion).

**Laura Gray** teaches English in Fulbright College at the University of Arkansas. Her teaching and research interests include Southern contemporary fiction and poetry. She began reading McCullers as a child. Gray received her MFA in poetry, and as a writer, one special service focus has been working in third world countries with undergraduates in project-based literacy studies using creative writing in development initiatives in Belize, Viet Nam and Kazakhstan.

**Alessandra Grego** was born in London (UK) and reared in Rome where she earned a PhD in English Literature from La Sapienza University. She has been Adjunct Professor of English Literature at John Cabot University in Rome since 2003. Her area of study are narratives of belief, which she has investigated in Victorian Literature (specifically George Eliot) and the novel in general, the function of myth in digital animation and popular culture in the 21st century, and digital humanities.

**Sarah-Marie Horning** is a PhD candidate in English at Texas Christian University where she works for TCU Press. She holds undergraduate degrees in English and Political Science and an MA in Literature and Cultural Studies from the University of Central Florida. Her papers and presentations have covered Southern women writers such as Flannery O'Connor, Carson McCullers, and Zora Neale Hurston.

**Katalin G. Kállay** teaches American literature at Károli Gáspár University in Budapest and also offered summer courses at the University of California in Santa Cruz. She received an MA. at L. Eötvös University in Budapest and defended her PhD. at the Catholic University of Leuven, Belgium. Her first book on nineteenth-century American short stories, *Going Home Through Seven Paths to Nowhere: Reading Short Stories by Hawthorne, Poe, Melville and James* was published in 2003 by the Hungarian Academy of Science. Her fields of research include nineteenth- and twentieth-century American fiction, especially Southern women writers, Hungarian literature in English, literary responses to the Holocaust and the relationship between philosophy and literature.

**Kerry Madden-Lunsford** is the author of the Maggie Valley Trilogy, which includes *Gentle's Holler*, *Louisiana's Song* and *Jessie's Mountain*, published by Viking. Her novel, *Offsides*, (Morrow) was a New York Public Library Pick for the Teen Age. *Up Close Harper Lee* made Booklist's Ten Top Biographies of 2009 for Youth. Her first picture book, *Nothing Fancy About Kathryn and Charlie*, was illustrated by her daughter, Lucy. Her picture book, *Ernestine's Milky Way*, is published by Schwartz & Wade of Random House. Kerry directs the Creative Writing Program at UAB and teaches in the Antioch MFA Program in Los Angeles. The mother of three adult children, she divides her time between Birmingham and Los Angeles.

**James Mayo**, Associate Professor of English at Jackson State Community College in Jackson, Tennessee, earned his BA in English at Middle Tennessee State University and his MA in English at the University of Idaho. He is the former president of the Carson McCullers Society and former editor of the society's newsletter. He has published work in various scholarly journals and reference works. As a way to relax, he and his wife spend their time and money renovating their 106-year-old farmhouse in which his father lived as a child.

**Liz Mayo** received her PhD in Textual Studies from the University of Memphis and is Professor of English at Jackson State Community College in Jackson, Tennessee. There, she has won the New Horizons in Teaching award and serves as the advisor for the JSCC Human Rights Club. She published in *The Chronicle of Higher Education* where she detailed her identity as a blue-collar scholar. She is a social justice warrior who has spent many hours marching with signs. She resides in rural West Tennessee on a 46-acre homestead in a 106-year-old farmhouse with her husband and two daughters.

**Annette Runte** received a PhD in German Literature after her graduate studies of German, philosophy and linguistics at the Universities of Bonn, Bochum and Paris. Having been a postgraduate at the first "Graduiertenkolleg" for Cultural Studies in Germany, she was a Professor of German and Comparative Literature at the University of Siegen from 1994 to 2016. She taught as a Visiting Professor at the Universities of Hanover, Graz and Rouen. There she was a member of the Research Group "Centre de Recherches sur l'Autriche et l'Allemagne." Special interests: German and French Literature from the 18th to the 20th century, Gender Studies, Autobiography, and Psychoanalysis.

**Shannon Russell** is Associate Professor of English Literature and Chair of the Department of English Language and Literature at John Cabot University, Rome. She received her D. Phil. from Oxford University where she was also a Post-doctoral Research Fellow. Her publications reflect her specialization in eighteenth and nineteenth century fiction. She is currently writing a book on Charles Dickens and Frederick Douglass.

**Emilia Salomone** teaches English language and culture at "Liceo Maria Montessori" in Rome. After graduating in "Foreign Languages and Literatures" from La Sapienza University, Rome, she translated N. Chomsky's *Knowledge of Language: Its Nature, Origin and Use* into Italian. She started teaching high school students in 1984 and has worked as a teacher since then. She has taken part in several international projects such as Italy Reads, eTwinning, Read On, Acer-European school-net Educational Netbook pilot, Comenius Multilateral Partnership.

**Mariarosaria Savino** is currently a Professor at De Nicola High School in Naples where she is Head of the Department of Foreign Language and Literature and Project Coordinator. She graduated with honors in English Language and Literature from the University "Orientale" in Naples in 1991. In 1996, she was qualified as a Primary school teacher, followed by qualifications in 2000 and 2002 as a High School teacher. Educational experience includes teaching courses at St. Giles College in London, International House in Newcastle, at the British Council of Naples and at the John Cabot University, Rome. Career highlights, throughout her 21 years of teaching, include experience as tutor and group leader for cultural exchange trips, tutorship in foreign language ministerial projects, responsibility for work / study projects, coordination as training tutor of recent teaching graduates and membership in evaluation committees.

**Sue Brannan Walker** is Professor Emerita at the University of South Alabama where she taught literature and creative writing for thirty-five years. She has served as President of the Alabama Writers Forum, the Alabama State Poetry Society, and the Alabama Writers Conclave. She is the editor and publisher of Negative Capability Press. From 2003-2012, she was Poet Laureate of Alabama. She has published ten books of poetry, a play, numerous book reviews, and critical articles. Her book *In the Realm of Rivers: Alabama's Mobile-Tensaw Delta* with a foreword by Edward O. Wilson, was published by New South Books as was *It's Good Weather for Fudge: Conversing with Carson McCullers. Let Us Imagine Her Name* was published by Clemson University Press, and her award-winning critical book, *The Ecological Poetics of James Dickey* was published by the Edwin Mellen Press.

**Glenn Willis** holds an MSC from the University of Edinburgh and is an Executive Committee member of the Carson McCullers Society.

*Note: As multiple papers submitted to the international conference in Rome, Carson McCullers in the World: A Centenary Celebration, the editors have chosen to retain the authors' original spelling and citation formating in this collection.*

www.ingramcontent.com/pod-product-compliance
Lightning Source LLC
Chambersburg PA
CBHW072049110526
44590CB00018B/3101